The International Library of Sociology

THE CHURCH IN
SOCIAL WORK

Founded by KARL MANNHEIM

The International Library of Sociology

PUBLIC POLICY, WELFARE
AND SOCIAL WORK
In 18 Volumes

THE CHURCH IN SOCIAL WORK

A Study of Moral Welfare Work undertaken
by the Church of England

by

M. PENELOPE HALL and ISMENE V. HOWES

ROUTLEDGE

First published in 1965 by
Routledge

Reprinted 1998, 1999 (Twice) by
Routledge
2 Park Square, Milton Park, Abingdon, Oxon, OX14 4RN
or
270 Madison Avenue, New York, NY 10016

First issued in paperback 2010

British Library Cataloguing in Publication Data
A CIP catalogue record for this book
is available from the British Library

The Church in Social Work
ISBN 978-0-415-17713-9 (hbk)
ISBN 978-0-415-60581-6 (pbk)
Public Policy, Welfare and Social Work: 18 Volumes
ISBN 978-0-415-17831-0
The International Library of Sociology: 274 Volumes
ISBN 978-0-415-17838-9

Publisher's Note
The publisher has gone to great lengths to ensure the quality of this
reprint but points out that some imperfections in the original
may be apparent

CONTENTS

Contents

TABLES

ACKNOWLEDGEMENTS

THIS study could not have been completed without the interest and co-operation of a number of people whose invaluable help we gratefully acknowledge.

Professor T. S. Simey, Charles Booth Professor of Social Science in the University of Liverpool agreed that the survey on which it is based should be sponsored by his Department and arranged for Miss Howes to be attached to the Department for the period of the investigation. At the same time a generous grant, sufficient to cover Miss Howes' salary for three years and other expenses incidental to the survey, was received from the Calouste Gulbenkian Foundation.

The idea of the survey originated with the Church of England Moral Welfare Council, and we owe a great deal to the then Chairman, the Bishop of St. Albans, and to members of the staff, notably Miss Ena Steel and Miss Eve Kennedy who together with the Reverend Gordan Dunstan and Miss Margaret Tilley, gave us every possible encouragement and help and did much to make our contacts with the workers in the dioceses as easy and friendly as they were.

Most of the field work was carried out in two selected dioceses, and the brunt of the inconvenience caused by the investigation fell on their organising secretaries who not only dealt with our seemingly endless requests for information but introduced us to committee members and workers and helped us in every possible way. Despite the extra work we caused them, outdoor workers and superintendents of homes made us welcome and gave us all the assistance they could, allowing us to examine records, accompany them on visits and, whenever possible, listen to interviews. The statutory officials whom we interviewed also received us courteously and dealt with the matters we raised helpfully and thoroughly, as did the sample of clergymen in the

Acknowledgements

northern diocese whom we interviewed with the approval of the diocesan Bishop.

In summarising the data and writing up our conclusions we were greatly helped by the constructive and penetrating criticism of our colleagues in the Department of Social Science, especially Professor Simey and Dr. C. H. Vereker. We should also like to thank Dr. Conor K. Ward, Lecturer in Sociology, National University of Ireland, for his advice and encouragement, and Miss E. Gittus for her help in connection with the preparation and analysis of the questionnaires. Owing to the differing categories of persons interviewed there were ten different questionnaires, some of which ran to several pages. Although not printed in this volume, copies can be made available on request.

Finally, we should like to express our indebtedness to Mrs. Brown and the typing staff of the Department for the patience with which they dealt with a succession of manuscripts, corrected and re-corrected by either or both of the co-authors, to Mrs. Thompson and Mrs. Martin for assisting with the typing of the final revision for publication, and to Mrs. Simmons for her help in checking this revision.

M.P.H.   I.V.H.

INTRODUCTION

THIS study is based on an enquiry undertaken in the autumn of 1958 at the request of the Church of England Moral Welfare Council (now Council for Social Work), one of the two constituent councils of the Church Assembly Board for Social Responsibility. The objectives of the enquiry, as set out at the time, were 'to examine the scope and character of the work undertaken by the Church of England under the general heading of moral welfare work, to relate it to the developments now taking place whereby statutory authorities (especially local authority health and welfare and children's departments), are taking increasing responsibility for family welfare, and to consider how far the work, as it is carried out at present, is the best response the Church can make to modern needs and conditions, or how far it should be modified or extended.'

The desirability of such an examination had been stressed for some time,[1] and during the latter part of the decade the need for it was accentuated by two parallel developments. In the first place, reassessments were being made of the scope and character of the social work undertaken by the two local authority departments whose work impinged most directly on that of moral welfare organisations. In 1955 a Working Party on 'Social Workers in the Local Authority Health and Welfare Services' had been set up under the chairmanship of Dr. Eileen Younghusband, and it was surmised that its recommendations would not only be far reaching in their effects on social work training, but would also endorse the expansion of local authority social work with families already taking place. The Working Party reported in 1959, and the possible effects of its recommendations both on the training of moral welfare workers and on provision for the care of unsupported mothers and other incomplete families, including

I

unmarried mothers and their children, are discussed in the body of this book. The second government enquiry initiated at this time was that of the Departmental Committee set up in 1956 under the chairmanship of Viscount Ingleby, its terms of reference being both to review the powers and procedures of juvenile courts and to make recommendations as to whether local authority children's departments should be given wider powers to prevent the suffering of children through neglect in their own homes. It was not until 1961 that the recommendations of this Committee were made public, but it was known that both social work organisations and individuals concerned about neglected children were pressing for the establishment in each local authority area of a family welfare service, which, if it were set up, might assume a major responsibility for social work with unmarried mothers and their children, as well as dealing with other marital and family problems hitherto regarded as being within the purview of moral welfare organisations.[2]

Parallel to these developments was the establishment by the Church Assembly of the Board for Social Responsibility and the incorporation of the Moral Welfare Council therein, which took place in 1958. This not only marked a new development in the relationship between moral welfare work and other forms of church work, but emphasised its wider social reference. On the one hand, therefore, changes were taking place in social work which might lessen the need for the Church to continue to participate in a form of social care with which it had become closely identified; on the other, the Church was alive to the possibility of modifying the nature and range of its interests in this field. In this situation an examination of existing moral welfare work was clearly desirable.

In undertaking this examination the first problem we encountered was that of nomenclature. 'Moral welfare' is a term which can be given different meanings in different contexts; more than this, it has become emotionally toned. It appears to have come into general use during the inter-war period to designate the social work in relation to sex, marriage and the family, which, at that time, was developing from the 'preventive and rescue' work and witness for 'social purity' of previous generations of church workers. 'Moral welfare' was a term which could be stretched to cover almost any activity which diocesan or local committees cared to undertake to further individual well-being and to uphold Christian standards of conduct in personal and family relationships. Much of the workers' time and energy, however, continued to be devoted to helping unmarried parents and their children, and the name has become associated with this particular type of social work irrespective of the agency undertaking it.[3] Not only outsiders, but moral welfare workers themselves sometimes perpetuate this misconception; for example, some of them spoke to us of the danger of the State 'taking over moral welfare work', meaning thereby the possibility of the statutory authorities assuming direct responsibility for social work with unmarried mothers and their children.

Originally adopted as an improvement on earlier phraseology, the term 'moral welfare' has long been subject to a considerable amount of criticism by both moral welfare workers themselves and others in contact with their work, but it has not been easy to find an alternative.[4] In 1961 the Board for Social Responsibility, with the permission of the Church Assembly, changed the name of the central council to Church of England Council for Social Work and similar changes in nomenclature have been made by certain diocesan and local associations. But the term 'moral welfare' is still widely used at the diocesan and local level, and it has been retained in this study to cover the casework, residential work and educational work relating to sex, marriage and the family undertaken by diocesan and local associations established for the purpose.

As defined above, moral welfare work is essentially social work undertaken in the name and on behalf of the Church, and its existence raises the question as to whether, in a modern welfare state with its own highly developed social services, there is any warrant for the Church's continued engagement in such work. In this context the designation 'Church' may be used in two distinct, although not necessarily exclusive senses. It may refer to the members of Christ's Body seeking to do His will and working for the advancement of His kingdom in whatever sphere of activity they are engaged. In that sense a Christian social worker carrying out the duties of her profession 'in His name' is the Church in action whether she is working under religious or secular auspices. The term 'Church' can, however, also be used to refer to a particular institution, and when the Church's

3

participation in social work is challenged, it is generally this institutional, and, in the present divided state of Christendom, denominational, usage of the word which is implied. We encountered little or no desire to question the validity of the participation of an individual professing Christian in social work, provided that she was loyal to her employers as well as to her own convictions and that she respected the disciplines and ethics of her profession as well as those of her Church. But the question which has been of major interest and importance throughout this survey is whether the continued corporate participation of the Church in social work through its own agencies set up for the purpose is and remains desirable.

This study is primarily concerned with the contemporary situation and its implications for the future, but this cannot be understood without some knowledge of the past. Tradition plays a significant part in moral welfare work and the pattern and organisation of the work is largely inherited from previous generations. Hence Part One of the study traces the development of moral welfare work from its beginnings to the present time and, compressed as it inevitably is, sets out to uncover significant trends and to assess the influence of creative ideas and outstanding personalities on the development of the work. The historical study showed that, at each stage of its development, the scope and character of the work had been modified in response to social change, and the effectiveness of the present day work can be measured, in some degree at least, by its relevance to the economic and social conditions of the mid-twentieth century. In Part Two, therefore, we draw attention to those aspects of the present situation which we regard as most significant in this connection. The present shortage of woman power is one important factor to be taken into account in any assessment of the total situation, and problems of recruitment and training are considered in Chapter 6.

Parts Three and Four of the study describe the organisation, scope and character of the work particularly as exemplified in two selected dioceses. This account is for the most part factual. The deductions drawn from our observations will be found in Part Five, where we have endeavoured to summarise and clarify the position in such a way as to facilitate considered judgment on the

Introduction

difficult problem posed at the end of our initial terms of reference, namely, how far moral welfare work as it is carried on at present is 'the best response the Church can make to modern needs and conditions'.

From the beginning it was agreed that the study would be limited in two respects. In the first place, it was designed as a survey of the work itself and how it was carried out, not as an overall investigation into the social problems which come within its scope, although it is difficult to keep the two entirely separate and some indication of the character of these problems is given in Chapter 4. Secondly, as it was impossible to make a comprehensive survey of the work throughout the country, it was decided to limit the field work for the most part to two dioceses, one in the Northern and the other in the Southern Province. We were fortunate, however, in that we were able to make contacts both with moral welfare workers from all parts of the country, and with members of the Commissions which had been set up by the Bishops of Manchester and Southwell to study the moral welfare work undertaken in their respective dioceses, and we learnt much from these contacts.

Within the two dioceses chosen for detailed investigation we first made contact with the workers themselves, and the fieldworker spent a week or more with each outdoor worker in turn, tracing the history of the association, reading case papers, accompanying the worker on visits and, where possible, listening to interviews. Either then or later she became resident in each of the homes within the dioceses, sharing in its life and work as a junior member of staff and recording her impressions. Contacts were next made with the statutory officials whose work was most closely akin to that of the moral welfare workers, and their views were obtained on the place of moral welfare work in the pattern of social work as they saw it. Meanwhile, we were attending moral welfare committee meetings and discussing with members and officials the organisation of the work and the role of the diocesan and local committees. The last major piece of field work, apart from the analysis we made of the background and subsequent careers of Josephine Butler House and London course students described in Chapter 6, was the series of interviews we undertook with a one-in-four sample of the clergy in one of the chosen dioceses. This was undertaken so that we could consider

5

moral welfare work, not only in the context of the social services, but as part of the pastoral ministry of the Church.

Throughout the investigation we sought to remain unbiased in the sense that we endeavoured to weigh up and present the material we collected as impartially as possible, but, over the years we were engaged in the work, friendships developed between ourselves and the workers, and we became increasingly conscious of the bond of shared religious faith and ideals. This meant that the report we presented to the Board for Social Responsibility on completion of the investigation was presented not simply as a document prepared by outside academic observers, but as an attempt to 'speak the truth in love' to fellow Christians serving the Church in a particular way, men and women whose devotion to their work had won our regard and respect.

We presented the report at a Board meeting held in September 1962, and it was suggested at the meeting that, if possible, arrangements should be made for its publication, since it was believed that both the factual material contained in it and the discussions of the wider issues made explicit by it were likely to be of interest to social workers and administrators as well as to clergy and laity concerned about the Church's responsibility in the field of social welfare. The revision of the report for publication proved a more exacting task than was envisaged at the time, partly because we were particularly requested to expand the historical introduction, which involved the collection and sifting of some new material, and partly because we decided to make a number of alterations in the text and rearrange some of the chapters, in part in order to make identification of places and persons more difficult. We have also changed the manner of presentation, but not to any extent the content, of the general discussion which concludes the study and which represents an attempt to examine some of the major issues raised by the Church's participation in social work.

PART ONE

Historical Development

I

RESCUE AND REFORM

I

FEW existing diocesan and local moral welfare associations were started before the closing years of the nineteenth century, but the work itself has a much longer history. There are indications that both homes for 'fallen women' and institutes for the care of foundling children[1] were in existence in France and Italy as early as the seventh and eighth centuries, and during the middle ages communities of 'Magdalens', the majority of whose members seem to have been women reclaimed from a life of prostitution, were to be found in a number of European countries. There is no evidence that any such communities existed in mediaeval Britain, but the record of a lay attempt to shelter and care for unmarried mothers has survived, namely that of London's famous Lord Mayor, Richard Whytyngdon, who in St. Thomas's Hospital, Southwark, in which he was interested, 'made a newe chambyr with VIII beddys for young women that had done amysse in trust for a good mendement.'[2]

At this time there seems to have been no general rejection of the illegitimate child,[3] and 'in the community obligations of mediaeval society a way could be found to provide for him'.[4] Where such care was lacking he might be sheltered in one of the religious houses, or in the school or hospital attached to it.[5] If not adequately cared for either in the community or by the Church, it was all too easy for the destitute child, whether legitimate or illegitimate, should he survive at all, to grow up into a vagrant or became a habitual beggar or thief.

Beggars and vagrants were common enough in the middle ages, but the economic and social changes which took place during the Tudor period added to their numbers. It was to deal with the

9

pressing problem of destitution, and the vagrancy which accompanied it, that the Tudor Parliaments passed the succession of Acts known collectively as the Poor Laws, and the unmarried mother and illegitimate child with no one else to care for them became the responsibility of the Poor Law authorities, at that time the parish officers.

Under the laws of Settlement, children born out of wedlock were chargeable to the parish of their birth. This ruling caused great hardship to their mothers, as women 'big with bastard child' were often harried from parish to parish by overseers trying by all means in their power to evade the cost of rearing the children when born.[6] The unwillingness of the parish overseers to carry the 'great burden' of maintaining these children, a burden which, it was alleged, was 'defrauding of the relief of the impotent and aged, true poor of the same parish',[7] was also responsible for the passing, in 1576, of what proved to be the first of a succession of Bastardy Acts, and its even harsher successor in 1610. The Acts condemned 'lewdness' and asserted that it should be punished, but their main purpose appears to have been to force parents of illegitimate children to pay for their upbringing,[8] since 'great charge ariseth upon many places within this realm by reason of bastardy, besides the great dishonour of Almighty God', as the 1610 Act phrases it, putting first things first.

The maintenance of the illegitimate child was at that time evidently regarded as the joint responsibility of the two parents, and in the eighteenth century so determined were the authorities that the putative father should be made to pay his share that legislation was enacted which made it possible for a single woman to charge a man with being the father of her child, whereupon, unless he could prove the contrary, he became liable to indemnify the parish for the cost of the child's upbringing. In default of this he could be committed to the common gaol or house of correction.[9] An alternative to being apprehended, and perhaps imprisoned, was to marry the girl, the resultant marriage being founded, according to the Commissioners appointed in 1832 to enquire into the administration of the Poor Law, 'on fear on one side and vice on both.'[10]

Whether the undesired consequence of a casual connection, or deliberately sought by a courting couple in order to expedite the wedding, since marriages were often long delayed by the economic and social circumstances of the time, pre-marital pregnancy was common throughout this period. In many instances the wedding took place before the child was born, but this did not always happen, and should the woman be left destitute, the parish overseers, reluctant as they might be to help, were bound to make some provision for her. When once it became clear that all efforts to bring about a marriage, or to secure maintenance from the putative father, or to remove the woman to another parish had failed, the treatment meted out to unmarried mothers and their children does not seem to have been unduly harsh by the standards of the time. According to the Poor Law Commissioners the amount of the order made on the father in respect of his bastard child varied from 7s. or 8s. a week to 1s., the average being about 3s. or 2s. 6d. in the towns and 2s. in the country, and should he fail to pay it was secured to the mother by the parish. As witnesses to the Poor Law Commission were at pains to point out, this meant that she might be better off than a respectable widow, whose allowance was commonly only 1s. 6d. a week. Whether legitimate or illegitimate, children with no one to care for them were usually boarded out with local families. Their treatment naturally varied from family to family and parish to parish, but in rural parishes, at any rate, they 'do not seem to have suffered from deliberate ill-treatment or neglect'.[11]

In London, however, the lot of the orphaned or deserted child left to the care of the parish was a sorry one, and few of those who came into public care under the age of three survived to reach adolescence.[12] But even this slender chance of life was denied to those infants whose mothers, in their shame and despair, left to perish by the roadside or on a dunghill. It was the plight of these infants that so aroused the pity and indignation of the retired sea captain, Thomas Coram, that he embarked upon his arduous and unremitting campaign to establish a hospital for their reception and care.

Thomas Coram was by no means the first, even in this country, to envisage the founding of an institution for the care of homeless children. Christ's Hospital, founded in 1552, was intended to provide for 'fatherless children, orphaned or illegitimate', but by the middle of the seventeenth century it had become respectable, and would only accept legitimate children. In 1713 Joseph

Addison printed an article in the *Guardian* (No. 105) which urged that provision should be made for foundlings, for, he lamented, 'what multitudes of infants have been made away with by those who brought them into the world and were afterwards either ashamed or unable to provide for them'.[13] It was, however, Coram who displayed the zeal and persistence necessary to overcome apathy and even hostility and bring the scheme to fruition.

The Royal Charter for the incorporation of the 'Hospital for the Maintenance and Education of Exposed and Deserted Young Children', the Foundling Hospital's legal title, was received in November 1739, and the first batch of thirty children were admitted in March 1741. The institution quickly justified its existence. By March 1756, 1,384 children had been received, rather more than one-third of whom survived, a mortality record which, poor as it may seem by modern standards, compared favourably with that of the poor law authorities.[14] But, in the words of Coram's contemporary and friend, Jonas Hanway, 'What were 1,384 infants to the thousands still drooping and dying in the hands of the parish nurses?,' or, for that matter, still being left on the dunghills by their desperate mothers, some of whom might have tried to get them admitted to the Foundling Hospital and failed. Demands for admission quickly outran accommodation, and early in the Hospital's career its governors encountered one of the most painful and difficult problems of social policy, for they had to decide whether to succour a few with some chance of success but leave the remainder to perish, or, on the other hand, to attempt to give assistance to many knowing that this might endanger the well-being of all.

The first attempt to deal with the situation was to introduce a system of balloting for places, a method of selection which, at a time when it was believed that no questions should be asked of the mother, was probably the fairest available. By 1756, however, the finances of the hospital were in a parlous condition and the governors petitioned Parliament for help. They were granted a subsidy of £10,000, but with the condition attached that all children under a certain age brought to the doors of the hospital must be admitted. This was the origin of the disastrous experiment of indiscriminate admission which, during the five years it continued, led to a great deal of abuse and seriously threatened the hospital's standards of child care. It was discontinued in 1761, and methods of admission which took into account the circumstances of the case were slowly introduced.

Not only the care, but also the training of foundling children, and their eventual apprenticeship were regarded as being among the prime objectives of the charity, for its founders and governors were businessmen as well as philanthropists and, well aware of the shortage of labour both in England and in the 'illimitable and untouched areas of the New World', they were indignant at the economic wastage as well as the moral iniquity of leaving infants to perish. This consciousness of the long-term benefits to be derived from the rescue and training of children who would otherwise probably grow up into thieves and vagabonds may help to account for the fact that it was laymen and men of affairs rather than clergymen and representatives of the Church who were active in this and related eighteenth century charities.

The Foundling Hospital was an early and enlightened attempt to deal with the problem presented by the illegitimate child, but it did not tackle the problem of illegitimacy itself. Coram and his friends were, indeed, accused of condoning profligacy by making themselves responsible for its visible consequences, and the grant to the Hospital from public funds was attacked by at least one contemporary on the grounds that it was likely to increase the evil it was seeking to cure, and 'There will unhappily be too much Reason for saying that this present Humanity will be future Cruelty'.[15] No social care was available for the mothers and, concerned as Coram might be about them, and distressed as he was by 'the morbid morality possessing the public mind by which the unhappy female who fell a victim to the seductions and false promises of designing men' was then left to face 'hopeless contumely and irretrievable disgrace',[16] he could do little to ease her burden except to see that when she brought her child to the hospital she was treated with consideration and respect. Like others in a similar situation, she was left to struggle to rehabilitate herself as best she could and, if unsuccessful, to drift into a life of prostitution.

Prostitution, with its attendant evils of drunkenness and venereal disease, was widespread in eighteenth century London. According to Jonas Hanway, writing in 1784, three thousand prostitutes then walked the streets; many of them were young, scarcely in their teens, and doomed to die before they were 24.[17] Some had been introduced to the brothel keepers by their mothers who then shared the profits, and they had no other way of earning a living.[18] At the beginning of the century societies 'for the Reformation of Manners' flourished, and were active in prosecuting women on the streets, keepers of disorderly houses and Sabbath breakers, but all this zeal did little or nothing to help the individual woman back to normal life. As time went on, advances in medicine led to increasing concern about the health problems associated with prostitution and the Lock Hospital was opened in 1746 for the treatment of venereal disease in patients of either sex. But, quite apart from any question as to the efficacy of the remedies then available, many women on being discharged had no alternative but to return to their former profession. It was not till forty-one years later, in 1787, that the Hospital's avowed intention of 'converting them to a more godly way of life' as well as treating their sickness, found practical expression in the opening of the Lock Asylum, the object of which was to provide some form of training for women patients discharged from the Hospital.

Meanwhile the earliest and most famous institution for the 'reception, maintenance and employment of Penitent Prostitutes', the Magdalen Hospital, had already been in existence for nearly thirty years. Opened in 1758, this institution can be regarded as a forerunner of present day moral welfare work, not least on account of the humanity of its founders and the catholicity of their concern. This was evinced in the wording of the Hospital's Constitution which made it plain that those responsible for the care of the penitents were expected to observe 'the utmost Care, Delicacy, Humanity and Tenderness; so that this Establishment, instead of being apprehended to be a House of Correction may gladly be embraced as a desirable, safe and happy Retreat from their Wretched and Distressful Circumstances'.[19] Penitents from all classes and backgrounds were admitted, only 'black women' being expressedly excluded.

As had been the case with the Foundling Hospital, whose work had helped to inspire them, Robert Dingley, the founder of the Magdalen and his associates in the venture were all laymen, but their motives were religious as well as humanitarian, and religious training was regarded as a fundamental part of the process

14

of reclamation. The Magdalen had its own chapel and chaplain and 'quickly won the respect and support of the Church'.

The success of the Magdalen Hospital led to the establishment of other charities with a similar purpose, particularly during the early years of the nineteenth century. The first of these appears to have been the Dalston Refuge, established in 1805, and this was quickly followed by the London Female Penitentiary established at Pentonville in 1807. Although information is scanty, there seems no reason to suppose that these homes were run on lines different from those of the Magdalen itself, and, as yet, the word 'Penitentiary' had not acquired its later unpleasant overtones. The early rescue homes seem to have been local projects, associated with a particular district such as Stepney or Westminster, and founded independently as the result of the concern of a benevolent individual or group. There is no evidence that they were connected in any special way with any particular church.

It was not long before similar homes were opened outside London, for example one at Bath which was established in 1808, 'upon a plan somewhat similar to that of the Magdalen Hospital in London'. Its object was 'to receive into close residence, protection, government and employment, with a view to reformation and restoration to their friends, or to prepare for placing in suitable services, a limited number of such deluded females as have wandered from the paths of virtue'. To these 'repentant daughters of vice and misery' the penitentiary afforded 'a friendly shelter from the storms of adversity and the goadings of conscience'. Like those of the Magdalen itself its 'internal arrangements' were formed 'on the basis of encouraging industry' as well as 'affording a penitential asylum to the outcasts of society' and no inconsiderable portion of the penitentiary's funds came from the profits of the work done by the 'unfortunate inmates'. 'Many females of distinction feel a gratification in thus affording them almost constant employment', concludes the account triumphantly.[20] The combination of piety, complacency and, withal, a genuine desire to help, so characteristic of nineteenth century rescue work, was already firmly established.

By the end of the eighteenth and beginning of the nineteenth century the rescue of fallen women had become a reputable, and in the case of the Magdalen itself, even a fashionable form of charity. By this time, too, it had already been recognised that, 'it is not only more charitable and humane, but less difficult and expensive, to prevent women and girls from being driven to Prostitution than to reclaim them when they are Prostitutes.' There is no evidence that Mr. Massie's rather grandiose 'Plan for the Establishment of Charity Houses for Exposed or Deserted Women and Girls', published in 1758, from which the above sentence is taken, ever came to anything, but in that same year Sir John Fielding founded a Female Orphan Asylum for 'Poor Friendless and Deserted Girls'. Two years earlier the Marine Society had begun to train vagabond boys for the sea, and by the beginning of the nineteenth century the Philanthropic Society was catering for the separate needs of boys and girls.

Such efforts, laudable as they were, could do little more than scratch the surface, and with the social and economic changes that accompanied the industrial revolution, and the instability and insecurity engendered by them, the needs of unmarried mothers and their children and friendless and homeless young women were, if anything, increasing. The drift of men from country to town in search of work not only disturbed the balance of the sexes in both town and country, but meant that out-of-wedlock conceptions that in previous generations would have been regularised by marriage now resulted in the birth of an illegitimate child. Moreover, as was the case with other categories of destitute people, the changes brought about by the Poor Law Amendment Act, 1834, tended to throw the unmarried mother back on her own resources, pitiable as these often were.

As we have indicated already, the Poor Law Commissioners were extremely critical of the existing Bastardy Laws. One criticism which could be made of these laws was that they might involve the imprisonment of an innocent man for an act which, whether it had been committed or not, was not punishable by English law, and that without a proper trial, since 'when the reputed father is brought by warrant before the justice, the magistrate has no power to examine into the merits of the case, but is bound by the express terms of the statute to commit him to the common gaol or house of correction, unless he gives security or enters into recognisance to give security'.[21] But in the eyes of the Commissioners the wrongful punishment of the innocent was a small matter compared with the overall effect of laws which, they asserted, sacrificed every other object to the indemnification of the parish concerned.

The guidance of nature has been neglected, the task of resistance has been thrown on the man instead of the woman; marriages in which the least fault is improvidence have been not only promoted but compelled; every possible inducement has been held out to perjury and profligacy, simply to save parishes from expense, and the direct effect has been to double or quadruple that expense— the indirect effect to augment it still more.[22]

The remedies suggested by the Commission were in keeping with both the *laissez-fâire* philosophy of the whole Report and the current widespread assumption that it was the woman's responsibility to resist temptation, not the man's to refrain from offering it, and that, should she succumb, the woman should suffer to the full the consequences of her fall. The Commission proposed the entire abolition of the existing Bastardy Laws; instead trust was to be placed 'in those checks and those checks only which Providence has imposed on licentiousness, under the conviction that all attempts of the Legislature to increase their force or substitute for them artificial sanctions have tended only to weaken or prevent them'.[23] In future an illegitimate child was to take his mother's settlement and she would be obliged to support him. This was the law with respect to a widow: 'an unmarried mother has voluntarily placed herself in the position of a widow; she has voluntarily become a mother without procuring to herself and her child the assistance of a husband or father. There can be no reason for giving to vice privileges we deny to misfortune.'[24] The punishment or restraint of the supposed father was regarded as useless or worse than useless, and it was the intention of the Commissioners that his part in the transaction should henceforth be ignored. During the passage of the Poor Law Amendment Act, which put their recommendations into effect, however, a clause was inserted empowering the parish to obtain a maintenance order against the putative father of a bastard child that had become chargeable to the rates. 'The clause was purely in the interests of the ratepayer, it was not intended to furnish a civil remedy to the woman or have a penal effect against the man,'[25] but, as time went on, the illogicality of the situation whereby the mother's right to claim affiliation depended on whether or not the child was chargeable to the parish became clear, and by the Bastardy Act, 1845, justices were given power to make an order against the putative father on the application of the mother supported by corroborative evidence. Although during the succeeding century the act was amended, its substance remained unchanged, and the law as it stands today embodies its principles and procedure.

The cold ruthlessness and lack of any kind of imaginative understanding of, or sympathy with, the unmarried mother which characterised the report of the Poor Law Commissioners was, to a large extent, a reflection of attitudes and assumptions held at that time by devout Christians as well as by the callous and indifferent. Nevertheless, the increasing distress of the poor was accompanied by a growing 'seriousness' among the 'employing classes' due, at least in part, to the stirrings of the Evangelical Movement, and although the cause of the betrayed and friendless woman or girl was not at this time taken up by any one person or group, there were those who, amid the all too prevalent self-righteousness, were prepared to approach these women with sympathy, charity and humanity, and to draw attention to their plight. In the climate of opinion of the time it must have taken some courage to make an unmarried mother the heroine of a novel and so seek to arouse sympathy for her, as Mrs. Gaskell did when she published *Ruth* in 1853,[26] and still more courage to receive 'fallen women' into one's own home in order to help restore them. This was the practice of a certain Mrs. Tennant of Clewer near Windsor, who in 1849 thus began the work taken over three years later by the Clewer House of Mercy, and expanded and developed by this Anglican Sisterhood.

Clewer was not the only community house to be established during this period, for the revival of the Anglican religious orders for women, which occurred as a result of a renewed appreciation of the Catholic tradition of the Church of England on the part of Tractarians and Anglo-Catholics, gave a new impetus to the foundation of penitentiaries and similar institutions. Thus the Wantage Sisters of St. Mary the Virgin started penitentiary work in 1850, only two years after their own foundation, and soon 'both they and the Clewer sisters were speedily engaged in this fruitful work of sheltering and training penitents'.[27]

Nor were new developments in rescue work confined to the Tractarian and Anglo-Catholic wing of the Church. As early as the 1830's a group of Evangelicals, whose fervent faith was by no means always the 'social anaesthetic' it has sometimes been decried as being, had founded the Female Aid Mission and opened a home for women.[28] As with the Anglo-Catholics, however, it was in the fifties and, in the case of the Evangelicals, in connection with the revivalist activities of this decade, that the work was developed on a larger scale. This was the period when organised rescue societies, such as that founded by Daniel Cooper in London in 1853, began both to supplement and promote the work of the homes. Missionary work was extended to the women of the streets and while some of these efforts, such as the 'London by Moonlight Mission', organised by Theophilus Smith, Secretary of the Female Aid Society, and his friends appear to have led on to work of a more permanent character, other attempts to seek out and save the lost by emotional appeals, whether individual or collective, seem to have been ill-conceived and unsuccessful.[29]

With the multiplication of effort which characterised the middle years of the century the need for co-ordination became increasingly apparent. In 1848 an article criticising the lack of co-ordination betwen the various charities in London and the provinces appeared in the *London Quarterly Review*. It called attention to the overlapping and waste of money which had resulted from the unrelated efforts to meet the needs of the unmarried mother and the prostitute, and in making the further point that 'the Church has no hold upon Penitentiaries' it raised a new issue, that of the role of the institutional church in controlling and guiding what had hitherto been largely spontaneous and individual efforts.

The article may well have been one of the influences which led to the formation of the Church Penitentiary Association three years later. From the time of its formation this association had strong connections with the Tractarian and Anglo-Catholic wing of the Church and the community houses were among the first to associate themselves with it. Its object was 'to promote the establishment and assist in the maintenance of Houses of Refuge and Penitentiaries for the reception and reformation of Fallen Women, Penitents and, when desirable, to facilitate the emigration of such women'. The Association pursued its aim mainly by distributing grants to such institutions as came within its ruling. This was that 'no House of Mercy is received into union unless it is under the management of self-devoted women with the ministration of a Chaplain of the Church of England in spiritual matters and its application is signed by the Bishop of the Diocese'.[30]

The Association evidently regarded itself as a promotional as well as a grant-giving body, however, its objective being that 'before long no Diocese ... will be without its Diocesan Penitentiary, its affiliated Penitentiaries and House of Refuge'.[31] The number of affiliated houses did indeed increase rapidly, but not rapidly enough to meet the growing demand, and running like a refrain through the early reports is the cry, 'We want more Houses. We want the assistance of self-devoted women to minister in these Houses,' while money was also needed both to enable every House to take its full quota of penitents and to open new Houses for those who had to be turned away.

More representative of the other wing of the Church, and indeed not specifically Anglican, was the Reformatory and Refuge Union founded in 1856 under the patronage of the Seventh Earl of Shaftesbury. The major concern of this charity was the prevention of crime and relief of destitution, but in 1858 a Female Penitentiaries Special Fund was opened 'for the purpose of assisting such asylums and penitentiaries and smaller homes as appear on careful inspection to be deserving of such encouragement'.[32] It was intended that, 'without interfering with the existing institutions, a centre of action should be provided, through which all might be assisted'. With this object in mind a Handbook was compiled 'containing brief accounts of fifty Penitentiaries and Homes for Females',[33] possibly the first Directory of Moral Welfare Work. Money from the Fund was also used to give direct practical help to women and girls in need and, despite its forbidding title, the Female Mission to the Fallen, as it came to be known, proved to be a far seeing and imaginative body which sponsored new developments in rescue work. Two of these, the appointment of paid 'street missionaries' and the provision of accommodation for mothers with their babies, were of special importance.

Although the concern of the Mission extended to attempted

suicides, foreign women and workhouse inmates, at the core of its work lay the activities of its paid women missionaries, whose numbers increased from two to eight in the first eight years of the Mission's existence, and later rose to ten. These missionaries, who worked under the general direction of a 'lady supervisor', were each responsible for a certain 'area of London, the purpose of their work being to seek out 'those who are desirous of abandoning their evil ways' and direct them to 'places of shelter'.[34] With this as their objective they were to 'go out into the streets at night, distributing tracts and speaking kind words to the unhappy creatures they met there'.[35] This initial approach was followed up in various ways 'Some are sent to Hospitals, others to Penitentiaries: the greater number to places of rough service where earning their own living and working their way back to respectability and good character seems to have a more salutary effect on some than Homes'.[36] The missionary forerunners of the outdoor workers of the twentieth century had already begun to realise that rehabilitation in the community was a possible, and in some cases a more hopeful, alternative to segregation from it.

This same forward looking approach was manifest in another piece of work supported by the Mission which seems to have passed almost unnoticed at the time, but which has developed into an important part of moral welfare work. Hitherto the only choice open to the unmarried mother whose family and friends had rejected her had been the workhouse with her child or the penitentiary without it. 'The joys and satisfactions of motherhood were not for those who had no right to be mothers, and the fate of the child was a secondary consideration'.[37] In the 1860's, however, two homes of a new type came into existence, apparently quite independently, but both supported by the Female Mission. The nature of their work is revealed in the comprehensive title of one of them, 'Refuge for Deserted Mothers and Home for their Illegitimate Infants'. Short term care was offered to the nursing mother and long term care, which might take the form of foster care,[38] was given to the child when, at the termination of this period, the mother went out to work, normally in domestic service. The mother was, however, expected and indeed required, to contribute to her child's upkeep, 'to the utmost limits of her power'. The homes were evidently subjected to criticism on the grounds that they were ridding mothers 'of a burden which they have brought upon themselves',[39] but the innovation made then has since been recognised as an early attempt to explore the possibility of rehabilitating the mother through her child.

II

By the middle of the nineteenth century rescue work of one kind or another was wide-spread particularly in London, but social conditions were such as to justify redoubled efforts. Mayhew estimated that in 1857 there were 80,000 prostitutes in London[40] and vividly described the night scenes in the Haymarket and other notorious London streets where, Ellice Hopkins tells us, 'Dr. James Hinton used to wander about at night and break his heart over the sights he saw and the tales he heard.[41] Nor was soliciting confined to the streets. In her old age Rebecca Jarrett recalled the Cremorne Gardens, a popular pleasure resort of the period, as she had known them in the 1860's. 'You could spend days in those gardens, drink as much as you like, and there were lonely walks; you could be lost for hours there. It was there I first saw the degraded life of immorality—not in the streets.'[42] Juvenile prostitution and procuring, suicide and attempted suicide, abortion and infanticide all took place on a scale which would have surprised respectable citizens, and with an impunity which was to shock the reformers and, when exposed by them, the whole nation.

It was a situation which existing rescue work, devoted as it was, was inadequate to remedy and indeed hardly touched. 'Self-devoted women', backed by concerned and compassionate men, were spending themselves in their efforts to rescue individual girls and women but were doing little or nothing to challenge the presuppositions on which rested the continuance of the evil they were endeavouring to combat.[43] The prostitution of a number of women in order to satisfy the sexual demands of men was, in general, looked upon as an inevitable part of the social order; the social and economic conditions which helped to promote this situation were ignored or thought too difficult to change, and the work of prevention was given less prominence than that of rescue. A new appraisal of the situation was needed, and during the last quarter of the century this was forthcoming, mainly through the new insights brought to bear on the problem by two remarkable women, Josephine Butler and Ellice Hopkins.

Neither of these two clear-headed and dedicated women was solely, or even primarily, interested in decreasing 'the social evil'. Their concern was a more radical one, the creation of a society with a single moral standard for both men and women, and closely allied to this, a legal and judicial system which should be impartial as between the sexes. At the same time, by specific reforms and practical measures of help, they sought to make it less easy for girls to 'go wrong', to hinder those who invited them to do so, and to substitute compassion towards them for the current hostility and condemnation. Their three points of attack were legal reform to make exploitation more difficult and less rewarding, educational work aimed at raising the tone of public opinion and increasing public understanding of the causes, social and economic as well as ethical, of prostitution, and, thirdly preventive work to improve the conditions of life of the most vulnerable women and girls and give them practical assistance before it was too late.

The longest and most controversial of the campaigns for legal reform was that waged to bring about the repeal of the Contagious Diseases Acts, a campaign to which Josephine Butler devoted her energies and talents and with which her name will always be associated.[44] In part a straightforward attack on the double moral standard and an assertion of the equal status of men and women, it was also, and perhaps primarily, an attack on the mores of a society which outlawed the prostitute so completely that even the common processes of justice were not considered applicable where she was concerned.

Another legal battle, and one in which both Mrs. Butler and Miss Hopkins were involved, was that which resulted in the passing of the Criminal Law (Amendment) Act, 1885. This Act, which raised the age of consent to 16 and made further provision for the protection of women and children and the suppression of brothels encountered much opposition, and was only passed after the sensational articles published by W. T. Stead in the *Pall Mall Gazette* under the title, 'The Maiden Tribute of Modern Babylon' had convinced the British public that girls of thirteen and under were being bought or kidnapped and sold

23

into virtual slavery at home or abroad in order to satisfy the lusts of men of wealth and influence.[45]

The revelation by Stead's 'Secret Commission' of widespread corruption, immorality and hypocrisy underlined the undesirable effects of the 'double moral standard' and the need for a change in society's attitude towards the sexual misdemeanours of men. Men had taken much of the initiative in organising rescue work among women, especially in the early days, but it had not hitherto been thought that they themselves might also need or indeed would respond to help and guidance in connection with their own sexual problems. The belief was widespread that it was impossible, or if not impossible, damaging to their health, for men to control their passions;[46] alternatively they were simply denounced as wicked seducers of helpless women, meriting condemnation but not amenable to reformation.[47] The credit for suggesting a less negative approach belongs principally to Ellice Hopkins who, with the support of a number of outstanding men both inside and outside the Church of England, first developed large scale educational work among men.

Born in 1836, the youngest daughter of a Cambridge mathematician, Ellice Hopkins early took an active interest in evangelistic and social work among the poor. But it was Dr. James Hinton, who wished to be remembered as a man 'who went mad over the wrongs of women', and died, it was said, of a broken heart, who persuaded her 'to give her life and unusual powers to the effort to rouse the world to a hatred of immorality and a higher standard of living'. He longed for her 'to rouse educated women, and through them their husbands and their sons to a sense of their duty with regard to the social evil'.[48] From then on, although frail in health, she spent most of her time 'holding meetings, organising practical work, agitating for greater legal protection of the young'. In 1879 she addressed the Church Penitentiary Association on the need for work among men and called for the establishment of 'a great National Society' of men 'pledged to the protection of women and children and to the propagation among their own sex of a high ideal of masculine conduct and responsibility'.

In due course her advocacy led to the foundation of the Church of England Purity Society and the White Cross Army (not specifically Anglican), both in 1883. Eight years later the two amalgamated to form the White Cross League, a movement which captured the imagination of large numbers of men and which, during the first years of its existence, spread very rapidly. It demanded from its members high standards of personal conduct and a 'chivalrous respect for womanhood'. By example and precept they were to endeavour to raise the tone of public opinion in matters of sexual purity and combat the prevailing double standard.[49] Meanwhile, Ellice Hopkins by her speaking and writing was endeavouring to rouse women 'to face the facts of their own womanhood and not to leave to chance the instruction of their sons about the "facts of life" and their responsibilities in this respect'.[50]

Apart from work among men, in which she was the leading figure, and her interest in the Criminal Law Amendment campaign, Ellice Hopkins was deeply concerned about the need to help wayward and friendless young girls in danger of drifting onto the streets. 'What chiefly strikes me,' she wrote in one of her numerous pamphlets,

is that on all sides we are leaving regular manufactories of degraded womanhood in full play, and then burdening ourselves with penitentiaries, rescue societies, hospitals, prisons, work houses, etc. to accommodate the results. Again and again I cry, were it not better at one tenth the expense and labour to close the manufactory? Were it not better to fence this terrible social precipice at the top rather than content ourselves with providing ambulances at the bottom.[51]

Hence she devoted a good deal of attention to founding Associations for the Care of Friendless Girls in the larger towns. They were to provide 'free registry offices, training homes, clothing clubs, etc.' as a means of keeping a hold on 'ignorant girls when first launched into the world'.[52]

The relationship between Josephine Butler, Ellice Hopkins and their associates, who were emphasising the need for a new approach to the whole problem of immorality and pressing for reform, and the men and women who continued to put their faith in the principles and methods of rescue work which had been developed over the century and which were by now firmly established, appear to have been somewhat ambivalent. In the initial stages of her campaign against the Contagious Diseases Acts,

Mrs. Butler received valuable support and guidance from Daniel Cooper, secretary to the London Rescue Society, who 'enlisted the help of all the societies with which he co-operated',[53] but there were other workers, equally sincere, who evidently felt that the publicity which the agitators drew upon themselves by their unwise conduct' was doing 'wide and fearful harm' to the cause of purity.[54] Neither Josephine Butler nor Ellice Hopkins underestimated the need for succouring or even providing institutional care for girls and women leading lives of vice and misery, but they were critical of the quality of the work done, and in particular of the harsh and rigid treatment often given to such girls in rescue homes and penitentiaries, treatment which, they stressed, punished 'not their sin but their penitence'.[55]

Criticism of this kind was not confined to the reformers and outsiders; some uneasiness was evidently felt by the more enlightened of those actively engaged in the work. For example, the writers of two textbooks on the subject, which appeared in 1885 and 1894 respectively,[56] both commented on the 'over strictness and mistakes in treatment in some homes', while Mrs. Bramwell Booth, in charge of the developing rescue work of the Salvation Army, was even more sharply critical of certain long-stay training homes she visited. 'No one over twenty-five was admitted, no girl with a baby of whatever age. Young women were kept in these places for one, two, or even three years. Bolts and bars; bare dismal rooms, high walls, no occupation except laundry work; she could not imagine herself becoming any better for a long stay in similar surroundings.'[57] Even by Victorian standards conditions in penitentiaries and similar homes were often austere and forbidding, and many girls, even those in dire need, must have hesitated to submit to the stern discipline, hard work and repellent uniforms they knew they would find there.

Nor was over-strictness the only feature of rescue work which detracted from its effectiveness. Despite the existence of the two co-ordinating societies already mentioned and the entry of the Salvation Army,[58] and its companion organisation the Church Army,[59] into the field, much of the work was still localised and run by small *ad hoc* committees, whose standards could and did vary,[60] and whose chronic shortage of money meant that many homes were largely dependent on the earnings of the laundry, an annexe to nearly every home. Classification, by this time accepted in principle, might in practice be sacrificed to the need to keep the home full and so balance the budget, or, on the other hand be applied so rigidly as to drive away cases which both needed and were looking for help, in particular mothers with their second illegitimate child. Moreover, even if the work had been systematically organised and standards improved it would still have been inadequate to meet the need.

It would be a mistake, however, simply to write off the considerable provision for helping women and girls, particularly by means of rescue homes, which existed at the end of the nineteenth century as harsh and punishing, incompetent and ineffectual. In the first place, in providing for a group almost totally rejected by contemporary society, rescue workers were tackling a job which few others would touch. Moreover, while hard work and strict discipline were the general rule, this did not necessarily rule out compassion for and a real desire to befriend those in need of help. 'You are not asking the women to come and join in a service, you are asking them to be your guests, that you may have the opportunity of making friends with them . . .' wrote the Rev. Arthur Brinckman about night services in his *Notes on Rescue Work*,[61] and a little later in the book he tells those running shelters that 'whoever is in charge should open the door . . . and make the coming inmate feel at home and welcomed at once'.[62] To some, at least, residence in a home brought a sense of security and a knowledge of being loved and wanted not hitherto experienced.[63]

While motives might sometimes appear mixed,[64] the basis of rescue work was religious; it was undertaken for the love of God and activated by a belief in the eternal worth of each human soul.[65] It was no accident that the streetworkers were known as missionaries, for their approach was markedly evangelistic,[66] while the atmosphere and routine of the homes to which the girls were sent emphasised the religious nature and purpose of the work.[67] But basically religious as it might be, the work was as yet in no sense the organised effort of the Church as an institution to grapple with a problem which those who cared saw as a slur on a civilisation allegedly Christian. The attitude of the Established Church to the repeal of the Contagious Diseases Acts had been equivocal, although Josephine Butler and her friends had won more support as time went on.[68] In the last decades of the century the Church had begun to play a more positive and active part in purity work among men, but the ambulance work among women was slow to receive official support. Neither the Church Penitentiary Association nor the Reformatory and Refuge Union, carrying as they did their party labels, could claim to speak or act on behalf of the Church of England as a whole, and while the value of the work being carried out by the Church Army was becoming increasingly recognised, it was that of an independent organisation.

In 1879, as the result of a petition presented by the Church Penitentiary Association, the Convocation of Canterbury appointed a committee to consider 'the question of prostitution, its alleged increase and the best means of recovering the fallen'.[69] Six years later, the Chairman of this 'Committee on the Recovery of Fallen Women', moved a number of resolutions, one of which was 'that it is desirable to invite diocesan conferences to use their influence for the maintenance and restoration of female purity by encouraging the initiation of industrial homes for girls and penitentiaries for fallen women' and another, 'that societies consisting of women as well as men should be formed for the purpose of ascertaining the condition of towns and villages in each diocese and reporting from time to time to the conference.'[70] Neither resolution escaped criticism and the debate appears to have had no immediate effect. It was not long, however, before dioceses began to appoint women organising secretaries for preventive and rescue work, London and St. Albans leading the way in 1890, Rochester coming next in 1894.[71] Slowly and tentatively the church was beginning to accept direct responsibility for the work done in its name, but it was not until another thirty years had passed that the first steps were taken towards the creation of a central organisation, and then it needed the wife of an Archbishop to support and guide them.[72]

Meanwhile the problem of finding and training an adequate number of suitable women to meet the demands of the work was already proving, as it has continued to prove, one of the most serious obstacles to its maintenance and extension. The only qualification required of the earliest workers was that they should be 'self-devoted' women, their primary objective the saving of souls. At that stage in the development of the work its difficulty eliminated the incompetent, and the social obloquy attached to all work for 'the fallen' guaranteed the motives of those who took it up. As time went on, however, these tests became less reliable. Women began to be attracted to rescue work because it offered them a home of their own, 'something to do', or even 'from the wish of obtaining training in laundry work' while the constant shortage of suitable workers meant that 'Institutions for the rescue of women find it impossible to obtain the class of workers they need, and are often compelled to accept the services of persons whom they know too well to be unsuitable'.[73]

By the end of the century it was becoming recognised that 'the work is one which eminently needs special qualifications and special training'.[74] Most of the training available at that time was what we should now call 'in-service'. The new recruit gained experience by working with a seasoned worker, with perhaps opportunities for visits to different types of homes and for some teaching and discussion. In 1898, however, St. Agnes' House was opened in London as both the central house of the Order of Divine Compassion, an order of women who devoted their lives to rescue and preventive work, and as a training home for students. Throughout the early years of the twentieth century St. Agnes' remained the only training house in the country, but in 1911 St. Monica's Refuge, Liverpool, moved to larger premises and the first training scheme in the north was started there by Miss J. E. Higson, who was both the worker in charge of the refuge and the first organising secretary to be appointed in the diocese of Liverpool.[75]

The courses offered by the two training houses were very similar. Within the framework of a more or less strictly disciplined devotional life they provided opportunities for practical experience with study of the theoretical background of moral welfare work.[76] At the end of their training students were regarded as fully qualified, but were sometimes given the opportunity of gaining further experience under the supervision of an experienced worker. After this they were sent, where possible, to dioceses where they could begin to organise the work on what was regarded as a proper footing.

The shortage of trained workers remained severe, however, and during the First World War two conferences were held which foreshadowed a more comprehensive plan. The impact of one of these, a conference designed to bring together experienced workers and enquirers and to help both groups in formulating 'more clear and specific statements of the ideals and principles underlying rescue work' and held in 1915, was later assessed by Miss Higson in these words: 'Though the Josephine Butler Memorial House was not opened until five years after this conference, I regard it as one of the first steps in a new attitude towards the "fallen" and a new conception of the training necessary for rescue work'.[77] Both the 'new attitude' and the new conception of training were needed to meet the new conditions created by the First World War which, whether the participants in this particular conference realised it or not, marked the end of one era and the beginning of another.

2

MORAL WELFARE WORK
BETWEEN THE WARS

I

IT was widely accepted at the time, and has been since, that the 'Great War' of 1914-18 marked the end of one era and the transition to another. But the economic and social changes which took place, although marked, and in some cases even revolutionary, were by no means all pervasive, and much that was characteristic of pre-war England survived the cataclysm of war and persisted as a conservative and stabilising influence in a rapidly changing situation. Hence, 'any analysis of the condition of Britain in the twenties must take into account these two characteristics, stability, more evident in some parts of the national scene than others, but never absent, and change, intruding everywhere, particularly in material conditions, but never all triumphant'.[1] In this respect moral welfare work reflects the characteristics of its time, for while in the work as a whole a new spirit and outlook was evident, and new methods were being evolved to meet new conditions and needs, yet, to some extent and in some quarters, old-fashioned ideas still persisted despite their inappropriateness to the new era.

A new approach was both necessary and unavoidable, for the effect of the war on the economic and social position of women, the conventions governing the relationships between the sexes, and on standards and values generally, was both marked and far-reaching, while although the disruption of family life was, perhaps, not as widespread or as noticeable as during the Second World War, yet it was serious enough and brought its own problems. Intensive recruitment, at first voluntary and later by means of conscription, drained the country of its younger men. This both robbed women of their husbands and sweethearts, and, as the war went on, forced them to undertake unaccustomed tasks in unfamiliar surroundings and conditions. They were called upon to replace the men in shops, offices and factories, on the land, and even as auxiliaries to the army itself. This gave the young women brought up in the sheltered conditions of the early twentieth century greater freedom and a more independent status than they had ever known, and although, when the armistice was signed, and the men demobilised, women workers were dismissed in large numbers,[2] all that had been gained in independence and in easier and freer relationships between the sexes was not lost. As the years went on openings for women workers increased again despite the overall problem of unemployment which was beginning to make itself felt, while middle-class girls began to make careers for themselves in the various professions now open to them and in business.

These new opportunities were all important for the women of that generation, for one legacy of the slaughter in France and Flanders was the large number of 'surplus' women, young widows faced with the prospect of years of loneliness and spinsters denied the probability of marriage.[3] Many of these women were able to find an acceptable substitute for marriage and family life in creative and satisfying work, including the developing profession of social work to which they made a notable contribution, but this did not meet the needs of more than a proportion of the women so placed, and there was a great deal of restlessness and frustration. This was reflected in the rather brittle gaiety of the period, in the straight boyish fashions which played down the wearer's womanliness, and, in apparent contradiction to this denial of her sex, the plea now beginning to be made vocal that motherhood should be recognised as the right of every woman whether married or not.[4] Meanwhile the spreading knowledge and use of contraceptive techniques, at least among the more educated, reduced the risk of unwanted children whether within or outside marriage and this in itself created an additional challenge to accepted beliefs and practices.[5]

Changes in the pattern of the birth-rate took place both during and immediately after the War. Between 1911 and 1918, the legitimate birth-rate decreased steadily from 23.1 per 1,000 of the population in 1911 to 16.6 per 1,000 in 1918. This was not altogether surprising in view of the absence of so many young husbands on active service, but it caused a certain amount of anxiety about the country's future,[6] and this, joined to a widespread, if rather confused and inarticulate, feeling that at a time when so many young men were being killed it was important to save the babies, stimulated the development of all forms of maternity and child welfare work. The culmination of these developments was the Maternity and Child Welfare Act, 1918, which empowered local authorities to make such arrangements as might be sanctioned by the Local Government Board (later the Ministry of Health) for the purpose of attending to the health of expectant and nursing mothers and children under school age. Local authorities were empowered by the Act to make grants to voluntary organisations, a provision which proved to be of considerable importance to organisations catering for the unmarried mother and her child, for this statutory assistance, with its attendant requirement of inspection, both made increased residential provision for mothers and babies possible and led to improvements in standards.[7]

Meanwhile attention had been drawn to the special hazards of the illegitimate child by no less a person than the Registrar General himself. During the war period, when the legitimate birth-rate was declining, the illegitimate birth-rate remained more or less constant at a proportion of about 1 per 1,000 of the population. With the concurrent fall in the number of legitimate births this meant that the percentage of illegitimate to all live births was increasing, and it rose from 4.2 per cent in 1914 to 6.3 per cent in 1918. But if a higher proportion of illegitimate babies were being born, a higher proportion of them were dying, and in his Report for 1916 the Registrar General drew attention to the disquieting increase in the ratio of illegitimate to legitimate infant mortality especially in the first week of life. 'The facts suggest,' he wrote, 'that infant welfare organisations might well devote special attention to the first few days in the life of the illegitimate child.'

The response to this challenge, which served to reinforce the experience of knowledgeable child welfare workers, was the formation of the National Council for the Unmarried Mother and Her Child.[8] This Council was brought into being at a conference of representatives of organisations concerned with the problem, held in February 1918, and from the first it set out to be a reformist and propaganda rather than a casework agency. It regarded its foremost task as that of educating public opinion, of teaching men and women to be constructive rather than deterrent in their approach to the unmarried mother and her problems. Its promoters emphasised that, whatever the faults and follies of his parent, the child was not to blame, and they contended that the best way to help both mother and child was to keep them together. Hence a guiding principle of the Council's work was that the separation of mother and child was to be tolerated only as 'an exceptional and deplorable necessity'.

The Council insisted, moreover, that the responsibilities of fatherhood must be recognised as well as those of motherhood, and schemes for the welfare of the unmarried mother must include means for bringing home this responsibility more effectively. Hence, one of its first tasks was to try to get the 5s. a week, the maximum amount then payable under an affiliation order, raised to a more realistic sum, and during its early years, efforts to bring about this and other changes in the law in order to improve the position of the unmarried mother and her child took up a great deal of its time and energy. At the same time however, the Council's staff, small though it was, had to deal with enquiries concerning individuals which soon numbered between 600 and 800 a year,[9] and the office became a recognised clearing-house for the whole country, its purpose being 'to put enquirers as rapidly as possible into touch with the people and organisations best able to give them the exact kind of help they required'. This involved co-operation with local associations 'particularly the Church of England Diocesan Associations', whose 'special competence in these matters was recognised'.

As already pointed out, it was the considered policy of the N.C.U.M.C. to ensure that, whenever possible, mother and child should remain together, the mother being assisted and supported in her efforts to maintain and care for her child, but during these same immediate post-war years a new movement was gaining ground which sought to provide a normal home and family for the child, but at the cost of complete separation from his mother. This was the movement to legalise adoption. As with the N.C.U.M.C. the movement gained impetus as a result of the

1914-18 war, since this had the concurrent effects of depriving a large number of families of their sons and of creating an increasing number of unwanted children, and it was in 1919, within a year of the foundation of the N.C.U.M.C., that, following a conference of the Associated Societies for the Care and Maintenance of Infants, a small committee was set up 'to investigate, report, and guide the opinion of the nation' in adoption matters.

By 1926 the efforts of the enthusiasts for this means of 'turning the "unwanted" into the "wanted" child'[10] had been crowned with success by the passing of the Adoption of Children Act of that year. This Act not only legalised adoption but laid down legal requirements and methods of procedure, and remained the basic legislation in matters pertaining to adoption until it was repealed by the reforming and consolidating Adoption Act, 1959.

Illegitimacy was not the only social problem associated with irregular sexual relationships which received attention during this period. The campaign led by Josephine Butler in the 1870's had put an end to a thoroughly misguided attempt to deal with the problem of venereal disease, but the problem itself remained unsolved. Not until the discoveries made by Wasserman and Erlich in the first decade of the twentieth century provided the means of scientific diagnosis and satisfactory treatment, could effective measures be taken by public health authorities to combat these diseases, but with the aid of the resources thus made available it became possible to envisage a nationwide prophylactic service. In 1913 a Royal Commission was set up under the Chairmanship of Baron Sydenham 'to inquire into the prevalence of venereal diseases in the United Kingdom, their effects upon the health of the community and the means by which those effects can be alleviated or prevented, it being understood that no return to the policy and provisions of the Contagious Diseases Acts of 1864, 1866 or 1869 is to be regarded as falling within the scope of the inquiry'.[11]

The Commission reported in 1916, and the widespread publicity which the Report received was itself symptomatic of the changing attitude towards the problem which the war was helping to bring about. Its recommendations were put into operation the following year by Local Government Board Regulations which made it obligatory for county councils and county borough councils to make provision for the free and confidential treatment of venereal diseases, 75 per cent of the cost being borne by central government funds. 'By the end of the year 1918 the Veneral Diseases Service had taken its place along with the Tuberculosis and Child Welfare Services as an essential part of the national provision for the care of the health of the people.'[12] Both compulsion to submit to treatment and compulsory notification of the disease itself were ruled out. Instead the service relied for its effectiveness on a combination of freely available confidential treatment and educational propaganda, and, whether or not as a consequence of the measures recommended by the Commission, the years following their introduction did in fact see 'a remarkable reduction in the mortality from and incidence of the venereal diseases'.[13] Follow-up measures formed part of the scheme, but it was not until considerably later that any almoners were appointed to V.D. clinics, and, until then, what little social work was done in this field was undertaken by moral welfare workers.

The First World War and the years immediately following were thus years of change and development in those aspects of individual and social life with which moral welfare workers were most deeply concerned, while new social and health measures were being evolved to deal with the changing situation. All this inevitably constituted a challenge to moral welfare work itself. 'Men and women are now planning reconstruction—they are discarding bad old methods that have proved useless and good old methods that have served their day—cannot we have the courage to do the same?' urged the Organising Secretary of the diocese of Southwark, Miss Morris, in 1918.[14] But changes of this kind would involve a re-appraisal not only of existing moral welfare work but of the attitude of the Church to sexual and related problems. There are indications that such a re-examination was in fact taking place in the Report of the Lambeth Conference 1920, and it is even more evident in the Report of the Conference on Christian Politics, Economics and Citizenship (C.O.P.E.C.) held at Birmingham in April 1924, which was an attempt by forward looking Christians of all denominations to consider the application of Christian social ethics to contemporary problems of human relationships.

When the Conference met it became obvious that there were

deep divisions of opinion between delegates on the two questions of birth control and divorce, both very much to the fore at the time, and the delegates took refuge in what appears to have been a compromise resolution. The Conference urged the churches represented 'to investigate and to consider with the intention of offering definite guidance to perplexed consciences, this and other relevant questions regarding marriage and parenthood. It would meanwhile lay emphasis on the privileges and responsibilities of Christian parenthood'.[15] But although differences of doctrine stultified the Conference's witness in connection with these two important issues, there seems to have been a wide measure of agreement on what the Churches' attitude should be with regard to other problems of sexual morality.

It would appear from both the C.O.P.E.C. pronouncements and the discussions which took place at the Lambeth Conference in 1920,[16] that not only specialist organisations such as the White Cross League and the Association of Moral and Social Hygiene, but the Churches themselves were calling for a new and more constructive approach to these questions. Inhibitions and prejudices died hard[17] but the desirability of creating a more enlightened public opinion in connection with such matters and the Churches' responsibilities in this regard were slowly being recognised.

One of the issues on which it was felt that enlightenment was badly needed was that of the possibility and desirability of a single standard of chastity for both men and women, and, as a corollary of this, a change in existing attitudes towards those who failed to live up to this standard. This would involve the exercise of 'greater understanding and forgiveness towards women, so that no longer would a "life sentence" be passed on girls who tripped on life's threshold',[18] while the hope was also expressed that 'those touched with the sympathy which shone in the life of Christ' might 'seek out and reclaim fallen men' as well as fallen women.[19] Existing rescue work for women was, it was believed, already being transformed by the new spirit that was abroad, an optimistic view that was reflected in the Report of the Committee on Problems of Marriage and Sexual Morality to the 1920 Lambeth Conference. 'In the case of those who have sinned' the authors of this Report wrote, 'methods of repression are largely discredited. It is recognised that the beauty and happiness of a

Christian life should be held before them and represented in the cheerful surroundings of the Home, and in a loving Christian fellowship, along with the discipline which is needed for building the character.'[20]

Unfortunately these statements appear to represent aspirations rather than realities, and another report, *Rescue Work—an Enquiry and Criticism* published for private circulation by the Committee of Social Investigation and Reform[21] in 1919, is less reassuring. It is a mixed and uneven document. The chapters dealing with different aspects of the work are by different contributors, and some chapters are simply short accounts of the writer's own work and the conclusions she draws from it, as for example a chapter headed 'Preventive Club Work' and an interesting study of prostitution in the Piccadilly area. On the other hand the long chapter on 'Rescue Homes' is based on something in the nature of a general survey and incorporates data derived from questionnaires circulated to a hundred Rescue Homes of all kinds and denominations. It is indicative of the current situation that this chapter takes up nearly half the Report; the work of the homes was evidently still regarded as central to the whole venture.

While the Committee recognised that much good work had been and was being accomplished by workers, both religious and secular, who are described as 'unflagging in their devotion', its general conclusions were critical, and it appears from what the authors of the Report have to say that there was still much to be done before it could truthfully be asserted that beauty and happiness were replacing harsh discipline and monotonous work in rescue homes. 'When we turn to the individual girl' was the Report's damning conclusion, 'we recognise that according to present day conditions, the system of so called "rescue work" leaves much to be desired. With the outstanding exception of the Salvation Army and one or two other small attempts, it seems to be based on the conception that the individual has committed the worst of crimes and the best way to "reclaim" her is to so arrange her life that it shall be spent in contemplation of the crime committed.'[22]

Penitentiaries (and the continued use of the word is itself significant) still approximated to 'a standard of extreme simplicity, almost of severity', with the tradition still persisting that 'comfort should be reduced to a minimum and that the "penitents" should learn through hardness to be "good soldiers" in the warfare of life rather than that goodness should be made attractive and life beautiful'.[23] Maternity homes 'with rare exceptions' excluded any but first cases, and when the time came for the girl to leave, the system most favoured was that of placing the child in the care of a foster-mother and sending the mother into domestic service. 'The most pitiable side of rescue work is the sufferings of the babies when the mothers go into service; the child is often passed from one woman to another and does not thrive, for an unloved child never thrives,' commented one worker, anticipating Dr. Bowlby's findings by thirty years. Even good work was hampered by lack of funds, for although grant aid from Poor Law or municipal authorities was available for creches, maternity homes and the treatment of venereal disease, many homes were still largely dependent on the 'alms of the faithful and the earnings of the wash-tub'. Salaries, when they were paid at all, were pitiably small[24] and heads of homes had to practise the strictest economy even sometimes, it would appear, to the detriment of the health of their charges.[25]

This was the Committee's indictment, but there were redeeming features. There were workers who showed not only understanding of and regard for individual girls, but evinced a real willingness to experiment in such matters as giving residents greater freedom and responsibility, substituting cubicles for open dormitories so as to ensure greater privacy, replacing ugly uniforms by more attractive and up-to-date clothes, and in general 'trying to make life as ordinary as possible, so that when they leave, the transition may not be too great a change', and they may 'go back to the ordinary daily life of the world healthier minded girls'.[26]

But these changes, good though they were, were merely tinkering. The real issue was whether in the changed conditions of the post-war world there was any place at all for rescue homes of the traditional type, and if not, what was to take their place. The opinion of the Committee was that, 'Rescue Homes *as* Rescue Homes, i.e., known by this or a kindred name and considered as places of refuge for "fallen women" with a stigma attaching to the inmates from the very fact of having been there, should not continue to exist.' What was required was a variety of residential

39

provision to meet particular needs. Such provision should include medical homes (for V.D. cases), residential hostels and temporary hostels for women workers and mothers with their babies, together with homes for mentally deficient girls and women.[27] These new residential provisions would embody 'the new spirit which is pervading rescue work and all work among young people, and a wise, humane policy of education and development'.[28]

It was a long time before these hopes were anything like fulfilled, and for many years the old and the new continued to exist side by side. This was noted by the Departmental Committee on Sexual Offences against Young Persons' in its Report published in 1926. 'There are Homes still managed on the lines of an old-fashioned penitentiary,' the Committee stated, and continued, 'Girls coming from such Homes are often lacking in initiative, so that when they leave they are at a loss because they miss the constant supervision to which they have been accustomed.' At the same time they recognised that 'many Rescue Homes have well-equipped premises and up-to-date schemes for education and training and allow scope for the development of personality;—from these, the after results obtained have been very satisfactory'.[29]

Although in the twenties new ideas were being discussed and practised in residential work, it was in the increasingly important outdoor work that the winds of change were blowing most strongly. A new generation of workers had grown up 'in the atmosphere of Christian social reform, of war work and the campaign for women's suffrage', and they held the old phraseology and many of the old assumptions in anger and contempt. Why they asked, did ' "the fallen" denote breakers of the seventh commandment (and only the seventh) where women were concerned, and heroes of the Great War, if it were men. If anyone needed "mercy" it was the slum landlord and the payer of sweated wages. It was society at large who should be the "penitents" for refusing to face and condemn the unjust conventions that poisoned social life.'[30] These workers called for a new attitude both towards the individual needing help and in the work as a whole, and during the succeeding years the new approach slowly gained ground, although the older tradition still persisted, at least in some circles.[31]

Perhaps the most important characteristic of the newer

approach was its greater flexibility, which, in turn, was associated with a clearer understanding of, and respect for, the feelings and wishes of the person helped. In contrast to the approach whereby 'the worker will try to get at the girl's better self, and lead her to wish, or at least consent, to be taken to a refuge as a means of entrance to a two year home . . .'[32] was that summarised by Miss Morris.

Whether a person is helped by being placed in a Home or by having work found for her is a matter of secondary importance; the great thing is that she should be helped according to her individual need. It is no good offering people help they cannot accept; and too often we talk as if doing what is right could only mean going into a Home or following the particular course we have mapped out. . . . In our zeal for speedy arrivals we forget that each soul must take its own way however long and tedious that may be.[33]

At this time not only was the outlook of many workers becoming more flexible, the scope of the work was widening both in ideal and practice, although it appears that it was largely centred on problems of personal conduct, and frequently, though not always, on problems involving irregular sexual relationships. Examples of cases likely to be brought to the notice of the outdoor worker are listed by Miss Cole as, women living by immorality, unmarried mothers, girls in 'acute temptation', patients suffering from venereal disease, plaintiffs or young witnesses in assault cases, 'troublesome girls' whose parents ask for assistance, and boy or girls 'with bad moral background'. Sources of referral were as varied as cases referred, and when discussing the ways in which help may be given she lays stress on the value of co-operation with other agencies, 'for wise co-operation is a tribute to efficient work'. The 'moral welfare worker' as she was now beginning to call herself, evidently regarded herself as a social as well as a church worker, and was prepared to adapt the resources and skills of this developing profession to meet the particular needs of her own cases. Through it all, however, she remained convinced that it was the love of Christ which she was showing forth in her work, and her ultimate aim was to put the girl in a right relationship, 'not only with her family, with industry, with friends, but with God.'[34]

One of the ways in which during this period the scope of

moral welfare work was being widened was the initiation in some dioceses of specialist help for child victims of criminal assault, children suffering from venereal disease and those 'with bad or immoral tendencies'. Southwark, where a Children's Committee and worker were appointed as early as 1914,[35] seems to have been the first diocese to make special provision of this kind, acting in conjunction with the London County Council Care Committees, and in London children's moral welfare work has developed along its own lines, a little apart from the main stream of moral welfare work. By 1918 a 'trained worker' had been appointed by the Liverpool Education Authority acting in conjunction with the Diocesan Association for Preventive and Rescue Work in that city and by 1928 children's workers were at work in the Isle of Wight, Manchester and Cardiff.[36] It was work which brought those undertaking it into close touch with other social, health and educational workers, and to some extent it both anticipated and reflected current public concern about both the welfare of children and young people in moral danger of one kind or another, and the inadequacy of existing measures for helping them. This concern issued in the setting up of two Inter-Departmental Committees, the one under the chairmanship of Sir Ryland Adkins to consider the special problems associated with sexual offences against young persons, the other with Sir Evelyn Cecil (later replaced by Sir Thomas F. Molony) as chairman, to review the whole question of the treatment of the young offender.

The Adkins Committee reported in 1926.[37] It dealt mainly with the prevalence of sexual offences against children and young people and with possible improvements in the existing law and its administration, but one section of the report was devoted to the welfare of the young persons offended against. Although tribute was paid to the special work undertaken by voluntary organisations to help child victims of sex offences, the after care of these children was described as 'spasmodic and unco-ordinated' and the committee was not convinced that specialist help was necessarily in the best interests of the child as it might result in too great an emphasis being placed on an incident which should be forgotten. Instead, the children and young persons concerned should be cared for 'under the general scheme of child welfare in each district'. Similarly, it was felt that, while a country holiday might be an excellent method of distracting the child's attention from the incident, removal to a special institution for long term care and training should not take place 'unless the necessity for this action is clearly established', for, 'to remove a child who has already suffered greatly as a result of the offence and send it to a Home is but to add yet another hardship to all that the child has already undergone.'[38] There were, however, cases where this regrettable necessity had to be faced, and in both Southwark and Liverpool the development of case work with assaulted children and their families brought home to the respective diocesan organisations the need for the establishment of small homes where psychologically damaged and disturbed children could receive loving individual care.

More far-reaching in its effects than the Report of the Adkins Committee was that of the Molony Committee on Young Offenders,[39] the recommendations of which were embodied in the Children and Young Persons Act, 1933. From the point of view of moral welfare workers, probably the most important recommendations were those concerning 'neglected children and young persons',[40] recommendations which were concerned to close the gaps in existing legislation. At that time it was still possible for children to remain for long periods 'in the worst possible surroundings and without any proper guardianship being exercised by their parents' since they could not be brought before the court unless and until they committed an offence. Child victims of incest could themselves be removed from the guardianship of their parents, but no similar action was possible in the case of other children in the home, nor could any statutory protection be given to girls 'entirely out of hand and in imminent risk of moral contamination'. The Committee was satisfied that 'a more consistent and comprehensive policy' was required, and the 1933 Act gave juvenile courts powers for dealing with children and young persons 'in need of care or protection', a category which included those 'in moral danger'.[41]

The legislation thus brought into being was bound to have long term effects on the scope and character of the work of moral welfare associations, particularly on what was then generally known as 'preventive' work. Cases which voluntary organisations had hitherto dealt with as best they could, would, in future, come within the scope of the new legislation since the children or young

43

people concerned could be brought before a juvenile court as 'in need of care or protection' and, if the case was proved, committed to the care of the local authority (usually the local education authority) under a 'fit person' order, or if necessary sent to an approved school. It looked as though the assumption of these new responsibilities by the statutory services might lessen those of the voluntary organisations, but there were also new possibilities of co-operation, while moral welfare associations had a continuing responsibility for the many cases which were still outside the scope of the law, or, it was thought, could best be helped without invoking its machinery. In the thirties moral welfare workers in many parts of the country were acting as part time probation officers, shelters were recognised as remand homes or 'places of safety' and girls found to be 'in need of care or protection' were sometimes sent to moral welfare homes for long term training instead of to approved schools. The workers of the period were evidently playing a real part in developments which were taking place in connection with the treatment of delinquents and near delinquents, and if sometimes, as with part-time probation work and the use of shelters as remand homes, their contribution was but to hold the fort until the statutory services were ready fully to take over, this was nevertheless necessary and valuable work, and work which, at that time, only an established voluntary organisation could undertake.

II

So far, in considering the development of moral welfare work in the twenties and early thirties, we have been considering it primarily as social work directed towards helping individuals faced with particular problems and in need of particular kinds of social care. But moral welfare work is not only social work; it is social work done in the name of the Church, and from this point of view the most significant development of the period was the gradual transformation of what was originally 'a small informal group of friends acting in an advisory capacity to field workers and others concerned with the problems with which they were dealing' into a properly constituted Board that had received recognition as part of the central machinery of the Church—the

Church of England Advisory Board for Moral Welfare Work.[42] Before the end of the period under review the Board was playing a leading part in the work as a whole, not only in this country, but overseas also.[43]

Much of the credit for this transformation must go to Edith Davidson, the wife of Randall Davidson, Archbishop of Canterbury 1903-1928.[44] As early as 1913 she invited a small group of organising secretaries and representatives to meet at Lambeth Palace; similar conferences were held in 1915 and 1917 and by February 1918 an advisory body was in existence which had agreed on a constitution for an 'Advisory Board' to be appointed by the Archbishops of Canterbury and York. This Board was to consist of ten members appointed by the Archbishops from a list of names submitted to them, and it was hoped that it would be of use to the dioceses in the following ways:—

(a) by collecting and imparting necessary and up-to-date legislative information.
(b) by reporting progress and development of new methods.
(c) by providing visitors and special speakers when required by the Dioceses.
(d) by advising on special difficulties and to decide when action is desirable.
(e) by arousing interest and undertaking work in new centres.[45]

There appears to have been some discussion as to the most appropriate name for the new Board, the one finally adopted being 'The Archbishops' Advisory Board for Spiritual and Moral Work'. Later its sphere of operation was made more specific by substituting 'Preventive and Rescue' for 'Spiritual and Moral', but by 1929 the committee was recommending that it should become the 'Archbishops' Advisory Board for Moral Welfare' on the grounds that this term was increasingly used in the dioceses. Two years later, in January 1932, a significant change of status had taken place and was marked by a new title—'Church of England Advisory Board for Moral Welfare Work'. By this time the Board had been enlarged and its constitution changed so that it was 'really representative of the dioceses' and relationships with the Church Assembly had been established. It was not until June 1934, however, that the Assembly put the Advisory Board on its

45

budget, giving it a grant of £500. The Board had been recognised 'as part of the central machinery of the Church'.

Meanwhile, the Board had more than earned this recognition by the extent of its influence and the range and variety of its interests.[46] Varied as these were, it is clear from the Board's minutes that throughout its formative years, certain questions constituted major and continuing concerns. They were, first the recruitment and training of workers, secondly educational work, including both the enlightenment of public opinion and the provision of information and instruction for young people, and, thirdly, the inclusion of men both as partners in the venture and as within the scope of the work.

The shortage of workers at all levels from kitchen matrons to organising secretaries has always been, and still is, one of the most important limiting factors in the development of moral welfare work, presenting, as it does, an even more intractable problem than that of finance. The two are to some extent interlocked, since moral welfare workers' salaries have generally lagged behind those of other workers in similar fields,[47] but financial considerations apart, the nature and difficulty of the work, the skills it requires and the demands it makes are such that it is unlikely ever to appeal to more than a relatively few educated women. Hence it is necessary to make the opportunities it presents as widely known as possible and to provide adequate training for those who do come forward, and as noted at the end of the last chapter, some steps in this direction had already been taken in the years before the First World War.

The attention of the Advisory Board was drawn to the need for wider recruitment, better salaries and more adequate training of workers even before it was properly constituted. What appear to be the earliest recorded minutes, those for a meeting held in November 1917, embody resolutions from a conference of Diocesan Organising Secretaries urging that 'the lack of workers being the most serious and pressing problem of rescue work', 'more organised efforts should be made by personal appeals to the various women's settlements, training centres and universities', and further, 'that the standard of training and salary of workers be fixed'.[48] Considering the diverse situations and standards in the dioceses and deaneries and the embryonic character and status of the Board, this last was indeed a bold request, and the meeting, while welcoming it in principle, not unnaturally decided that it required 'further thought and consideration'. At the same time the Secretary was asked 'to urge upon Diocesan Secretaries the inadequacy of present salaries and the need for increasing them in the future in order to attract a better type of worker'. With this resolution began the efforts of the Board and its successor, the Moral Welfare Council, to induce diocesan and local associations to pay their workers salaries generally recognised as adequate and appropriate. In time this led the Board to work out and circulate salary scales for different types of workers which they hoped would be adopted throughout the country.

But if workers were to receive professional salaries they must be professionally competent, and parallel with the Board's concern about workers' salaries went its increasing involvement in schemes for their training. The pioneer efforts in this direction already described[49] were inadequate to meet the needs of a time when 'changes in social conditions were demanding a wider training with a social service background which would appeal to the educated woman,'[50] and when, 'while it might not always be necessary to agree with or adopt modern methods,' it was 'surely fatal to ignore them'.[51] Hence, in October 1918, a sub-committee was appointed to draw up a scheme for training workers, with the significant proviso that 'a certificate be part of the scheme as it would be a safeguard against the half-trained worker'.

It was at this juncture that the plans for establishing a training house in Liverpool as a fitting memorial to Josephine Butler, which by this time were beginning to materialise, were brought to the notice of the Advisory Board, who were asked to support the venture and appoint members to its Committee of Management. The Board, while disclaiming all responsibility, financial or otherwise, acceded to the request for representation on the House Committee and allowed a fund to be opened from the central office to benefit Josephine Butler Memorial House, St. Agnes' House and a training home in Rochester.[52] Josephine Butler House was opened in April 1920, and at its July meeting the Board decided that the two training houses, St. Agnes and the Josephine Butler Memorial House should be recognised as 'affiliated training houses'. From then onwards close relationships were maintained between the Board and Josephine Butler House, especially as Miss J. E. Higson, who was the moving spirit in all that happened at this time, took so prominent a part in both ventures.

Miss Higson has told her own story in *The Story of a Beginning, an Account of Pioneer Work for Moral Welfare*. She was indeed a pioneer, and it is characteristic of her that when in 1918 it was resolved 'that in order to make the fullest use of the Advisory Board, a full time Organising Secretary be appointed' she should leave her beloved St. Monica's and the work in Liverpool to take over this new responsibility. Two years later she was back in the north as the first warden of the Josephine Butler Memorial House, but she was not allowed to remain there undisturbed for long. Her talent for public speaking, making contacts and arousing interest could not go unused, and although for the next few years her prime responsibility was the establishment and running of the House, part of her mandate as warden was that she should go about 'appealing for workers and commending the whole work', and opportunities for this grew 'at an alarming rate'.[53]

So great was the task of general education and enlightenment coming to be that it demanded a full time worker, and in 1928, convinced that this was the best contribution she could make to the cause of 'social purity', Miss Higson resigned the wardenship of Josephine Butler Memorial House to become the first lecturer to the Board.

That after the organising secretary the first full-time member of staff to be appointed by the Board should be a lecturer, is an indication of its concern for propaganda and educational work. As early as 1922 a Propaganda Committee was set up, 'to plan the launching of a national appeal in the cause of social purity and to recommend methods of developing and extending the work of the Board.'[54] Their first efforts at enlightenment were directed towards the clergy, who were frequently ignorant of the work and might well be prejudiced against it,[55] but whose understanding and help were needed, for it was becoming abundantly clear that 'one most important line of advance would be much closer co-operation between parish priests and rescue workers'.[56] A start was made with lectures in theological colleges and by 1933 thirty-six colleges were having yearly lectures, including at least one Methodist college.[57] But one, or even two, lectures a year, given by special lecturers supplied by the Board could do little more than arouse the student's interest; much more was needed if he was to be equipped to deal with the social and personal problems he was likely to meet in his first parish. In 1930 the Board tried to bring this home to the leaders of the Church by sending a resolution to the Lambeth Conference urging the importance of 'improving the training of candidates to Holy Orders by including therein a definite course of instruction in the ethics of sex relations and some knowledge of the practical methods of dealing with those faced with moral difficulties'.[58] Whether or not the Conference's Committee on the Ministry of the Church did in fact consider this resolution, they do not appear to have acted on it, and in any case it is doubtful if it was what was required. Something deeper and wider than 'instruction in the ethics of sex relations' was called for, and it is interesting to compare this resolution with an approach made to the Central Advisory Council on Training for the Ministry rather more than twenty years later.[59] This asks them to consider how 'the theology of personal relations which is basic to all subjects dealt with in Moral Welfare lectures in theological colleges, could be more fully integrated into the normal theological teaching'.

Important as it was to inform the clergy and enlist their support, this was only one aspect of the challenge confronting the Board.

While we *say* that education is the most important side of our work, with the exception of a few of our Organising Secretaries who attempt very limited work in this way, we are doing practically nothing by means of positive teaching for the individual or by influencing public opinion.... We are pouring money into rescue work with comparatively little effort for preventive and educational work. I am aware all the time of opportunities which are being lost while propaganda from undesirable sources is increasing,

lamented Miss Higson to Mrs. Randall Davidson at the time when she was considering giving up the wardenship of Josephine Butler Memorial House to become the Board's first lecturer.[60] Something more than dissemination of information about the nature, scope and objectives of moral welfare work itself was needed, and in June 1930, the suggestion was made to the Board that the 'Propaganda Committee' should enlarge its terms of reference. In future these were to be 'to foster the educational side of the Board's work by the preparation and distribution of literature, the delivery of lectures and by other suitable methods, to keep in touch with present day thought on moral questions, to prepare from time to time memoranda for submission to a Consultative Panel of experts and to make periodic reports'. At the same time it was suggested that 'Educational' would be a better title for the Committee than 'Propaganda', and the suggestion was adopted.

The development of educational work emphasised the desirability, indeed the necessity, both of utilising the services of men as well as women in moral welfare work, and of bringing men and boys as well as women and girls within its scope. During the first three years of its existence, the Advisory Board was composed entirely of women, but within three months of its formation was expressing its desire 'that definite work among men and boys ought to be the aim of this Board'.[61] There appears to have been considerable resistance to overcome, however, and it was not until 1922 that men were first appointed to the Board and men and women could work together at what was essentially a common task.[62] During the next few years attempts were continually being made to encourage the development of work among men and boys, work which was intended to be both educational and remedial, and would cover unmarried fathers and 'other men in moral difficulty' as well as 'cases of perversion and abnormality'. But, apart from the appointment of men workers in one or two dioceses, for example, Liverpool, little was accomplished until 1938, when, almost on the eve of the Second World War, the Board appointed Dr. G. L. Russell, a priest with medical as well as theological training, to work with men and boys for an experimental period of three years.[63]

The Archbishops' Advisory Board was not the only church organisation undertaking personal and educational work among men and boys. The foundation and early work of the White Cross League has already been briefly described, and during the war and post-war years, when the Church's 'rescue' work, hitherto almost entirely confined to the reclamation of 'fallen women', was broadening its scope to include educational and personal work of all kinds, the League, although continuing to emphasise its mission to men, 'was necessarily compelled more and more to become engrossed with the general principles of sexual morals and conduct, and therefore with larger questions of marriage and the family'.[64] It is a significant coincidence that it was in 1922, the year men first became members of the Archbishops' Advisory Board, that the bye-laws of the League were altered to allow the enrolment of women as full members. There were now two organisations at work in the name of the Church; one originally wholly, and still mainly, concerned with women, one mainly concerned with men, but both now concerned with educational work and the wider issues of sex morality generally. Friendly co-operation between the two bodies had been established, but the situation was anomalous. Discussions and negotiations continued for a number of years, issuing in a scheme for the fusion of the two bodies into the Church of England Council for Moral Welfare work. This Council came into being in the spring of 1939, just in time to receive the impact of the Second World War.

3

DEVELOPMENTS DURING
AND AFTER THE
SECOND WORLD WAR

I

THE Second World War, like the first, brought a series of social changes and problems in its train, some anticipated and prepared for, some exaggerated in anticipation, some underestimated and some unforeseen.[1] The one in which moral welfare workers were most deeply involved was that of the increased incidence of illegitimate births with all its personal and social implications. This problem was not entirely unforeseen, but both the proportions it assumed, which were greater than during the earlier war period, and its complexity, appear to have been underestimated.

During the 1914-18 war, as we have already seen, there was a marked increase in the percentage of illegitimate births to all live births, but this increased proportion was due to a decline in the legitimate rather than to an increase in the illegitimate birth-rate. Compared with the years immediately before the war there was some increase in the number of illegitimate babies born, but this increase was not great, and there was a decline in the number of illegitimate live births per 1,000 single and widowed women of child-bearing age. During the years 1911-14 there were 150,399 illegitimate live births, 8 per 1,000 single and widowed women of child-bearing age; during the years 1915-18, 152,543 illegitimate live births or 7·9 per 1,000 such women. During the Second World War there was a marked increase in both numbers and incidence, from 25,633 or 5.9 per 1,000 single and widowed women of child-bearing age in England and Wales in 1940 to 63,420 or 16.1 per 1,000 such women in 1945.[2] Whatever the explanation, and many were put forward, here was a social problem which was to tax existing resources to their limit and in the end lead to the enunciation of a new government policy concerning the unmarried mother and her child.

At the outbreak of war available resources were, when measured against the problem itself, meagre, inadequate and unco-ordinated, and as in other branches of health and social work, the situation was made worse by the panic measures taken at the start of hostilities which resulted in the requisition or closure of several moral welfare homes and the dispersal of workers to other tasks.[3] By and large the tendency in government circles was to play down the special needs of the unmarried mother. It was argued that illegitimacy was not a special feature of war time society, and while the Ministry of Health allowed no discrimination against unmarried mothers, it was equally opposed to granting them favours.[4] Hence, apart from the special arrangements made for girls in the Forces, which appear to have worked well, unmarried mothers had to make do with the services provided for their married sisters. It was soon realised, however, that in certain cases this was causing both considerable hardship to the girl and her baby, and worry to the officials concerned, and quite early in the war the Ministry asked for the co-operation of voluntary bodies, including both the National Council for the Unmarried Mother and her Child and the Church of England Moral Welfare Council. These organisations were willing to help in every way they could but there were difficulties in the way of full co-operation. One of these was the overall problem of the continuing serious shortage of beds in moral welfare homes, but a more fundamental issue was the discrepancy which soon became apparent between the requirements of the situation as seen by both the girls themselves and statutory officials who were making arrangements for them, and the approach of much pre-war moral welfare work.[5]

Compared with cases previously handled by moral welfare workers war-time unmarried mothers were in the main independent and self-reliant young women. Even if distressed at the situation in which they found themselves, they were conscious of the fact that as soon as they had recovered from their confinement they could easily obtain work which would command good wages, and they reacted strongly against what they regarded as the over-rigid discipline and unnecessary emphasis on religion characteristic of the more old-fashioned homes. New methods were required to meet their needs, and while this was recognised by the Church of England Moral Welfare Council, diocesan and local workers and committees might be slow to accept the implications of the situation, reluctant to change with the times, or, even if anxious to do so, find this difficult with war-time shortages of staff and equipment. Thus homes perforce remained open which were regarded by the officials making use of them as 'much too rigorous' and imposing 'unreasonable discipline and too heavy work', and 'where the diet, heating and sanitary arrangements may be of too low a standard for a woman in advanced pregnancy'.[6]

A year after the ending of hostilities the research organisation, Political and Economic Planning made similar criticisms.

The standards of the homes and the workers sponsored by these bodies[7] are extremely variable and uncontrolled even by the central organisations with which they are associated. Some of the homes are excellent, but many are extremely old-fashioned in building and personnel. Some work on free modern lines, others have locked doors, open all letters, remove pocket money and notepaper. The latter are virtually prisons and the more self-respecting girls would not want to enter them even if they needed them badly.[8]

It was the continued existence of this type of home, however few they might be, and however much genuine kindness and desire to help might lie behind the strictest regime, which lent colour to the belief that moral welfare work contained a strong punitive element and that this element was inseparable from a religious approach.

Along with the accusation of archaic restraint and punitive discipline went the allied criticism that moral welfare workers were taking advantage of the girl's need of care to impose unwanted religious teaching and practices upon her. In the words of the P.E.P. broadsheet, 'There is a tendency to combine moral welfare work with compulsion to attend religious services, moralising and attempts at making converts for particular religions. Unmarried mothers should not have to pay the price of a pseudo-conversion for the help they receive, and from the point of view

54

of the mother's resettlement such methods are not only objectionable but also ineffective.'⁹ The validity of this particular criticism, in as far as it applied to Church of England homes, was challenged in a letter sent to P.E.P. by the then General Secretary to the Moral Welfare Council, Miss Ena Steel. The letter questioned the statement about compulsory religious observance and denied that attempts were made 'to make converts for particular religions', but the writer added the significant sentence '. . . there are religious and moral aspects of the problem and we should not be doing *our* job if we did not try to provide ways of meeting these particular needs'.¹⁰ This, in effect, reasserted the proposition that moral welfare work was the expression of religious conviction, with religious as well as social ends. Traditionally it was a long term process which aimed at nothing less than complete spiritual and social rehabilitation, if this was at all possible, and committees and workers were not finding it easy to adjust their aims and methods to a situation in which what was asked for was temporary shelter, adequate physical care and as speedy a discharge as possible. It was divergence of aim which underlay the constant arguments between workers and officials about length of stay and rules of admission, and although scarcely recognised at the time, it raised a question which was to be much discussed after the war, and is at the heart of this study, 'If moral welfare work adapts itself completely to secular expectations, what is its distinctively Christian contribution?'

By the mid-war period it would seem that, despite misunderstandings and mutual criticism, inevitable in a difficult and rapidly changing situation in which all, officials and workers alike, were subject to very considerable strain, relationships between the Ministry of Health, local authorities and voluntary organisations caring for unmarried mothers and their children had been established on a reasonably firm and friendly footing and the three parties could work together in partnership. This is shown by the fact that when, in 1943, the Ministry formulated its policy with regard to the care of illegitimate children this partnership was recognised and commended.

Circular 2866, in which the Ministry's policy is set out, acknowledged the 'successful work of voluntary agencies and moral welfare workers attached to diocesan and other religious bodies',¹¹ but, as was patent to all, these bodies were neither large enough

55

to do all that was needed, nor were their services acceptable to all unmarried mothers. Statutory responsibility must be taken; the Poor Law, hitherto the girl's last resort should all else fail, was not the appropriate body to undertake it, and, in any case, its demise had been foreshadowed by the Beveridge Report published at the end of 1942. In this situation the Minister placed responsibility for the care of unmarried mothers and their children where it most appropriately belonged, with the local authorities responsible for maternity and child welfare, who were asked to give 'very early and urgent attention to this matter'. Statutory bodies were not, however, expected to take action alone. According to the Circular, the Minister considered that in most areas 'the most promising line of attack would be that the welfare authorities should co-operate with and reinforce the work of existing voluntary moral welfare associations', and it was suggested that every welfare authority should formulate a scheme for the purpose. Furthermore, since the range of work would be wide, 'the appointment of a trained worker, experienced in the special problems she will have to handle will probably form an essential part of the organisation and administration of the scheme.'[12]

Circular 2866 was a landmark both in the care of unmarried mothers and their children, and in the relationship between statutory and voluntary bodies working in this field. Published on 16th November, 1943, its effect appears to have been immediate, for the December Quarterly Leaflet of the Moral Welfare Council, which reprinted it in full, recorded that it 'has led in all parts of England to consultations between Medical Officers of Health and Moral Welfare organisers and committees. Schemes are being considered, and in some areas new or additional grants to moral welfare associations are already being discussed'. 'So far,' the Editor continued, with a touch of satisfaction, 'we have heard of very few instances where the Local Authority has appointed its own worker, whereas several have asked that diocesan moral welfare workers should carry out the duties outlined in par. 5' [of the Circular]. By March 1945, 339 authorities in England and Wales had submitted schemes; 210 of them were working with voluntary bodies, 50 had appointed qualified workers and others had placed a health visitor in charge of the work.[13]

Developments during and after the Second World War

Implicit in the recommendations of Circular 2866 was the assumption that mother and child should remain together, and only in special cases, for example, where the mother was very young or the wife of a man not the father of the child, was it suggested that the worker should give advice about legal adoption. The Ministry's adherence to this policy, which was in accordance with current ideas and methods of working, was reaffirmed in an address given by Dr. Dorothy Taylor, then Senior Medical Officer, Maternity and Child Welfare to the Ministry, at a conference of the National Council for the Unmarried Mother and her Child, held in 1945. 'I emphasise the fact,' she said, 'that in the Ministry we are anxious to pursue a policy which would enable the mother to keep her child with her.'

Although this policy was generally accepted by health and social workers, the merits of the alternative of adoption were attracting attention, reinforced by a tendency, which was to become even more marked after the war, for much social work to become child centred, that is, to make what were believed to be the psychological needs of the child paramount in all cases. The divergences of opinion which accompanied these developments evidently caused heartsearchings and differences among moral welfare workers, but there was general agreement that if adoption was to be accepted as a possible, and in many cases a desirable procedure, it must be properly carried out with effective safeguards to ensure the welfare of the child. By this time a good deal of evidence had accumulated to show that the Adoption of Children Act, 1926, had not succeeded in providing these safeguards. The passing of the Act had led to the proliferation of adoption societies and agencies, not all of which were above reproach, and in 1939 the Adoption of Children (Regulation) Act prohibited any body of persons other than a local authority or an adoption society registered by such an authority from placing children for adoption. It also attempted to control that social worker's bane, the 'third party' adoption, by providing that the welfare authority must be informed of such private placements. Implementation of the Act was postponed by the war, but, as might have been expected, war-time conditions resulted in an increase in the number of adoptions, and it became clear that the situation was getting out of hand. Hence in June 1943 the Act was put into operation. It would appear that some moral welfare workers, at any rate, were already arranging adoptions within the terms of the existing legislation, but the passing of the new Act meant that if adoption work was to continue and develop, associations must come into the open and register as Adoption Societies. This inevitably raised the question as to whether or not this was going back on the overall policy of keeping mother and child together if at all possible, and the comment in the December *Quarterly Leaflet* is interesting as an indication of the reasons which led some associations to register. 'We are interested to note that some Diocesan Moral Welfare Associations and certain Local Associations and Homes have registered as Adoption Societies under this Act,' the comment runs :

> They have done this sometimes at the request of the local authority, not necessarily because they want more adoptions, but because they are desperately anxious to ensure better ones than those that are often arranged. Many workers feel that registration will be the means of putting them in touch with unmarried mothers whom otherwise they would never have known, and that in some cases an alternative to adoption will be welcomed. In all cases they can offer some period of personal help to the girl and her family.

Both Circular 2866 and the Adoption of Children (Regulation) Act were designed to meet peace-time as well as war-time needs, and by 1943 plans for post-war reconstruction were getting under way in all branches of social service. The Beveridge Report had already been published, the Minister of Education's White Paper, 'Educational Reconstruction', the forerunner of the Education Act, 1944, was presented to Parliament in July 1943, while the first government proposals for a comprehensive health service were brought out in February 1944. The time was apposite for moral welfare work to examine its own presuppositions and its place in the new scheme of things, and an opportunity for such an examination was provided by the setting up by the Church of England Moral Welfare Council in May 1943 of a Commission 'to investigate the whole content of training for moral welfare work'. This had been asked for by the organising secretaries, and the desirability of some clarification of the scope and aims of the work was reinforced by an article written by a sympathetic but critical social worker in another field of social work. This writer, after expressing the 'grave anxiety' of many family caseworkers about 'the casual attitude of both the individuals concerned and the general public to the matters of irresponsible sex relationships and the personal and social problems to which this was giving rise', asked, 'What is the remedy and why have earlier methods apparently proved so ineffective?' The answer given was that 'to caseworkers certain causes present themselves—one is the isolation from general social work of the moral welfare worker and her committee. This seems due to a failure on the part of both to adapt function and methods to changing times'. The writer goes on to plead for 'a re-statement of the scope and function of moral welfare work, coupled with an active propaganda policy and a willingness for general co-operation not only in casework, but in matters of social policy and reform'.[14]

Both the Interim and Final Reports of the Moral Welfare Council Training Commission[15] include attempts at such a re-statement. They make interesting and stimulating reading, and much of what is said is still relevant in the changed conditions of the present time. The assessment of the existing situation on which the Final Report was based emphasised that, although moral welfare workers did not lack work, the character of their work was rapidly changing, and changing in a way that was likely to continue and perhaps accelerate. 'In some directions,' the Commission observed, 'it may seem as though their special field is narrowing, in that a large proportion of their cases are maternity cases, and there is a tendency for Refuges and Training Homes to turn into Mother and Baby Hostels.' The commission attributed this change of emphasis to three main factors, more adequate statutory provision, better understanding of problems involving sexual relationships and greater readiness among social workers to deal with such cases in a general setting along with other personal and social problems. These were changes which moral welfare workers had themselves helped to bring about, but they were having the long-term effect of narrowing their own field of work, and already the question was being raised as to whether some day it might not be eroded away altogether. 'In particular,' noted the Commission, 'many people think that sooner or later all local authorities will appoint their own officers, not because the authority thinks ill of moral welfare work, but because, unless there is some unforeseen reversal in present trends of thought, it will come to regard the care of illegitimate children as its own responsibility not to be handed over to people it cannot ultimately control.'

The Training Commission declined to accept that the end was in sight. 'There is no doubt,' they said, 'that in other directions new developments and opportunities are apparent and the work is receiving increasing recognition,' but they stressed that other social workers would only be prepared to co-operate fully with moral welfare workers if the latter were adequately trained. 'Social workers are not convinced that "religion" makes up for deficiencies in other fields.'

While this was accepted by the Commission, they did not lose sight of the fact that the moral welfare worker is a church as well as a social worker. Rather they considered that 'in many ways this fact needs re-emphasis at a time when moral welfare is not a matter of extending kindness or "mercy" to outcast girls, but of dealing with sophisticated young people who have discarded or never known Christian moral sanctions.' In the new situation the task of the moral welfare worker might be to 'bring spiritual help to people whom social security had not saved from moral bewilderment and doubt'.[16] But however relevant to the situation this ideal might be, it was evidently a long way from actual practice. 'Many workers are acutely conscious that they have little or no time for spiritual teaching and help. Some feel ill-equipped to offer such help, even if time were available, and a few doubt whether religious teaching should have any part in their work at all,' reported the Commission, and in commenting on this and the kindred problem of relationships with the clergy, their report adds, 'There is much to put straight here, and our emphasis on the need for better theological training is very relevant to this aspect of moral welfare.'

It was to the question of training that everyone returned. On the one hand the moral welfare worker's specialised, and, in the eyes of many social workers, inadequate, training hindered the development of a 'definite and co-operative policy by all the agencies dealing with moral welfare in all its aspects;'[17] on the other, the inadequacy of their theological background was hampering moral welfare workers in both their advisory and educational work, and their relationships with the clergy and other church workers. Hence, what was required to meet the situation was that moral welfare workers should receive more adequate training as both social and church workers. To achieve the former the Commission considered that as a general rule their training should include the Social Science Certificate, since the attainment of this qualification was 'good training in itself and also necessary for the due recognition of moral welfare in the set up of statutory and voluntary social work'; to achieve the latter it endorsed the recommendation of the Archbishops' Commission on Training for Women's Work in the Church[18] that a central college should be established for women training for all branches of church work. This college should be associated with a university and 'concentrate on a good education in theology and the Christian interpretation of life.'[19] Students training for moral welfare work would take a social science course covering two years and specialise in moral welfare work for one. Study in basic theology would extend throughout the three years of training, but the greater part would be carried out during the third year and integrated with the moral welfare training. 'The Commission is strongly of the opinion that it is not possible to give adequate training in moral welfare unless theology forms an integral part of the course.'[20]

In the event the proposals of the Archbishops' Commission to set up a new central college was never implemented as planned, and the task of adapting moral welfare training to meet postwar requirements fell back on Josephine Butler House, which in June 1947, moved into a larger house with accommodation for thirty students. It was hoped by this means that not only would more students be able to pass through the House, but 'the time and scope of their training might be extended'. Courses of training lasting two or three years, which in exceptional cases might be reduced to four terms, were offered. They were designed to meet the practical needs of varying kinds of work, and it was possible to combine the specialised training in moral welfare with a social science course at Liverpool University.[21] It was at this juncture, also, that the idea began to take shape of providing a special short training course for older women with relevant experience, women who, possibly because of family and other commitments, were unable to take advantage of any of the courses offered at Josephine Butler House. The 'London Course' as it came to be called, appears to have been thought of originally as an 'emergency' course, but it quickly proved to be of such value as a form of training and a means of entry to the profession for older women that it was continued beyond the immediate post-war period.

Although in an address to the Moral Welfare Council in November 1947, Miss Eileen Younghusband suggested that the low salaries paid to moral welfare workers were not the main reason why students rejected moral welfare as a possible career,[22] they were a considerable source of anxiety to both the workers themselves and the Moral Welfare Council, especially in view of the swiftly rising cost of living which continued and even accelerated after the war. As we have seen, the Council, ever since its inception as the Archbishops' Advisory Board, had sought, although not always successfully, to induce diocesan and local associations to accept salary scales with maxima and minima for different categories of work. In 1944 the matter was taken up again, and the Council recommended a revised scale, a scale which, with due regard to the jealously guarded autonomy of the dioceses, was set forth not as one which must be accepted, but as a guide within which salaries might be fixed. The minimum yearly salaries proposed, organisers and diocesan lecturers £275, outdoor workers £220, lagged slightly behind those paid at that time in comparable professions, but the maxima, organisers and diocesan lecturers £350, outdoor workers £300, were considerably lower.[23] More important than the exact amount recommended was the basis on which salaries were determined, and in the light of future developments it is interesting to note that, 'the Sub-Committee considered and set out as a principle, that the salaries of women workers in the Church, like those of the clergy, will not be on the same level as in secular professions.'[24] This principle with all that it implied, was to come up for discussion more than once during the next fifteen years.

II

Throughout the period under review developments were taking place in general social policy and administration which were to affect the role of the moral welfare worker quite considerably. In addition to developments in the statutory services, which will be discussed in some detail in a later chapter, the establishment of the National Marriage Guidance Council meant the creation of a nation-wide voluntary service whose work impinged on that of moral welfare associations. Started in 1938 and revived and reconstituted on a national basis in 1943, the National Marriage Guidance Council and its associated local councils quickly became established not only in London, but also in the provinces and soon received statutory recognition and grant aid.[25]

The initiation and rapid development of this new marriage guidance service raised the question as to how closely moral welfare associations could identify themselves with it. Although primarily concerned with unmarried parents and secondarily with young people drifting into promiscuity or in moral danger, moral welfare workers, by the very nature of their work, were frequently in contact with families where marital relationships were strained and unsatisfactory, and from time to time they were called in to help where married couples were drifting apart through ignorance and misunderstanding. Then, as now, this appears to have been a comparatively small part of their work; nevertheless not only workers but committees and councils felt that they had an overall responsibility for maintaining Christian standards of marriage and family life, and they asked themselves how far was this also the aim of the National Marriage Guidance Council and its associated local councils.

From the start the National Marriage Guidance Council was a broadly based movement including, as well as Christians of all denominations,[26] people with no specific religious affiliations, but all those associated with the movement were expected to accept its general principles and aims. These, whether as originally set out, or as revised in 1952, would seem to be unexceptional, and, except to those who regard all forms of scientific contraception as sinful,[27] in line with Christian teaching on marriage and sex relations. Despite all this, the fact that the movement was not specifically Christian led some local moral welfare committee members and workers to question the desirability of associating themselves with it. In other areas, however, there was close co-operation from the start, members of local associations and diocesan boards served on their local marriage guidance councils and the two worked in close association.[28] In 1946 the Church of England Moral Welfare Council defined its own policy when it decided not to attempt to set up a separate Anglican Marriage Guidance Service as the Church of Rome had done, and as was advocated in some quarters, but to co-operate in the work of the National and local marriage guidance councils as far as it proved possible. Two years later, in 1948, the Lambeth Conference Committee on Discipline in Marriage took the same line. 'We welcome,' they said, 'many efforts now afoot, in England, the United States and elsewhere to provide marriage guidance. Church people should as far as possible take part in them, qualifying to become advisers of others by their firm understanding of the Christian principles involved.'[29]

Meanwhile, as Dr. Russell had reminded the Church of England Moral Welfare Council in 1946 when it was discussing the recommendations of the Denning Committee, there is a sense in which the Church has its own marriage guidance service in that 'every parish priest has a pastoral duty to the married and those about to be married', and he went on to emphasise the responsibility of moral welfare councils 'to see that they are equipped for their task'.[30] It was recognised that the requisite grounding in moral theology could only be given in the theological colleges, but this was considered to be no more than a beginning, and the Moral Welfare Council regarded itself as having a responsibility which 'it may share with others but which it cannot evade'[31] for post-ordination training. In subsequent years this responsibility was in part discharged by a series of short residential courses sponsored by the Church of England Moral Welfare Council with the co-operation of the National Marriage Guidance Council. They started with one at Hawarden in September 1956 and between that date and October 1960 about 270 parish priests attended such courses.[32] Over the same period the Moral Welfare Council's staff maintained and developed their contacts with the theological colleges as far as their heavy commitments allowed, and the appointment in 1958 of a psychiatric social worker with special responsibility for training, made it possible to help ordinands to become more aware of the casework approach to problems of personal relationships and what is involved in it.

Education of the clergy was regarded as vital, since 'the

pastoral ministry of the Church of England rests, and ought to rest, primarily upon its parish priests',[33] but it was not considered to be the only educational responsibility of moral welfare councils whether central or local, and throughout the post-war years much concern was expressed about the need for the further development of educational work among young people themselves. This is work which for the most part must be undertaken at a diocesan or even local level, and will be discussed in that context later,[34] but the Church of England Moral Welfare Council had its own contribution to make, not least through its publications. In this it had inherited a lively tradition from the White Cross League, and one of the Council's most popular publications, *The Threshold of Marriage*, up to 100,000 copies of which have been sold, was first issued by that organisation in 1932, although it has been revised more than once since. During the post-war period, moreover, it is possible to trace a shift in emphasis in the Council's educational work, away from sex education as such and towards the consideration, along with others, of the bearing of Christian teaching on patterns of personal relationships in the context of contemporary thought and modes of life. As the Annual Report for 1957 put it:

The Church has pioneered much in its day, from what used to be called 'sex education' to immediate preparation for marriage.... In the current situation, however, it is suggested that the function of the Church's specialists is not so much to purvey family life education at every level as to sit down with teachers and social workers whose professional duty this is, and help them to master principles, to assess ends and to fashion appropriate means....

But the Church of England Moral Welfare Council regarded its responsibilities as extending beyond the furtherance of more effective communication of the Church's teaching on matters relating to sex, marriage and the family. It was concerned not merely to help communicate but also to help formulate such teaching, and during the post-war period certain members of staff, in particular, played an active part in the preparation and drafting of reports on these issues.[35] An exceptionally important opportunity for discussion of this kind occurred when the Archbishop of Canterbury requested the Council to convene a group of distinguished theologians, sociologists, and other experts, to prepare a report on Problems of Population and The Effects of Social Change on Family Life, to be presented to the 1958 Lambeth Conference. The Report issued by the group, *The Family in Contemporary Society*,[36] described by one churchman,[37] as 'the most realistic and challenging Church report I have ever read', showed how stimulating and fruitful such discussions might be and how much could be accomplished by such co-operation.

The preparation of this major Report occupied much of the time of the staff of the Church of England Moral Welfare Council during this period, but there were other important and urgent matters demanding their attention and calling forth all their resources of conviction, intellect, persuasion and diplomacy. The most controversial of these was probably that of the reform of the laws relating to homosexuality and prostitution.

It was as early as 1952 that the Council's Education Committee, stimulated by one of its lecturers, Dr. Sherwin Bailey, approved the calling together of a small group of clergymen, doctors and lawyers to undertake unofficially and privately, a full investigation of the problem of homosexuality. The results of this enquiry were published in 1954 in a document called *The Problem of Homosexuality*. This report (which is now out of print) appeared at a time when a number of notorious cases had brought the problem to the notice of the public and it received general approval as 'an attempt to deal responsibly, honestly and charitably with a problem, the magnitude and character of which had scarcely been realised'.[38] It reiterated a demand, also being made in other responsible quarters, for a government enquiry, and in August 1954, the Home Secretary, Sir David Maxwell-Fyfe, appointed a Departmental Committee to look into the matter. The same Departmental Committee was also asked to examine 'the law and practice relating to offences against the criminal law in connexion with prostitution and solicitation for immoral purposes', and Sir John Wolfenden was appointed Chairman to guide it in its double task.

Moral welfare work originated as work for the reclamation of the prostitute, and the teaching and inspiration of women such as Josephine Butler and Ellice Hopkins, who had attacked not simply the evil itself, but the presuppositions about relationships

66

between men and women which tolerated its continuance in a professedly Christian society is passed on to each generation of workers as part of their heritage. Nevertheless, by this time, little was expected, and except in special areas and circumstances, little was being done in the way of 'rescue' work of the old direct type. There were various reasons for this, among them the changes in the character of prostitution itself, of the type of girl undertaking it, and of her reasons for adopting it as her profession, while women police, whose widespread employment had been among the reforms the Archbishops' Advisory Council had supported in the inter-war years, were now carrying out, though in rather a different way and with a different purpose, the street patrolling once undertaken by the early 'missionaries'. Moreover, Josephine Butler had herself founded an organisation, the Association for Moral and Social Hygiene, to continue her campaign against the regulation of vice and all that this implied, and this association was usually ready to take the initiative when protests had to be made or reforms were advocated in conection with the working of the law concerning solicitation and kindred offences. Hence, when called upon to make recommendations to the Wolfenden Committee, the Moral Welfare Council made its own recommendations with regard to homosexuality, but associated itself with the recommendations made by A.M.S.H. with regard to prostitution. It was realised, however, that 'such is the responsibility of the Church of England Moral Welfare Council' that 'both the Departmental Committee and the nation might look to it for some statement on the subject', and a Memorandum was prepared which attempted to review the problem in general, and to examine historically the Christian attitude thereto. This Memorandum forms the second and shorter section of a report, *Sexual Offenders and Social Punishment*, the greater part of which consisted of the Council's evidence on the problem of homosexuality.[39] But the Council did not stop there. Its Memorandum had pointed out that 'an examination of the history and practice of prostitution ... shows plainly enough that it is perhaps less a female than a male problem; yet students of the subject have generally neglected the latter aspect, and have persistently treated the whole question from the standpoint of the women concerned'.[40] The Council's next contribution to the attack on this social evil was, therefore,

67

the formation of a small working party to study the male client.
The Wolfenden Committee reported in September 1957.[41]
The proposals for the reform of the law relating to homosexual
offences, being very similar to those put forward by the Church
of England Moral Welfare Council, were welcomed by this
body, but those relating to prostitution (and in particular to soliciting) were regarded as 'unsatisfactory in many respects and
hardly calculated to deal adequately with the evil.'[42] Steps were
immediately taken to give as wide publicity as possible to the
Council's views, and activity was redoubled when the Street
Offences Bill was presented to Parliament a few months later.
The Bill was in some respects a piece of panic legislation, pre-
cipitated by public concern at the admittedly scandalous spec-
tacle of open immorality in streets and parks in central London
and some of the larger towns, and it bore the marks of its origin.
The Government's objective was to 'clean up the streets'; other
considerations were set aside so that this objective might be
achieved quickly, and despite protests and constructive proposals
for amendment from a number of quarters, including the
Council, the Bill, imperfect and even unjust in some respects as
it was, was rushed through Parliament and became law in
August 1959.[43] On the other hand the Government refused to
take action on the Wolfenden Committee's recommendations
with regard to homosexuality, and the manifest injustice of the
present law remains.

The part played by the Moral Welfare Council in connection
with these two related questions of homosexuality and prostitution
has been described at some length as it illustrates its role as a
pressure group. The issues dealt with by the Wolfenden Committee also raised the general question of the relationship between
law and morality,[44] a matter of fundamental importance not
only to the Moral Welfare Council but to the Church at large,
and the Council made its own contribution to the clarification of
this issue by publishing a pamphlet, *What is Unlawful?* by Mr.
Quentin Edwards, Barrister-at-Law. The same issue was raised
again in rather a different context when a small group of lawyers
and theologians, with a member of the staff as secretary, tackled
the question of suicide, and set out its conclusions and the arguments on which they were based, in a pamphlet, *Ought Suicide
to be a Crime?* published in 1959.[45]

Developments during and after the Second World War

It would seem from the above, that although a moral welfare caseworker employed by a local association might be spending the greater part of her time coping with the problems of unmarried mothers and their families, the purview of the Church of England Moral Welfare Council and its staff was much wider, and during the fifties was, if anything, widening. The problem of bringing the concerns of the Council home to local associations and getting them to participate in them was not always easy, but it was continually being attempted, not least through the Council's Quarterly Review, *Moral Welfare*, (now *Crucible*), which also had a wide general circulation.

The widening scope of the Council's work brought it into close touch with other Councils of the Church Assembly.[46] By 1956 the Assembly had already undertaken a thorough examination of the structure, functions and finances of its constituent committees, one result of which was a proposal to set up a Council for Social Responsibility within the compass of which the work hitherto undertaken by the Moral Welfare Council would be included. This far-reaching proposal naturally resulted in a great deal of keen discussion within the Council itself as well as in the Assembly, but agreement was reached, and, on the last day of 1956, a statement was made welcoming the proposal to create a Social Responsibility Council for the Church of England and expressing the readiness of the Moral Welfare Council, 'subject to the continued acceptance of the essential principles of its present work', to be comprehended within it.[47] At its autumn session the following year the Church Assembly resolved that a Board for Social Responsibility be set up, and in January 1958 the Moral Welfare Council became a constituent part of the new Board, together with the Assembly's Social and Industrial Council.

It is clear from its Annual Report for 1957, the last Annual Report it was to issue as an independent body, that the Moral Welfare Council considered participation in the proposed new set up as 'a further step in the integration of moral welfare work within the life of Church and Nation', the continuation of a process already taking place. Over the years of the Council's growth, from its beginning as the Archbishops' Advisory Board to its status as a full Council of the Church Assembly, its main responsibility, 'the co-ordination of thought and action in relation to sex, marriage and the family in the Christian life' had become integrated with 'the study and service of the society in which the Christian life is lived', and the new arrangement was regarded as a recognition of this, a response by the Church to an evident need. The integration of a well-established organisation, with its own character, reputation and field of interest, within a new and experimental set up, somewhat uncertain of its scope, direction and purpose, was not an easy matter, but despite the difficulties which have been encountered, the experiment was potentially a creative one, in line with current trends and needs, and with possibilities of interesting developments in the future. It is a development which could both carry further the Council's commitments and concerns, and open the way to new and wider spheres of both influence and action.

PART TWO

The Present-day Setting

4

SOCIAL CONDITIONS
AND ATTITUDES

IN the first three chapters of this study we traced the development of the Church's moral welfare work from its beginnings in the eighteenth century and earlier to the present time; here we consider the social conditions and attitudes which form the background of the present day work.

The situation today is paradoxical. In some respects it is more satisfactory than previous generations could have dared to hope. Full, or almost full employment has been maintained in most parts of the country and with it the prosperity of all but comparatively small sections of the population, while young people are not only healthier and given better educational opportunities than their forerunners, but on leaving school find it easier to obtain work carrying wages sufficient to leave a considerable margin for discretionary spending.[1] Yet this period of material prosperity is also one of unease and of social and moral uncertainty, and, if the economic and social setting of moral welfare work today is different from that of the past, the problems which confront the workers are no less numerous or urgent.

This situation is reflected in the position with regard to illegitimacy, the social problem with which moral welfare workers are most continuously involved. Illegitimate births have been recorded by the Registrar General since 1842, both in numbers and as percentages of all live births. This latter criterion taken by itself may give a somewhat distorted view of the situation, but it is a useful measure of long term trends. As such its most noticeable feature is its stability. Despite the economic and social changes of the last 120 years it has, apart from a steep rise during each of the two world wars, fluctuated little from year to year. In 1845 illegitimate births were 7% of all live births, thereafter the percentage slowly but steadily declined, reaching 4% in 1899 and remaining at about that figure until the First World War and immediately afterwards when it rose to more than 6%. During the inter-war period it hovered between 4·1 and 4·6%, but during the Second World War rose sharply to 9·3%, the highest recorded figure, in 1945. With the return to normal conditions it dropped again and during the first half of the 1950's remained fairly steady at 4·7 or 4·8%. Towards the end of the decade, however, both numbers and percentages were increasing and in 1960 there were 42,707 illegitimate births, 5·4% of all live births.

In considering the significance of illegitimacy as a social phenomenon it is necessary to take into account not only the number of children born illegitimate but also the number of pre-marital conceptions legalised by the mother's marriage before the birth of the child. Each year since the implementation of the Population (Statistics) Act, 1938, which made it possible to calculate the number of children conceived before marriage, the number of pre-maritally conceived maternities[2] has considerably exceeded that of illegitimate ones. In 1938 it was twice as many (64,530 compared with 27,440), but during the war the two totals came nearer together, and it is likely that an important factor in the rise of the illegitimate birthrate during this period was that such contingencies of war as the transfer of men abroad prevented the solemnisation of marriages which otherwise would have taken place.[3]

Since the war the proportion of extra-maritally conceived maternities legitimated before the birth of the child in England and Wales each year has been appreciably below the proportion so legitimated in 1938. Throughout the fifties it remained approximately 60%, compared with 70·2% for 1938, and in 1960, the middle year of the survey, 60,972, that is 58·5% of the 104,253 maternities conceived extra-maritally during that year, were legitimated before the birth of the child, leaving 43,281 maternities in which the child was born illegitimate. The 104,253 extra-maritally conceived maternities constituted 14·4% of all maternities and represented 35·5 such maternities for every 1,000 unmarried women of child-bearing age 'at risk'. The corresponding figures for 1938 were 91,970 extra-maritally conceived maternities which constituted 13·2% of all maternities taking place that year and 18·6 per 1,000 women 'at risk'.⁴

Over the last few years there has been a good deal of concern not only about the increase in the number of illegitimate births to women of all ages but especially about the number of young girls who become unmarried mothers. The Annual Report of the Chief Medical Officer of Health for 1960 included a table which showed that, according to his statistics, the number of illegitimate maternities occurring in girls under 17 rose from 887 in 1956 to 1,872 in 1960, that is almost doubled during these four years.⁵ According to the Registrar General, during 1960 approximately 1,500 girls under 17 conceived a child outside wedlock but married before the birth of the child so that in all, in that year, about 3,400 girls between 12 and 17, that is just under 2 out of every 1,000 girls in this age group, conceived a child outside wedlock, but despite the fact that the minimum age for legally valid marriage is 16, nearly half these girls married before the child's birth.

Between the ages of 17 and 20 the number of unmarried mothers rises sharply and according to the Registrar General's figures there were, in all, 7,939 illegitimate maternities in this age group in England and Wales in 1960. In addition there were 23,536 maternities within nine months of marriage, making a total of 31,475 out-of-wedlock conceptions.⁶ By relating numbers of illegitimate and extra-maritally conceived maternities occurring to all girls and women under 20 to the girls and women of that age group 'at risk', the Registrar General calculated that in 1960 there were 6·79 illegitimate maternities and 17·7 extra-maritally conceived legitimate maternities for every 1,000 such girls and women.

Despite the widespread concern about 'teen-agers' the number of both illegitimate maternities and pre-marital conceptions is greatest between the ages of 20 and 24. In 1960 there were 13,874 illegitimate maternities in that age group, constituting 18·84 per 1,000 women 'at risk', while pre-maritally conceived legitimate maternities numbered 28,589, or 38·64 per 1,000 women 'at risk'. After the age of 25 numbers and proportions of both illegitimate and pre-maritally conceived maternities start to decline, pre-maritally conceived maternities more rapidly than illegitimate ones, and after 30 the decline is accelerated. Even so

1,499 women over 40 gave birth to illegitimate children in England and Wales in 1960. Many of these women were, no doubt, living in stable partnerships with men not their husbands but an older unmarried woman not in that position may present the social worker with an even more difficult problem than a younger woman.

A child is born illegitimate if his parents were not married at the time of his birth, but this event may cover a wide variety of situations. There is a marked difference in all but legal standing between the position of a child born to a couple cohabiting on a permanent basis and that of the child whose parents had no more than a passing relationship with each other and who has no father in any but the biological sense. It is believed that about one-third to one-half of the children born out of wedlock are born to mothers living in a comparatively stable relationship with the father,[7] but it is from the remaining half to two-thirds that the moral welfare worker is most likely to draw her cases.

While the overall figures supplied by the Registrar General make it possible to estimate the extent of the social problem of illegitimacy and so help to maintain a sense of proportion, more detailed studies are required to reveal its different facets and to obtain some idea of the factors which may be contributing to its extent and character. Comparatively few detailed studies of unmarried parenthood have been published, however, and those that there are vary considerably both in their approach to the problem and in the conclusions reached.

At one extreme are those studies which regard the causative factors in unmarried motherhood as almost entirely psychological. A well known and influential study of this kind is that of Professor Leontine Young, Professor in Casework, School of Social Administration, Ohio State University.[8] According to Professor Young unmarried motherhood is the outcome of an unconscious drive to have a baby without making any permanent relationship with the father, and this pathological condition derives from a faulty family background, usually one in which one parent has dominated the home.

To say that her [the unwed mother's] behaviour is the result of immorality or free choice is to ignore all the evidence. The logical and seemingly inevitable result of her psychological development is an out-of-wedlock child and, like a sleep-walker, she acts out what she must do without awareness or understanding of what it means. . . . She must have the baby no matter what it means for herself or for others, but she is completely unconscious that this is so.[9]

A different but equally unreservedly psychological approach is that of Dr. Donald Gough of the Tavistock Clinic, London. As the result of close contacts made with a group of girls in a mother and baby home, Dr. Gough advanced the proposition that unmarried motherhood is rarely accidental and elaborated his thesis by continuing,

When discussing unmarried mothers we are talking of a very special group of girls who have not only 'got into trouble' but who have failed to adopt any of the alternatives (savoury or unsavoury) to unmarried motherhood. A girl in our society who starts a pregnancy with a man whom she is neither willing nor able to marry has shown herself to be a disturbed personality and I think that we are entitled to look upon the illegitimate baby as the living proof of his mother's emotional difficulties.

Illegitimate conception is, moreover, not only the result of the girl's emotional problems, but is her attempt to 'communicate these problems to those whom she thinks can help her with them.'[10]

To both these observers unmarried motherhood would appear to be a psychopathological rather than a social problem, the unmarried mother a mentally sick person whose neurosis sets her apart from others of her own age, sex and social background. This may well be true in some cases, and many social workers would echo Virginia Wimperis' cautious summing up of the position, namely that '*among* unmarried mothers . . . there are an important number who are in general terms neurotic, immature and not fully responsible for their actions'.[11] It does not necessarily follow, however, that this diagnosis is correct for the majority of girls who bear children out of wedlock. Both Dr. Young and Dr. Gough seem to have based their conclusions on studies of selected cases. Dr. Gough's cases were girls who had not only sought the help of a social work agency, itself a selective process, but had been found to be in need of residential care. Dr. Young states that the random sample of 100 cases from an unmarried mother agency she took as the basis of her study excluded two specific groups, adolescents under the age of 18 and 'girls coming from a social background where illegitimacy is more or less socially acceptable'.[12] Less selective studies in which the conclusions are validated by statistics rather than by case illustrations have drawn attention to the importance of the sociological as well as of the psychological aspects of the problem, and some studies have given them precedence.

A local investigation of this kind, and one based on a wide range of cases, is that of Miss Barbara Thompson who analysed the records of all women who gave birth to illegitimate children in Aberdeen during the four years 1949-52.[13] It was an unselected group of 582 women, including those married, widowed and divorced (together nearly one-third of the total), as well as single women. It was, moreover, possible to compare the backgrounds of the single women having their first babies with those of 1,750 legitimate first maternities which occurred during the year 1952-53. As the result of her investigations Miss Thompson reached the conclusion that the most marked feature of the incidence of illegitimacy in Aberdeen was its association with 'unskilled, unattractive or menial occupations', and the same appeared to be true of pre-marital conceptions. Both illegitimacy and pre-nuptial conceptions occurred predominantly among the lower social classes. Not unexpectedly there was some association between illegitimacy and broken and unhappy homes;[14] more unmarried mothers than married women had had an abnormal family life, and 'many of the case histories described by Young could be paralleled from the Aberdeen records'. But, Miss Thompson commented, 'this explanation did not fully cover the "epidemiology" of illegitimacy in Aberdeen', and she concluded,

Illegitimacy, like delinquency, thrives when social values, cultural as well as material, are low. Insecure family life, poor and over-crowded homes, lack of constructive aims and outlets, lack of general planning ability and permissive attitudes to extra-marital relations may all contribute to the occurrence. Such factors rarely occur in isolation, and it would be difficult to assess their relative importance in causing or favouring a high illegitimacy rate.

Miss Thompson's findings are based on data from one Scottish city, but the importance she attached to social conditions and attitudes as predisposing factors is a feature of other British studies

78

of illegitimacy. It is very marked in an intensive study of a series of 62 adolescent primigravidae attending an ante-natal clinic at a city maternity hospital undertaken by the Department of Psychiatry, Manchester University. As the result of their investigations, which included home visits by a psychiatric social worker as well as psychiatric and psychological interviews, the investigators reached the conclusion that pregnancy followed naturally enough from the pursuit of adolescent practices normal to the society of which these young people were part. In 36 (76%) of their subjects it arose from the choice of a mate, usually of the same occupational level, and deliberate association with him. With the remaining 12 girls the precipitating factor was the common exposure to risk of post-pubertal girls working and amusing themselves in a large industrial town. That intercourse resulted in conception seemed little more significant than biological chance.[15] Judging by the girls' own accounts and the visits made by the investigators, their families did not present an unduly pathological picture. Such adverse emotional and psychological factors as were found were combined with much family feeling and realism, and the girls accepted them in much the same way as they accepted the rather indifferent physical health of their parents, that is as an unavoidable, if irksome, part of the business of living. The authors concluded that, as far as these adolescents were concerned, extra-marital pregnancy was far more likely to have been the result of normal teen-age behaviour than of psychological abnormality.

On a rather different basis from these two local investigations are the studies which have been made by Cyril Greenland, Senior Psychiatric Social Worker, Crichton Royal Hospital, Dumfries. As the result of a preliminary ecological study he reached the tentative conclusion that his data 'did not appear to support the view that unmarried mothers as a whole, apart from having conceived out of marriage, differ in important respects from other women of the same age and social class. If there is a difference it is in their relatively higher reproductive capacity which has a physical as well as a psychological basis'.[16] In order to carry the investigation further Mr. Greenland then embarked on an analysis of 3,444 cases of pregnant women dealt with by the National Council for the Unmarried Mother and her Child in 1953.[17] The limitations a study based on records kept for practical rather than research purposes and cases which may not be representative, are admitted by the investigator, but he claims that it produced a framework of data which makes it possible to examine certain theoretical and practical aspects of illegitimacy.[18] On bringing together the various factors which, from the available data, appeared to have 'some relevance to the general problem of unmarried motherhood and the circumstances which cause these women to seek help', he found that 'no special psychological features emerged', but he did point out that 'the research undertaken here would tend to be insensitive to problems of that kind'. It proved possible to put forward a tentative hypothesis that a combination of events such as residence away from home and occupations which make for greater opportunity for intimate contact with men, coupled with a high index of fertility expose younger unmarried women to an increased risk of antenuptial conception.[19]

Since the findings of the post-war investigations into the problem of illegitimate maternity outlined above differ so markedly, any general observations about the nature of the problem and the factors likely to predominate in any particular case can only be very tentative. Social workers can make a valuable contribution to our knowledge of the subject by the careful recording and, where feasible, objective investigation of their own cases and, given appropriate encouragement, advice and assistance, moral welfare workers have already shown their willingness and ability to do this. A particular instance of this participation was in connection with a follow-up study of illegitimate children whose mothers retained responsibility for them. Inspired by the late Miss Celia M. Joy, and encouraged by the then general secretary to the Church of England Moral Welfare Council, a number of workers throughout the country undertook to follow-up the first five of their clients who gave birth to illegitimate children in 1952 and retained responsibility for them. Contacts were maintained until 1958 with 163 out of the original 180 mothers selected for study and although, as was also the case with other studies already referred to, the numbers included in it are small, the study adds to our knowledge both of the types of adjustment made by mothers to their situation and of the care received by the illegitimate child during the first five years of his life. Perhaps the most valuable contribution this study has to make to our understanding of the

Social Conditions and Attitudes

problem of illegitimacy is that it reveals so clearly that 'there is not one problem—that of the mother and her illegitimate child—but a wide variety of situations each with quite different problems', and that 'there are probably greater differences in the living arrangements within this group of mothers than there are between them and ordinary families'.[20] In discussing what happens afterwards, as well as what leads up to the birth of an illegitimate child, generalisations are likely to be misleading.

A question raised by this and other studies based on social workers' records is whether and in what respects unmarried mothers seeking help from social work agencies differ from other girls and women in the same dilemma. On the basis of a comparison between the figures given by the Church of England Moral Welfare Council of cases handled in 1952[21] and the Registrar General's statistics for 1953, Greenland concluded that 'it is usually the younger unmarried woman who needs and seeks the help of the moral welfare agencies'.[22] He also considered that the girls seeking such help were likely to have 'very special difficulties which often include the broken home and mental instability', but, like two of the correspondents who wrote commenting on Dr. Gough's article,[23] he apparently regards the girl's pregnancy and the circumstances surrounding it as much the cause as the consequence of her emotional difficulties. Be that as it may, the girl who reaches the moral welfare worker frequently brings with her a number of inter-related problems, practical, social and personal, and the more light that can be thrown on the sociological and psychological factors which have combined to precipitate her condition and which affect her attitude and that of her family and social group to the situation in which she finds herself, the more effective will be the help the social worker is able to render.

The responsibility of the moral welfare worker and the Church in whose name she works goes beyond helping individuals, however, and the incidence and distribution of extra-marital pregnancies must be considered not only in terms of personal well-being but as a pointer to current patterns of hetero-sexual behaviour. Its significance in this regard is difficult to assess as the situation is complicated by the existence of practices about whose incidence we have little precise information. The Registrar General's totals of illegitimate maternities may be regarded as

81

reasonably, if not wholly accurate, but, by themselves, extra-marital conceptions taken to term do not give any reliable indication as to the extent of extra-marital intercourse. Both the number of successful abortions, whether legal or illegal, and the extent to which unmarried persons make use of contraceptives are largely matters of conjecture. Contraceptives are relatively easy to obtain,[24] and it is at least possible that, although the proportion of maternities conceived extra-maritally remains below pre-war level, extra-marital intercourse is more widespread.

A possible pointer to the extent of such intercourse is the incidence of venereal disease, but in considering the social implications of its fluctuations medical factors, notably the response of the organism responsible for the disease to differing methods of treatment, have to be taken into account. Thus the marked decline which followed the end of the Second World War could be regarded as being to some extent due to the return of more stable conditions, but it was also partly due to the discovery that penicillin was an effective agent in combating venereal infections. In the early 1950's high hopes were entertained that these 'ancient scourges of mankind' might be eliminated, but unfortunately such hopes were set too high. The reports of the Ministry of Health for 1958, 1959 and 1960 all refer to increases in gonorrhoea 'sufficiently marked to cause anxiety'.[25] In part these increases appear to have been associated with the development of strains of gonoccocii with increased resistance to penicillin.[26] But in his report for 1959 the Chief Medical Officer suggested that social factors were also involved. He considered that 'in large centres of population immigrants living in difficult circumstances still contribute greatly to the high prevalence of gonorrhoea and are particularly prone to multiple infections', but added, 'there is evidence too of an increasing number of infections resulting from promiscuity among young people'.[27] The following year he referred again to 'the increase of promiscuity, and therefore of venereal disease, among young people under the age of 20', and quoted as evidence a report from the Advisor in Venereology to the Liverpool Regional Hospital Board which stated that 471 males, 8·6% of all males attending V.D. clinics in Liverpool, were between the ages of 14 and 19. Also attending were 388 girls between 11 and 19 who constituted 37·4% of all females attending.[28] An analysis made by the British Co-operative Clinical

Group of the Medical Society for the Study of Venereal Diseases showed that the number of young men between 15 and 24 treated for gonorrhoea in clinics[29] in England and Wales had increased between 1957 and 1961 from 4,999 or 17·5 per 10,000 of the population in that age group in 1957 to 8,142 or 26·0 per 10,000 in 1961. Young women treated numbered 2,316 or 8·3 per 10,000 in 1957, 4,123 or 13·7 per 10,000 in 1961.[30] As with young unmarried mothers there appears to have been a proportionate increase over the last few years greater than can be accounted for by the increased numbers in the relevant age group, but the evidence given is incomplete, the actual numbers quoted are small and amount to only a fraction of the young people in the age groups cited.

Associated with the problem of venereal disease is that of the extent and character of professional prostitution.[31] It was anxiety about the spread of this social evil, especially in London and the larger towns which led to its inclusion in the terms of reference of the Wolfenden Report and the passing of the Street Offences Act. As the Wolfenden Committee admitted[32] we have no exact means of knowing whether or not the problem really is more serious at the present time than it has been in the past and, apart from the sociological study undertaken in the early fifties, *Women of the Streets,*[33] there is little first-hand information available as to its characteristics and causative factors. Whatever may have been the situation in Victorian England, poverty can no longer be regarded as in itself a cause of prostitution, and the research worker engaged in the study mentioned above considered present day prostitution to be 'a way of living consciously chosen because it suits a woman's personality in particular circumstances'.[34] It is suggested that these may include a past history of recurrent failures in personal, family and community living, which have produced feelings of unimportance and apathy and so have rendered the girl vulnerable to people and opportunities offering apparent compensation in this way of life.

The United Nations Study on Traffic in Young Persons and Prostitution, 1959, suggests that in many countries the professional prostitute now has a competitor in the promiscuous woman[35] and, among young people in particular, it may be difficult to distinguish between promiscuity and the practice of prostitution. Reliable information is lacking as to whether promiscuous behaviour in this country is restricted to a small section of the community or is more widespread, and it is hoped that the extensive investigation now being undertaken by the Central Council for Health Education into the sexual behaviour of young people will help to supply it. Such information as we have at present is based on impressions, albeit sometimes the impressions of knowledgeable observers, or on questions addressed to small groups. Sensational publicity has, moreover, done much to shock susceptibilities and inflame prejudices[36] and it is not easy to maintain a sense of proportion. With all these reservations, however, there would appear to be certain characteristics of the contemporary situation which make it particularly difficult for young people to maintain the high standards of extra-marital chastity traditionally expected by the Church.

The earlier onset of puberty, which combines oddly with increased length of schooling and widens the gap between sexual maturity and marriage, is sometimes adduced as a factor which helps to account for the apparently more widespread heterosexual intercourse among young people. It is, however, counteracted to some extent by the present increase in the number of teen-age marriages made possible by full employment with higher rates of pay. About 6% of the bachelors and no less than 26% of the spinsters who married in 1960 were under 20 at the time of their wedding. Figures published by the Registrar General show that during the fifties about 27% of these teenage brides, compared with about 15% of brides in their early twenties were pregnant at their wedding. In general, teenage couples are 'likely to be worse housed and soon become more encumbered with children than their elders'. This may help to account for the fact that whatever their duration, marriages where the bride was in her teens run about twice the risk of ending in divorce as those contracted later. 'Even with this greater risk, however, these figures suggest that over 80% of all teenage marriages will remain intact and unbroken compared with more than 90% of those with older brides.'[37]

Another demographic change which is taking place and which may well have some bearing on the relationships between men and women is the change in the sex-ratio. About 106 boys are born alive for every 100 girls, but they seem to be less well fitted to survive than their sisters, and in 1911 the numbers had evened out between the ages of 5 and 9, after which there was an excess of girls. Improvements in living conditions and medical care have improved the boys' chances of survival and in 1959 it was not until between the ages of 30 and 34 that the balance of the sexes was achieved[38] so that in the late teens and twenties, when desire is most potent and competition most keen, it is the men who are now likely to be unattached, a situation which may be conducive to restlessness and frustration.

Biological and demographic changes are not in themselves sufficient to account for changes in patterns of behaviour and, in any case, are gradual in their operation, but they have been accompanied by changes in the general climate of opinion which, as the Crowther Committee has pointed out,[39] now allows boys and girls 'much greater freedom to live their own lives without adult supervision' but at the same time 'deprives them of the security which comes from a well-understood knowledge of what is right and what is wrong'. Lacking coherent guidance, and living in an era of rapid social change, young people understandably model their behaviour on that of their contemporaries rather than of adults, and the development of a teenage cult has been encouraged by the affluence which makes young men and women a profitable commercial market. Adults can thus be indicted not only as 'the first to cast doubts on the rules', but also on the grounds that 'society does not know how to ask the best of the young' and 'as a whole is not much more concerned with them than to ask them to earn and consume'.[40] In no sphere is this double betrayal more clearly manifest than in the sphere of sexual morality. 'Young people are given no firm guidance from above, since their elders are bitterly divided on this issue. But the one thing which is impressed on them from the earliest age is that sex is of transcendental importance.'[41] What has been described by one theologian as 'the erotic obsession of the twentieth century'[42] is reflected in serious writing and discussion as well as in advertising, television, films and the popular press, and, although manifest in a different way, it may be as much a preoccupation of the middle-aged as of the young.

There is, then, a sense in which adolescent behaviour now, as always, results from and reflects the mores of the society of which the young people form a part. It is a society in which the more rigid conventions of the immediately preceding generations have been relaxed and, within wide and flexible limits, social relationships between men and women are free and to a considerable extent uninhibited. Within these limits, which, it has been suggested, cover extra-marital intercourse but usually exclude extramarital pregnancy without the prospect of marriage,[43] the atmosphere is one of easy-going tolerance, while the widespread tendency to question the validity of established standards of behaviour is accentuated by the availability of the means whereby the age-old connection between sexual intercourse and the procreation of children may be broken at will.[44] At its best increased freedom in the relationships between men and women, as in other relationships, can make for greater maturity of outlook and more responsible behaviour; at its worst it can lead to stultifying confusion of thought and deteriorating standards of conduct.

The response to the complexities of the present time made by those church leaders and thinkers whose views on the subject have been made public would seem to be almost as diverse as those of writers who do not 'profess and call themselves Christians'. From within as well as from without the Church, traditional teaching and discipline on matters relating to sex and marriage have been criticised as imposed, legalistic, restrictive and punitive,[45] while these views have, in their turn, been subject to vigorous criticism.[46] The very sharpness of the controversy can be regarded as in itself a measure of deep and widespread concern as to what guidance the Church should give the modern generation on these issues, a concern which manifests itself in the thoughtful and prayerful attempts which are being made by both individuals and groups[47] to re-examine Christian ethical teaching in the light of modern knowledge and to assess the contemporary situation with the help of insights derived from the Christian gospel.

When such an attempt is made two contrasting approaches become apparent. One works deductively from accepted principles; the other 'from the individual case in all its concrete details with no other general principle than that of being guided by love', that is to say by 'the closest possible relationship of mutual responsibility with the other people involved'.[48] The outcome of the first approach, carried to its logical conclusion would be strict adherence to a defined moral code, although this would not necessarily preclude understanding of and tenderness towards those who transgress it; the outcome of the second a 'new

86

morality' in which personal relationships would be paramount, responsible freedom the ideal and 'nothing prescribed—except love'.[49] One of the most urgent tasks now facing Christian thinkers is to evolve a synthesis which will do justice to both these points of view. To few would this be of greater help than to the Church social worker. Her daily work brings her in contact with sordid tragedies involving the wreckage of young lives resulting from the misuse of freedom, but she is made equally aware of the damage done by unforgiving self-righteousness associated with rigid adherence to a narrow moral code. As a caseworker her ultimate concern is with individuals in their uniqueness; as a church worker she is expected to uphold the standards and values of the religion she professes. Her dilemma is a real one, and in some respects her position is more difficult than it was when, although the situations she had to deal with were as tough or tougher, both she and her clients had a greater certitude as to what were accepted standards of behaviour. Today she is inevitably involved in both the ethical problems and uncertainties of contemporary life and thought and the changing and apparently contradictory responses of the leaders of the Church to the social and moral challenge of the present situation.

5

CONCURRENT DEVELOPMENTS
IN SOCIAL WORK
AND POLICY

IN the chapter just completed we were describing those aspects of twentieth century life most closely related to the type of problem with which the moral welfare worker has to deal. In this chapter we propose to discuss those changes in social policy and administration which already have had some, and in future are likely to have more influence on the scope and character of moral welfare work.

For the most part these are developments which are taking place in the health and child care services, and an early and important development of this kind was the issue by the Ministry of Health, in 1943, of Circular 2866, *The Care of Illegitimate Children*. As already pointed out in Chapter 3, this Circular drew the attention of local maternity and child welfare authorities to the desirability of formulating and administering schemes for dealing with the difficulties encountered by unmarried mothers and their children, and suggested that 'the appointment of a trained worker experienced in the problems she would have to handle' might well form part of any such scheme. Whether or not they made this appointment, authorities were encouraged to 'co-operate with and reinforce the work of existing voluntary organisations'.

The immediate steps taken by local authorities to implement the Circular have already been outlined.[1] They revealed a marked tendency on the part of authorities to rely on existing moral welfare organisations and workers rather than to appoint their own specialist staff, and this tendency has been maintained.

Concurrent Developments in Social Work and Policy

Reporting in 1959, sixteen years after the issue of the circular, the Younghusband Committee observed that 'there is less tendency to take direct responsibility for this service than for some others with which we are concerned'.[2] At the time when the Committee were making their investigations, the returns of only sixteen local health authorities in England and Wales listed staff specifically appointed for this type of work. As the Committee pointed out, any real comparison with early figures was impossible because of the reduction in the number of responsible authorities brought about by the National Health Service Act (which took away from the municipal boroughs and county districts their maternity and child welfare responsibilities and concentrated them in the hands of the county councils), but they estimated that, between 1945 and the date of the enquiry there had been a relative decrease of nearly 50% in the number of local health authority workers specialising in the care of unmarried mothers and their children.[3]

The Younghusband Committee made no attempt to account for this relative decline. The decrease in the illegitimacy rate during the early fifties, the shortage of suitable workers and the tendency, which will be discussed later in the chapter, to play down specialist provision and substitute more general family care, may all have contributed to it. Circular 2866 had been a war-time measure, an attempt to deal with a situation which was becoming desperate as illegitimacy rates soared, and many local authorities were no doubt content, when the war-time crisis was past, to revert to their well established practice of relying on the district health visitors to deal with those cases in which no urgent social needs were apparent, while referring to the voluntary organisations cases presenting special difficulties or needing residential care.

The different arrangements which might be made by local authorities, and the varying modes of co-operation with moral welfare associations, as well as the general trend away from direct provision by authorities in recent years, were all illustrated in the two dioceses of the present survey. Between them these covered the areas of two county councils in the south of England and part of one in the north, besides seven county boroughs, one of which was a large city. Only one of the three county authorities within the survey dioceses had at any time appointed its own

89

specialist social worker, and none of the county boroughs had taken this step. The county which made the specialist appointment was one of the two southern counties, the council of which showed a general preference for administering its social services directly, appointing and utilising its own staff for the purpose, rather than making use of voluntary organisations. In accordance with this general policy, the council quickly followed up Circular 2866 by appointing a trained and experienced almoner who was to be responsible for work with unmarried mothers and their children throughout the county. This appointment was followed by others and at one time the county was employing five full-time and one part-time worker. By this time the scope of their work had been widened to include the welfare of patients suffering from tuberculosis and venereal disease as well as the care of unmarried mothers and illegitimate children. At this period, too, the county council was running its own mother and baby home, which was opened in 1948, but this venture does not appear to have been wholly successful. The home proved expensive to run, partly perhaps because of the wide fluctuations in the number of cases utilising it at any one time, and it was finally closed down in 1954. For the next five years beds were reserved in a private maternity home, but this did not prove to be a satisfactory arrangement either, and when, in 1959, the diocesan moral welfare association opened a new mother and baby home in which the arrangements were made sufficiently flexible to allow for difficult and emergency cases, the county reserved four beds there, an arrangement which was in operation at the time of the survey.

The almoner service also appears to have encountered difficulties and the number of almoners employed by the county for the various purposes mentioned above was allowed to decline, so that by the time of the survey only one was still employed and she was nearing retirement. She retained her original responsibility for unmarried mothers while those in connection with after-care had been expanded to include mental-health work. In consequence she had limited the area in which she herself undertook casework with unmarried mothers to the northern and eastern parts of the county. In other areas the county had an agency agreement with the moral welfare associations whereby the almoner remained responsible for the approval of all maintenance grants for mothers going into homes but the moral welfare workers undertook the social casework. The county council paid an annual grant to the diocesan moral welfare council, which the latter distributed to the various local associations affiliated to it, including those covering the area dealt with by the county almoner. Thus in certain districts, at the time of the survey, the county council was helping to finance what were virtually two parallel services. Nor had the moral welfare associations concerned apparently made any attempt to modify the scope and character of their work so as to relate it to that of the county almoner and the two services were maintained side by side.

The position taken up by the health authority in the other county within this diocese was quite different. No attempt had been made to bring in a specialist social worker to care for unmarried mothers and their children; the policy had always been, so we were told, 'to support to the fullest extent the diocesan moral welfare societies'. The health official who made this statement was one of several officials in different parts of the two dioceses surveyed who pointed out that in many cases of unmarried motherhood the girl and her baby were absorbed into her family, and who believed that in these cases all that was required was the practical help and advice of the health visitor. 'We don't particularly want to do anything, or for moral welfare workers to do anything, if there is no need,' was a typical expression of this way of looking at the situation. Only one local health authority referred all extra-marital pregnancies which came to the notice of its officials to the moral welfare worker for social help; in other areas it appeared to be the practice to refer only those cases where the family was non-existent, unsatisfactory or unsympathetic and it was believed that the girl was in real need of residential accommodation and social care, together perhaps with women and girls needing or wanting advice on obtaining an affiliation order or placing a child for adoption. For the general run of cases the health visitor was regarded as 'the key to the situation'. Nor was it the common practice to appoint special health visitors for this kind of work. This policy had been tried in one of the smaller county boroughs, but it had subsequently been abandoned, the reason for this being, according to the borough's superintendent health visitor, that a special appointment of this kind singled out unmarried mothers, and, on balance, the advantage lay with an arrangement whereby each district health visitor handled her own cases.

The most pressing need of many unmarried pregnant girls is for somewhere to stay during the weeks immediately before and after their confinement. Provision for the confinement itself is the responsibility of the hospital service and, although we made enquiries from a number of medical officers of health on this point, we received no indication that, in their view, unmarried mothers were inadequately catered for. One medical officer stated that there was a shortage of maternity beds generally in his area, but commented that in this situation 'unmarried mothers get preferential treatment and are, in fact, in a better position than married expectant mothers'. A possible reason for this apparently preferential treatment, we learnt in another connection, is that there are likely to be more obvious social reasons for making a place for an unmarried mother than for a married woman, and a hospital would be prepared to take these into account when allocating beds.

While the regional hospital boards and management committees provide hospital care for unmarried as well as for married women, the provision of accommodation before and after confinement comes within the scope of the local health authorities and, as with the social care of unmarried mothers and their children, few authorities undertake this responsibility themselves. The majority leave it to the voluntary organisations, a policy apparently accepted by the Ministry of Health who, in a recent commentary on the general situation, gave the impression that, for whatever reason, they are reluctant to take any active steps to modify the present position. 'The rising number of illegitimate births,' the statement reads, 'is likely to increase the demand for provision for the unmarried mother; the voluntary organisations experienced in this work will, no doubt, continue for a long time to make the major contribution.'[4]

The position of local authority children's departments with regard to the care of unmarried mothers and their children differs from that of the health departments in two respects. In the first place, the aim of the local authority maternity and child welfare services is the promotion of the health of mothers and young children and social care is a means to that end; on the other hand children's departments are concerned about the overall psychological and social adjustment of neglected and deprived children, and their physical health is regarded as but one component in this well-being. The majority of child care officers are regarded, and regard themselves, as social workers, and in as far as they concern themselves with the care of the unmarried mother and her child, they are concerned about her social rather than physical needs. In this respect their function with regard to these mothers and children is much more akin to that of the moral welfare worker than is that of either to the function of the health visitor. It is perhaps significant that in our discussions with health officials it was referral from the health department to the moral welfare worker which was at issue; in discussions with child care officials the question usually raised was whether and, if so, under what circumstances, cases should be referred by the moral welfare worker to the children's department.

The second feature which differentiates the position of the children's department from that of the public health authority is that the former has no specific responsibility for the care of unmarried mothers and their children as such comparable with that laid on health departments by Circular 2866. Leaving aside their responsibilities in connection with adoption, local authority children's departments derived their authority at the time of the survey from two major enactments, the Children and Young Persons Act, 1933, and the Children Act, 1948, together with their subsequent amendments. The former Act, whose immediate impact on the scope and character of moral welfare work has already been described,[5] made provision *inter alia* for the protection of children and young persons under 17 who, although they might not have committed offences, were falling into bad associations, were in moral danger or were beyond control or, (after the passing of the Children and Young Persons (Amendment) Act 1952) were 'being neglected in a manner likely to cause them unnecessary suffering or injury to health'.[6] The 1952 Act also laid on local authorities the duty to 'cause enquiries to be made' in those cases where they received information 'suggesting that any child or young person might be in need of care or protection' unless satisfied that 'such enquiries are unnecessary'.[7] The Children Act, 1948, made statutory provision covering children deprived of proper home life. It gave the county and county borough councils overall responsibility for the care of such children and directed that each county council and county borough council should appoint a children's committee and officer to undertake this responsibility. The major task assigned to the newly formed committees was that of providing alternative care for children whose parents were unable, temporarily or permanently, to provide proper care for them, but the committees were also assigned statutory duties in connection with adoption, child life protection, and children and young persons in need of care or protection 'within the meaning of the Children and Young Persons Act, 1933'.

We found marked differences of opinion both between officials and moral welfare workers and between the officials themselves, as to whether and under what circumstances unmarried mothers under 17 should be regarded as young persons possibly 'in need of care or protection' and therefore a responsibility of the children's department. The children's officer of one county expected moral welfare workers to notify her of all unmarried pregnancies where the girl was under 17, as was the practice of the health visitors in this county. The children's department would then investigate the circumstances; if the local moral welfare worker was already in touch with the family she might (though not necessarily) be asked to continue her work with it, but if she wished the children's department to pay for residential accommodation the girl in question had to be received into care. Where there had been no previous contact with a moral welfare worker, the children's department would take full responsibility for the case, make arrangements for residential accommodation should this prove necessary, visit the family while the girl was in the home and undertake after-care which, if it was in the girl's interest, might continue until she was 18, or even longer.

Other local authorities were more flexible in their approach. They did not expect moral welfare workers to refer to them all cases of young unmarried mothers, and when cases came to their notice from other outside sources they would either deal with these themselves or refer them to a moral welfare worker, the decision in such instances depending, according to one authority, on such matters as 'age, home circumstances, previous knowledge of the girl concerned and whether or not a serious offence had been committed'.[8]

The situation with regard to teen-age unmarried mothers is

complicated by the fact that carnal knowledge of a girl under 16 is an offence under the Criminal Law Amendment Act, 1886, so that what is involved is not simply the welfare of the girl and her infant, and the possible need of her family for social work help, but a decision as to what action should be taken with regard to laying information before the police, and whose responsibility that should be. It seemed from our investigations that children's departments were, in the main, both flexible and sympathetic in dealing with cases of this kind and had sufficiently good relations with the police to ensure that criminal proceedings were only taken when such action was really appropriate. Nevertheless there were moral welfare workers to whose notice a case might have been brought in the first instance who were very reluctant to have the decision taken out of their hands. They were sensitive to the distress that the possibility of any contact with the police might cause the girl's family, and felt strongly that they had a duty to respect the confidence of those private individuals, the family doctor, for example, who had referred the case to them without any inkling that such a referral might ultimately result in police proceedings. With the increase in the number of girls becoming pregnant in their early teens this issue of private trust and public responsibility is likely to become more widespread and acute and appears to be already under discussion in social work circles.

Although so far in this chapter the discussion has centred on the extent and nature of local authorities' responsibilities for unmarried mothers and their children considered as a specific category of persons, such responsibilities are regarded by the authorities concerned as part of their responsibilities for wider sections of the community. Maternity and child welfare services are designed to promote the health care of all mothers and young children in the authority's area, while children's departments exist to meet the needs of all deprived children and they undertake 'preventive' work in many different kinds of cases. To the former service, the unmarried mother is a young mother with special needs and problems, but before all else a young mother to be treated as far as possible like all young mothers; to the latter service she is an adolescent girl in a particularly difficult situation, and perhaps presenting particularly difficult social and psychological problems, but in many respects not unlike other adolescent girls with difficult problems and to be dealt with accordingly. This gives rise to the question as to whether, and how far, it is necessary or desirable to maintain for unmarried mothers, a specialised service with its own specially trained workers and its own separate provisions.

This particular issue was considered by the Younghusband Committee in connection with their discussion about the scope and character of the work undertaken or likely to be undertaken by social workers employed by health and welfare departments. The conclusion they reached was that, 'From the social aspect and the need for social work by local authorities, it does not seem to us desirable or necessary to single out unmarried mothers to any greater extent than circumstances make inevitable.' The Committee regarded the unmarried mother primarily as a woman endeavouring to bring up a child or children without the support of a husband and father, and pointed out that she is not alone in this position. Widows and deserted wives are also 'unsupported mothers', and in these categories, as among unmarried mothers, there are some women who are 'socially maladjusted' and 'mentally dull'. Hence, 'apart from medical or health conditions and arrangements for the confinement,' the committee saw 'no advantage in isolating the care of [unmarried] mothers either from similar work with unsupported mothers or from the work of a family caseworker employed by the health department'.[9]

The recommendation of the Younghusband Committee that for the purposes of social care unmarried mothers should not be singled out 'any more than circumstances make inevitable' reflects the current emphasis on general and family casework which is regarded as generally preferable to the specialised treatment of narrowly defined categories of need. Much has been, and still is being accomplished by the specialised social services, but, as time has gone on, it has become increasingly obvious to many social workers and administrators that 'specific forms of help to meet specific needs' are no substitute for 'comprehensive and lasting help to the whole family'.[10] This change of emphasis has been accompanied by an ever increasing awareness on the part of social workers that, whatever the particular administrative setting of their work, some attempt to rehabilitate and strengthen the family is an essential concomitant to their job of dealing with the needs and problems of the particular individual who has come into their care. Hence over the last decade children's departments have been exploring the possibilities of 'preventive work' and in some areas appointing special officers to undertake it, while local health authorities are also paying increasing attention to this aspect of their work. By some health authorities the rehabilitation of 'problem' or 'near-problem' families appears to be regarded as a natural development of the role of the health visitor, working in co-operation with other voluntary and statutory services,[11] but in others social workers have been appointed specifically for this purpose.[12]

An inevitable, if regrettable, accompaniment to these developments has been a certain amount of inter-departmental rivalry,[13] but perhaps more significant than these rivalries have been the efforts made to devise better means of co-operation. Co-operation is one of the key words of modern social work and 'case conferences', 'liaison committees' and 'co-ordinating committees' abound. In many areas they have done valuable work[14] but they have their limitations. Both their structure and organisation and the use made of them vary considerably from area to area and it has been argued that, valuable as co-ordination may be, 'more than co-ordination is needed,'[15] the 'more' being the employment by local authorities of 'general purpose social workers', or even the creation, in some areas at least, of a local authority family casework service. According to one pamphlet advocating the creation of such a service, it would be an extension of the work of the local children's department operating through a Family Committee, and would 'offer a casework service to families in which the welfare of children was endangered and others that sought its help'. This would include 'help to unmarried mothers in planning for the future of themselves and their children' and would provide mother and baby homes, 'thereby relieving the Health Department of their responsibility.'[16]

The pamphlet just quoted was prepared as evidence from the Fabian Society to the Committee on Children and Young Persons which met under the chairmanship of Viscount Ingleby to consider both the constitution, jurisdiction, procedure and powers of juvenile courts and further, 'whether local authorities responsible for child care in England and Wales should, taking into account action by voluntary organisations and the responsibilities of existing statutory services, be given new powers and duties to prevent or forestall the suffering of children in their own homes'. The recommendations of this committee were incorporated in the Children and Young Persons Act, 1963, whose implementation is likely to have a marked effect on the scope and character of the work of local authority children's departments and, because of this, on the future of voluntary organisations working in related fields.

The section of the Act most relevant to the future of moral welfare work is Section 1 which imposes a duty on county and county borough councils 'to make available such advice, guidance and assistance as may promote the welfare of children by diminishing the need to receive them into, or keep them in care or bring them before a juvenile court'. The section is widely drawn and 'confirms and significantly extends the existing powers and duties of local authority children's departments', that is the departments through whom the new powers are to be exercised and on whom the new duties are laid. The circular issued by the Home Office announcing the date on which the section was to come into operation, from which the above quotation was taken, both made it clear that the new legislation had been drafted so as to 'give scope for initiative and experiment by local authorities',[17] and also gave some indication as to the lines along which it was hoped the service will develop. It pointed out that, 'the section does not give power to intervene in family difficulties or domestic problems unless there is some reason to suppose that these may create a risk of children having to be received into or committed to the care of a local authority.' Liaison should be maintained with such statutory services as the National Assistance Board, and 'the Secretary of State hopes that the Council (i.e., of the county or county borough) will maintain close liaison with voluntary organisations in their area active in the field with which the section of the Act is concerned'.[18] By Subsection (2) of Section 1 of the Act local authorities may, if they so wish, make arrangements for voluntary organisations to give advice, guidance and assistance on their behalf, which arrangements 'may include contributions to voluntary organisations in respect of additional expenditure incurred by them on preventive work'. It was also stated that 'many voluntary organisations which are not directly concerned with the care of children may also be able to help with

Concurrent Developments in Social Work and Policy

preventive and rehabilitative work', while from the point of view of this study, one of the most interesting and significant paragraphs in the circular was that which explored the possibility of closer liaison between the local authority and the churches in its area. Here it was suggested that 'Section 1 of the Act should widen the scope for fruitful co-operation with the clergy and congregations of various denominations in work contributing to the welfare of children'. It would seem that what is envisaged is co-operation with 'clergy and congregations' rather than with church organisations undertaking professional social work, although such an organisation might well be considered a voluntary organisation covered by Subsection (2) of the Act.[19]

At the time of writing it is still too soon to forecast with any degree of precision the ways in which individual local authorities will utilise their expanded powers and discharge their new responsibilities, but taking both this legislation and the impact of the recommendations of the Younghusband committee on local authority health and welfare services into account, it appears likely that the next decade will see a considerable expansion in the work with families undertaken by local authorities. Inter-departmental rivalries may complicate the issue, but the most serious problem to be faced in this, as in so many social work developments, is likely to be the recruitment and training of an adequate staff. It was the shortage of trained staff in local authority health and welfare departments which led to the setting up of the Younghusband committee, while, despite the strenuous efforts that have been made by the Central Training Council in Child Care to recruit and train both fieldworkers and residential staff, the number of child care officers in the local authority service with no social work qualification at all rose from 346 (34% of the total number of officers employed) in 1956 to 546 (39%) in 1962, and 53% of the unqualified staff were appointed between 1957 and 1962. In 1962 the number of child care officers with full professional qualifications was only 374 that is, 26% of those employed, while 40% were completely untrained.[20] The difficulty of staffing children's departments is further complicated by the rapid turnover of trained staff, many of whom are young graduates in their early twenties who soon leave to marry and look after their own children.

The Younghusband Committee recognised that the numbers

of students graduating from university social science departments and taking post-graduate training courses was unlikely to come anywhere near to meeting the demands of social service departments, all of which were crying out for new workers. Hence they recommended the establishment in colleges of further education of two year courses which would provide a general social work training and lead to a National Certificate of Social Work. By 1962 eight such courses had been started and more were expected to follow. Up to the present the majority of students taking these courses have been men and women already in local authority employment, but as the courses expand and multiply a good deal of this backlog should be taken up, and there should be more places for new entrants.

These courses were started primarily to meet the pressing needs of local authority health and welfare departments and directed towards their work, but the possibility of extending and adapting them so that they can be utilised by men and women wishing to specialise in some other branch of social work have not been overlooked, and courses on similar lines for potential child care officers, sponsored by the Home Office, have already been started at both the North-west Polytechnic and in conjunction with the Department of Extra-mural Studies in the University of Manchester.

It is hoped that the Younghusband and similar courses will make it possible to recruit men and women who may be good potential social workers but who are unable to satisfy university entry requirements, thus increasing the number of 'middle-grade' workers who will be able to undertake the bulk of the work. Graduates with additional professional training will still be required to carry the most difficult cases, advise and help other members of staff, supervise newly appointed workers and assist with in-service training, and the number of university post-graduate professional training courses offered by the universities has increased of recent years. Another noticeable development in university training over the last decade has been the tendency to substitute 'combined' or 'generic' courses for the earlier specialist ones. These courses are based on the assumption that the presuppositions which caseworkers have in common are as important, if not more so, than the settings which divide them.

All this means that the moral welfare worker of today not only moves in a world of rapidly changing social conditions and attitudes, but that these changes have been and are being accompanied by policy developments and administrative changes which challenge her to re-think her role as a social worker. No longer a lone pioneer braving public opprobrium to rescue the outcast and with few or no social worker colleagues, she is now a representative of a well established and generally accepted voluntary organisation for social service. It is, however, a voluntary service which has survived into an era in which the emphasis is on statutory provision, and one, moreover, in which social work is becoming recognised as one of the professions and professional standards and training are becoming increasingly desirable. The question of training is of crucial importance, and before going on to consider the work itself we propose to examine the situation with regard to the recruitment and training of moral welfare workers.

6

THE RECRUITMENT AND
TRAINING OF WORKERS

WE have now outlined the historical development of moral welfare work and briefly discussed those aspects of the contemporary situation which are most relevant to the consideration of its scope and character. Before going on to describe the work itself we propose to say something about the recruitment and training of workers, for if the Church is to continue to engage in social work not only must it attract a sufficient number of persons able and willing to devote themselves to this form of service, it must both ensure that they are of sufficiently high calibre to achieve the required professional standards and see that they receive adequate and appropriate training.

One of the noticeable features of moral welfare work during the first half of the present century was the continued concern of both individual leaders such as Miss Higson, and of the Archbishops' Advisory Board and its successor the Church of England Moral Welfare Council, for both the recruitment of an adequate number of women of good intellectual calibre and their proper training. The foundation of the Josephine Butler Memorial House in 1920 was an early concrete expression of this concern, while the 'London' course, a six month course for older women, was started in 1946 to meet the acute shortage of workers during the period immediately following the Second World War. In order to obtain as much information as we could about the women coming forward to train as moral welfare workers we examined the records of all London course students completing the course between its inception in 1945 and July 1959, together with those of the Josephine Butler House students who completed their training between the time the House moved into its present

The Recruitment and Training of Workers

premises in 1947 and July 1959.[1] During these years 142 students successfully completed the Josephine Butler House training and 180 the London course, so that in all 322 women were given some kind of preparation for moral welfare work during the period under review, rather more than half of whom took the London course.

In order to discover any changes which might be taking place in the characteristics of students and in their subsequent careers over the period we divided them into three groups according to year of entry. Group I consists of those students who attended the London courses held during the years 1945 to 1949 and J.B. House students who started training between 1946 and 1949. Group II are the J.B. House and London course students who started training between 1950 and 1953. Group III consists of those students who embarked on their training from 1954 onwards and completed it by 1959, that is it includes the 1958 entrants to the J.B. House course but, since this course normally lasts for two years, not those entering in 1959. London course students for 1959, are however included since this course lasts less than a year. Numbers in these groups were as follows:—

J.B. House			London Course		
Group I	1946–49	42	Group I	1945–49	50
Group II	1950–53	51	Group II	1950–53	54
Group III	1954–58	49	Group III	1954–59	76
		142			180

Since the periods of time covered are not of equal length, numbers in the three different groups are not strictly comparable, and it was necessary to establish the number of students entering each course each year in order to discern trends. The number of students embarking on the London course each year between 1945 and 1959 fluctuated between 7 and 18, the averages for the periods covered by the above three groups being 10 for the period 1945-49, 13·5 for the period 1950 to 1953 and 12·7 for the years 1954-59. The 1960 course trained 12 students and 13 were in training in the autumn of 1961. Josephine Butler House had its largest influx of students in the years immediately after the war and in 1949 entrants rose to 23. Numbers declined to an average of about 12 entrants each year during the early 50's and latterly

103

CWS 8

the average intake each year has been about 10. This was the number of students who completed the Josephine Butler House training in 1960, and during the session 1961-62 there were 9 students in the first and 9 in the second year of the course. Moral welfare work is generally regarded as being unsuitable for the young and inexperienced and the minimum age of entry for Josephine Butler House is normally 23.[2] The London course was designed primarily for women over 40 with good relevant experience, younger candidates being expected to undertake the longer J.B. House training if at all possible. In fact a sprinkling of students under 40 all of whom, except one, were over 30, were accepted for the London course during the years under review. The age distribution of students of the two courses taken together over the period studied is shown in the following table.

TABLE I

Age at Entry of J.B. House and London Course Students

	J.B. House	London Course	Total
Under 25	26	1	27
25 and under 30	36	—	36
30 and under 35	35	5	40
35 and under 40	19	18	37
40 and under 45	—	43	43
45 and under 50	18	53	71
50 and over	—	58	58
Not recorded	8	2	10
	142	180	322

From these figures it is apparent that over the period it was the older rather than the younger woman who was coming forward to train as a moral welfare worker. Two-thirds of those who successfully completed one or other of the courses and whose ages were recorded were over 35, 55% over 40. There appears to have been some increase in the proportion of younger students of recent years, but taking both courses together only about 46% (57 out of 125) of Group III were under 40. It is difficult to see how even the present coverage of moral welfare work could be maintained without the opportunities for older women provided by the London course.

In view of the attention now being given to the need for providing openings for older married women, it is interesting to note that 16 of the 180 students who took the London Course were married women with husbands living and 31 were widows. In both the 1958 and 1959 courses single women were in the minority.

One of the recurrent problems in the selection of candidates, particularly older candidates, for social work training, is the weight to be attached to educational attainments. While, on the one hand, there must be some evidence that the candidate has the ability to undertake academic work involving at least a certain amount of abstract reasoning and independent thought, on the other, rigid insistence on an examination qualification appropriate to adolescence and usually taken between 16 and 19 may debar candidates of real maturity of outlook as well as considerable practical ability. Hence even some universities, while requiring 'A' level passes as a condition of entry to the degree, and in the case of younger candidates to the certificate or diploma courses, are more flexible in their attitude towards certificate or diploma candidates of mature years, sometimes substituting an entrance test of their own for the more orthodox requirements.[3]

There are no minimum educational requirements for entry to Josephine Butler House, but an essay test forms part of the selection procedure. This flexibility may be compared with the position adopted by the recently started Younghusband and external child-care courses. Although the Younghusband Committee recommended that the minimum entry requirements should include passes in appropriate subjects at 'O' level or its equivalent,[4] this was not insisted upon in the first courses to be started. Nor was it made an entry requirement for the child care course started by the Manchester University Extra-mural Department in 1961. Detailed comparisons as to the calibre of the candidates will not be possible until the Younghusband and other similar courses have been running for some years, but an important difference has already become apparent in that competition for both the Younghusband and non-university child care courses is very keen,[5] which means that selectors have a large number of candidates to choose from; while candidates for moral welfare training are few and the need for workers great, which makes it difficult to refuse any but the clearly unsuitable, and this places considerable responsibility on the shoulders of the selectors.

The educational background of the 322 students taking the J.B. House and London courses over the period surveyed is set out in Table II (p. 107):

It will be seen from this table that, for nearly one-tenth of the students from both courses taken together, there was insufficient information for precise classification, while another tenth were educated privately, to what standard we have no means of knowing, although it would appear from the records that many of them were highly educated and cultured women. Of the remaining 259, 112 or 43% remained at a grammar school sufficiently long to take School Certificate or G.C.E. 'O' level, while only 40 or just under 16% passed through the Sixth Form and reached Higher School Certificate or G.C.E. 'A' level. There are indications that in as far as educational standards can be measured by examination successes they are improving. Both numbers and percentages of the London course students with a secondary grammar education up to School Certificate or 'O' level rose during the years under review from 9 students or 18% of the total in Group I to 26 or 34% of the total in Group III. The number of Josephine Butler House students reaching this level of education remained constant over the period, but the number reaching 'A' level, admittedly very small, was twice as high in Group III as in either of the other groups.

Comparatively few women with university qualifications trained for moral welfare work during the period under review: 21 at J.B. House and 13 by means of the London course. One of the 21 Josephine Butler House students had obtained a social science degree prior to entry, 11 degrees in other subjects, seven a social science certificate or diploma and two a certificate or diploma in other subjects. Seven London course students were graduates, six held university diplomas or certificates.

From this examination of educational standards reached by entrants to both Josephine Butler House and the London course, it would appear that not only is it the older, but also the less academic woman who is coming forward to undertake moral

TABLE II
Schooling of Moral Welfare Work
Trainees 1946-1959

	Elementary or Secondary Modern		Central or Technical		Secondary Grammar to S.C. or 'O' Level		Secondary Grammar to H.S.C. or 'A' Level		Private Tuition		Information Incomplete		Total		
	J.B.	L.	J.B.	L.	J.B.	L.	J.B.	L.	J.B.	L.	J.B.	L.	J.B.	L.	Total
Gp. I	7	18	3	4	18	9	4	7	5	7	5	5	42	50	92
Gp. II	10	16	6	6	19	16	4	8	2	5	10	3	51	54	105
Gp. III	12	21	3	6	19	26	8	9	1	13	6	1	49	76	125
Total	29	55	12	16	56	51	16	24	8	25	21	9	142	180	322

The Groups in this table are those already set out

welfare work, but many such women have professional qualifications of considerable value in the work which, it is worth remembering, includes residential work of various kinds as well as casework. The different types of non-university training, including technical training, obtained by students both university trained and non-university trained prior to entry are listed below, Church Army training being excluded. Some students had taken more than one type of traininig, and where this was so both types were listed.

	J.B. House	*London Course*	*Total*
Nursing: Hospital	14	36	50
Nursing: Nursery	5	4	9
Teaching	9	11	20
Secretarial	28	37	65
Domestic Science	7	14	21
Social Welfare Work	10	17	27
Missionary	3	5	8
Theological or Church work	8	25	33
Other	25	19	44
None Recorded	51	61	112

Secretarial work and nursing easily predominated, but there were evidently a number of women who transferred to moral welfare work after training for some other form of educational, social or church work.

On the basis of the information available it is impossible to do more than speculate as to the motives which have led students to give up their existing work, sometimes at considerable financial risk, to train for moral welfare work. We did, however, try to obtain some indication as to how students in training at the time when we made the investigation first heard about the work; this was obtained informally from 12 of the 13 students taking the 1961 London course and 10 out of the 18 students at Josephine Butler House. The majority (9 out of 12) of the students taking the London course had known about moral welfare work for many years prior to coming forward to train for it, but for most of these students some kind of catalyst had been needed to make them realise that moral welfare could be their work and that it was possible to obtain training for it. In five cases the connection was made as a result of reading an advertisement about training in a paper, two trainees read advertisements for jobs in their own localities and on application were told about training, while another three had learnt about the possibilities of moral welfare work in their previous occupations. Only two of the 12 appear to have had little or no knowledge of the work before being led to consider it as a possible vocation; one of these learnt about it through an advertisement in a church newspaper, the other through hearing the local organising secretary speak at a Youth Council Meeting at which she was present.

The picture presented by the ten Josephine Butler House students was more varied. Only one, a vicar's daughter, said she had known about the work for a long period—'since my early teens'; the others learnt about it in a variety of ways. In some cases the student was already thinking of taking up some form of social work. One student wrote, 'I had felt the need for some time to do work with people in less fortunate circumstances than myself, and hoped to do work with deprived children, but after a chat with my vicar learnt about moral welfare,' while another had been a nursery nurse and as such had come across a number of unmarried mothers and wanted to do more to help them. A student who was searching for an opportunity for working for the Church, looked through the advertisements in the *Church Times*, together with her vicar, to find out what were the various forms of church work in which women were needed. Moral welfare work particularly appealed to her.

Twenty-seven of the 142 Josephine Butler House, and seven of the 180 London course students, about whom we obtained particulars were non-Anglican. Of these, two London course students and eight at Josephine Butler House were Roman Catholics; the remainder belonged to some other church or domination. The replies of two J.B. House students, one a Baptist, the other a Roman Catholic, throw light on the service the House can render to students from other churches. The latter wrote, 'For a number of years I had been working (part-time) in the Legion of Mary. . . . It seemed wise to train before settling permanently. J.B. House was so well spoken of by one or two Catholics whom I knew had trained there that it seemed the best place in which to get a good comprehensive training in moral welfare work.' The Baptist student became interested in moral welfare work as far back as 1956, but withdrew the application she made then as 'the more I saw of the work the more it appeared that the majority of openings were for members of the C. of E. and little was done by the nonconformist churches'. Later, however, she decided that even if she did not eventually take up moral welfare work, the Josephine Butler House training would be an invaluable preparation for other kinds of social work with adolescent girls, in whom she was particularly interested.

Perhaps even more important as a determinant of future standards of work than the backgrounds of prospective students is the nature and quality of the training they receive, although, of course, the two cannot be entirely separated. As has been pointed out by Miss Chrystobel Blackburn, formerly Warden of Josephine Butler House,[6] training for moral welfare work is based on the assumption that the worker has a dual task. 'She is a specialist caseworker within the general field of family casework, and is accepted as such by the Church and by voluntary and statutory social workers in this country,' but she is also a Christian educationalist in the widest and deepest sense of those words. 'Through the medium of her work she seeks to interpret Christian belief and practice to men and women, married and unmarried, who are trying to find satisfying Christian relationships,' and she is 'no less concerned to commend Christian principles and values to those who are grappling with moral and social problems such as prostitution and the problem of venereal disease. . . .' The objective of the training is to equip the student to discharge these functions in the contemporary world'.

Josephine Butler House students usually undertake a training lasting two years. At the time of the investigation this included lectures and classes in Social Administration, Psychology and Biblical Theology, together with a second year course in which an attempt was made to relate Christian doctrine to the contemporary problems the student was most likely to encounter in her future work. Individual tutorials and group discussions supplemented specialist lectures on the principles and practice of moral welfare and general social casework. These are now being developed into a properly integrated course in Social Work. At that time one of the resident staff was a graduate in Theology, another a trained and experienced moral welfare worker. Arrange-

ments for the teaching of Psychology and Social Administration
were made with the University of Liverpool, Department of
Extra-Mural Studies, and in both these subjects the lecturers
were of university standing. During term time practical work was
carried on concurrently with the theoretical work. First year
students spent successive short periods, regarded primarily as pro-
longed visits of observation, in a number of different statutory
social service agencies; second year students spent three days a
week for one term in a family casework agency or with a statutory
social service such as probation or child care. Residential experience was obtained during the vacations, and all students were
given two months' supervised casework experience with a mcral
welfare worker before completing the course.

When the Younghusband Report was first published both the
Josephine Butler House Training and Selection Committee and
its Council gave a good deal of attention to the question as to
whether the training given at the House could be regarded as
comparable with the training courses which the Younghusband
Committee proposed should be established, and which, if completed satisfactorily by the student, would lead to the award of a
National Certificate in Social Work. Allowing for differences in
vocational emphasis, it would seem that, although the social
studies coverage of the Josephine Butler House course, at the
time of the survey, was not dissimilar from that of the Younghusband courses which had already been established, less
emphasis was placed on the theory and practice of social casework.
The desirability of moral welfare workers possessing a nationally
recognised social work credential is accepted by those responsible for their training and, at the time of writing, the
implications of this for the planning of the course were under
consideration.

For the majority of students training at Josephine Butler House,
theoretical and practical work at the Younghusband standard is
likely to be the most they can achieve, and some find the amount
and quality of the academic work already expected from them
stretches them to the limit of their powers. The Younghusband
courses and the qualification it is hoped they will confer are,
however, designed primarily for what the Report designates as
'middle-grade' social workers, on the assumption that for the most
part the consultant and specialist, as well as the more senior

administrative posts, would be filled by candidates who have obtained a university social science qualification followed by a year's professional social work training.

From its early days the link between Josephine Butler House and the University of Liverpool Department of Social Science has been a close one, and for many years it was possible for suitable students to take a three year House course which interlocked with the Social Science Certificate course at the University, the two courses running concurrently. Such an arrangement sometimes imposed a considerable strain on the student, and at the time of the investigation those candidates of sufficient ability were being encouraged to take the Social Science course in the first instance, during which time they could live at the House as boarders, following it by a year's moral welfare training. This enables the student to take fuller advantage of the university course and gives her more time and freedom to join in student interests and activities. At the same time it means that the training given by the House is more in accordance with the general pattern of social work training.

Of the 142 students passing through the House between 1947 and 1959, 22 took the Social Science Certificate course, six in Group I, nine in Group II and seven in Group III. If we add to these 22 the 21 who on entry already possessed a university degree, diploma or certificate, it would appear that just under 30% of the Josephine Butler House students received some kind of university education either prior to entry or as part of their training. In 30 cases, 21% of the whole number of students, the university qualification was in Social Science.

Whether, at the conclusion of the course, Josephine Butler House students take up some form of social work sponsored by the Church or enter one or other of the statutory services, they are known to be trained and commissioned by the Church and are in some sense its representatives; hence the depth and extent of their understanding of the Christian faith and their ability to relate it to the challenges and problems encountered in their daily work are all important. The theological and related teaching given at Josephine Butler House seeks to provide background knowledge of Biblical teaching and Christian doctrine, supplemented by study and discussion of their application to contemporary social needs and ethical problems, both general and particular.

During their two years in the House, students are, then, expected to combine general social work training, including the background studies such as Social Administration which this involves, with theological studies sufficiently detailed for them to qualify for the Inter-diocesan Certificate of Recognition of the Council for Women's Ministry in the Church. There is, moreover, a third requirement. The Trust Deed of the House lays it down that the curriculum 'shall always include definite teaching with reference to the furtherance of abolitionist principles to the end that every student and trained worker shall be equipped to meet and combat such existing or proposed legal, medical or social methods for dealing with prostitution or venereal diseases, as may be in fundamental unity with the principles underlying State Regulation of Vice. . . .' Nor does her 'moral welfare' training in the narrow sense end there. She is also expected to become acquainted with the legal and administrative, as well as with the sociological aspects of such problems as juvenile promiscuity, illegitimacy, adoption, guardianship of infants, marital disharmony and breakdown. She must be in a position to discuss the general issues arising from them as well as to apply principles to particular cases. This is her specialism, comparable with the special instruction in the administration of the child care services given to child care students or the medical social work training of the almoner. It is a difficult and disturbing one, controversial in character and highly charged emotionally. It requires both skill and sensitivity on the part of the staff to help students to see things in proportion and maintain a detached and balanced outlook, and it is fortunate that the staff/student ratio is sufficiently large to make regular individual tutorials possible.

In all, then, the course is quite a demanding one, both intellectually and emotionally, particularly for those unaccustomed to academic work, while despite the pre-training experience (usually residential) which is always insisted upon, some students are also unprepared for the social conditions they will encounter and the nature and difficulty of the problems they will meet. A further new, and sometimes searching, experience for many students is the community life they now must share. Josephine Butler House is a community with a strong religious emphasis and its own ethos and tradition, participation in which is regarded as part of the training. This is, without doubt, a joy and a strength to many who pass through the House and it is impossible to attend a moral welfare workers' gathering of any sort without finding evidence of this. Nevertheless, life in a close-knit single sex community has its drawbacks, and its suitability as the setting of social work training lasting in most cases for two years may perhaps be questioned.

At the time of the investigation the London course differed in many ways from that taken at Josephine Butler House. It was a non-residential course, consisting of two months theoretical and a minimum of four months practical work. Supervision might, however, continue after the completion of the course and the award of the Certificate be deferred. Started as an emergency course, and handicapped by inadequate finance and lack of suitable accommodation, factors which seriously hindered its development, it has nevertheless achieved much. Although the theoretical part of the course was always of short duration, the teaching given was intensive and undertaken by persons of repute in their own spheres. Its objective was not so much to give students a great deal of detailed information as to encourage them to be flexible in their thinking, understand broader issues and appreciate the importance of long term trends, and for some, at least, it has brought about 'a reorientation of their thinking habits', as one of the 1961 group expressed it. Good as this was, it could not wholly counteract the fact that the course was a short one, nowhere near the length of the recognised social work training courses. Perhaps the course it most resembled was the Home Office probation training course specially designed for older men and women with an adequate educational background and relevant experience.[7]

The training given at both Josephine Butler House and by means of the London Course is general in character, designed to equip the student to take up whichever type of moral welfare or related work she is most interested in. The first appointments of 274 out of the 322 students included in the investigation were in moral welfare work of some kind. The nature of these posts is shown in Table III on page 116.

The most significant feature of this table is that 176, or 64·5%, of these posts were in outdoor work, and only 86, or 35%, were residential, the remaining 12 being combined posts. Moreover, it was the London course students rather than those from Josephine Butler House who were taking up residential work (56 compared with 30). The majority of the younger women training for social work with the Church evidently regard themselves as potential caseworkers rather than residential workers.

Both Josephine Butler House and the London course were started to meet an urgent need for more trained moral welfare workers, but it has always been recognised that some among those undergoing training might find that their interest and vocation lay elsewhere, possibly in some other kind of statutory or voluntary social work. In that event they are encouraged to make a free and responsible choice. This is perhaps easier today than in the past, partly because of the greater number and variety of available social work posts of all kinds, and partly because nearly all students are now able to obtain grant-aid from their local education authorities and thus do not need help from diocesan funds with the moral, if not legal, obligations involved.

Table IV, (p.117) gives some indication as to the extent to which students taking either a Josephine Butler House or a London course between 1946/47 and 1959 took up work other than moral welfare on leaving.

The great majority of students, just over 75% of Josephine Butler House, and 93% London course, that is 85% of the whole group, took up moral welfare appointments on completing their training and, despite the wider opportunities now open to students, these proportions changed very little over the years. Josephine Butler House students were readier, and since they were younger and have had a more general and longer training, probably found it easier, to obtain some other form of church or social work than those who completed the London course. This tendency was even more marked in the case of the 22 Josephine Butler House students who, in addition to the House Certificate, obtained a Social Science Certificate from Liverpool University, only thirteen of whom obtained moral welfare appointments. In all, however, both the numbers and proportions of those who took up other forms of social work immediately on completing training were small and, especially if it is remembered that some students are nonconformists who do not always find it easy to obtain 'moral welfare posts', no more than would be expected in

TABLE III

Nature of First Appointment in Moral Welfare Work of J.B. House and London Course Students

	Organising Secretary		Outdoor Work		Combined Indoor and Outdoor		Residential				Totals		
							Supt.		Asst.				
	J.B.	L.	J.B.	L.	J.B.	L.	J.B.	L.	J.B.	L.	J.B.	L.	Total
Gp. I	4	—	18	26	2	2	5	9	2	6	31	43	74
Gp. II	5	6	19	29	2	1	5	13	7	5	38	54	92
Gp. III	—	4	24	42	3	1	4	14	7	9	38	70	108
Totals	9	10	61	97	7	4	14	36	16	20	107	167	274

TABLE IV

First Appointments of all Students completing the Josephine Butler House and London Courses

	Moral Welfare		Other Social Work		Other Church Work		Other or Not Recorded		Totals		
	J.B.	L.	J.B.	L.	J.B.	L.	J.B.	L.	J.B.	L.	Total
Gp. I	31	43	3	1	4	1	4	5	42	50	92
Gp. II	38	54	2	—	5	—	6	—	51	54	105
Gp. III	38	70	4	—	1	1	6	5	49	76	125
Totals	107	167	9	1	10	2	16	10	142	180	322

any group of people trained for one specialism but with work in related fields open to them.

Entry into a profession on completion of training does not, however, rule out the possibility of subsequent movement away from it. The next table attempts to throw light on the extent of this movement by setting out the subsequent careers of those 107 Josephine Butler House and 167 London students whose first appointment was in moral welfare work.

This Table shows that over the years just over 20% of the Josephine Butler House and about 24% of the London course students who obtained moral welfare posts on completion of their training have since left the profession, but this does not necessarily mean that they have been attracted to other forms of social work. Only ten of the 22 Josephine Butler House students who, at the time the analysis was made, appeared to have given up moral welfare work, were occupied in social work; four were engaged in some form of church work, and the remaining eight either married and at home or employed in some other form of work.

Six of the London course students who gave up moral welfare work at the end of their first appointment took up some other form of social work, three church work, while six became nurses or teachers or were married and unable to continue in full-time work. This leaves 25 of the London course students unaccounted for, but ten are recorded as having retired or died while others appear to have remained at home, at any rate for a period, possibly because of domestic commitments, and their present occupation is unknown.

From this analysis of the information made available to us it would seem that an appreciable, but not an unduly high, proportion of students trained at Josephine Butler House or by means of the London course, gave up moral welfare work either immediately after the completion of their training or after some experience of the work. A few—four in all from Josephine Butler House and eleven from the London course—returned later. In the case of the eleven London course students, six who left and returned had left because of home ties; two had retired but resumed work again, one part-time; two returned after a period in some other form of church work and one after a period in some kind of social work (unspecified).

TABLE V

Subsequent Careers of Students whose First Appointment was in Moral Welfare Work

	Moral Welfare First Appointment		Move from Moral Welfare and not returned by 1961		Move from Moral Welfare, but returned before 1961		Remained in Moral Welfare to 1961	
	J.B.	L.	J.B.	L.	J.B.	L.	J.B.	L.
Group I	31	43	10	17	2	7	19	19
Group II	38	54	10	16	2	3	26	35
Group III	38	70	2	7	—	1	36	62
Totals	107	167	22	40	4	11	81	116

119

The Present-day Setting

This picture of the recruitment, training and careers of Josephine Butler House and London course students over a period of twelve to thirteen years shows that the numbers starting training were few, nine or ten each year at Josephine Butler House, rather more for the London course, and the majority were older women. There was little wastage during training, but a persistent, if small, drift away afterwards, occasioned not only by the attractions of other work, but by home ties, marriage and retirement. This means that the ranks of the Church's moral welfare workers were not being strengthened by more than 15-20 long-term workers with any kind of recognised moral welfare training each year, and this in a situation in which general social work standards are continually rising, the work becoming more intensive and training counting far more.

Since it appears that it is lack of suitable young recruits rather than subsequent wastage which is mainly responsible for this dilemma it is important to ask why they are so few. In as far as it is trying to attract younger women, the Church is operating in a highly competitive market. Young women interested in people and anxious to serve their fellows are in demand as teachers, nurses, almoners, probation officers and child care and mental health workers, to list only those professions most nearly akin to moral welfare work, and the increased number of girls taking advantage of the more advanced education now available to them, and hence available for social work training, is offset by the increased number of early marriages. Many of the young women entering the social work professions are sincere Christians looking for work which, as well as being interesting and worth while, will provide an opportunity for service. Yet, compared with other forms of social work, there appear to be two serious disincentives to moral welfare work. The first is the salaries paid, the second the status, scope and nature of the work as the student sees it.

The salary scales recommended by the Church of England Council for Social Work at its meeting in the autumn of 1961 and comparable salaries for other forms of social work are set out in Table VI. It will be seen that the starting salaries recommended in 1961 for outdoor workers were at least £100 lower than those of social workers in comparable professions and with comparable training and there was an even more noticeable discrepancy in career prospects. An organising secretary, at the height of her

The Recruitment and Training of Workers

TABLE VI

Salary Scales—Moral Welfare Workers and other Social Work Professions Summer, 1962

MORAL WELFARE

Interim Scale Recommended by Church of England Council for Social Work Autumn, 1961.

Organising Secretaries: £750–£30–£870 (Large dioceses may go beyond this figure)

Outdoor Workers: £550–£25–£750 (Extra increments for senior
posts of special responsibility
and London weighting)

Indoor Workers: (12 beds or more)

Superintendents: £490–£25–£665 (including full board and
lodging)

Assistants: £285–£25–£425 (including full board and
lodging)

OTHER SOCIAL WORKERS

Almoners—Whitley Council Scales from April, 1962
Basic grade £720–£840
Almoner in sole charge—£840—7 years £1,035
Head almoner II £930—6 years £1,105
Head almoner III—£1,040–£1,180
Head almoner IV—£1,070–£1,310

Child Care Officers—(including 3½% increase recommended Summer 1962)
Basic grade £700–£1,010 with a bar at £930 for unqualified workers unless they have had at least five years experience in child care work.
We were informed that university students who had satisfactorily completed a child care or applied social studies course could obtain a starting salary of £850. The scale for senior child care officers is approximately £1,000–£1,180.

Probation Officers—(including increase recommended Summer 1962)
Starting salary at 22, £640, at 28, £825. Maximum salary in the basic grade, £1,050.
Senior Probation Officer—In sole charge, £1,160–£1,285
Working under a Principal Officer, £1,100–£1,225.
Salaries of Principal Probation Officers are higher again.

Local Authority Social Welfare Workers
Welfare Assistants (unqualified), £435–£665.
Social Welfare Officers, £690–£1,010 with a 'qualification bar' at £950.

powers, carrying heavy responsibilities and perhaps with many years experience behind her would, if her diocese adopted the scale recommended, receive a salary similar to that of a probation officer entering the service at 28, or a young graduate with a year's professional training taking up her first post in child care. Posts carrying comparable responsibilities in child care, almoning or in local authority health and welfare departments were worth, in monetary terms, £200 or £300 more per annum than senior posts in moral welfare work. The discrepancy is as great or greater if the moral welfare worker remains a caseworker throughout her career and does not take on any special administrative responsibility. In this event her maximum salary as recommended would be £750, compared with £1,050 in probation, £1,010 in child care, £1,035 in almoning and £1,050 in a local authority health and welfare department.

If moral welfare workers' salaries are one possible disincentive to young women interested in social work but undecided as to which particular branch to specialise in, another may well be the nature and scope of the work itself, as they see and understand it. Workers in the field claim that their work is no narrow specialism but a form of family casework, a claim which will be examined later, but in most areas illegitimacy is the presenting problem in a large proportion of the cases handled, and unless very carefully supervised, students going to a moral welfare agency for practical experience may come away with the general impression that the work consists mainly of arranging for unmarried mothers to go into homes. Many students are, moreover, ambivalent in their attitudes towards irregular sexual relationships, as these may be regarded as the natural and accepted thing by some of their fellows, and they are peculiarly sensitive to any suggestion that they are seeking to impose their own moral values on anyone else. They are, therefore, inclined to shun work which both brings them in to close contact with such problems and, since it is carried on in the name of the Church, involves the acceptance of and adherence to certain standards, however 'non-judgementally' applied in relation to particular cases. Similar situations are, of course, met with in child care and in work with problem families, but the local authority provides a more neutral, and hence, to some, a more acceptable setting. There are a minority of young Christians whose desire to undertake social work on behalf of the

Church is sufficiently strong to counteract its financial disadvantages compared with other social work specialisms, and who are attracted by the work precisely because, since it is Church work, they can openly commend Christian values and teaching, but they are relatively few in number, nor does there appear to be any real likelihood of the present trickle of entrants increasing markedly.

Moral welfare work today is largely being sustained by older women,[8] many of them the 'surplus women' of the twenties, now in their fifties and sixties, others women, possibly married women with grown-up children or widows, who have entered the profession late in life. With the present marriage rate and the numerous career opportunities available to women today it is unlikely that the present generation of elderly spinsters who have given up the greater part of their working lives to the work, kept it alive through all the difficulties of the economic depression of the inter-war years and the demands and strains of the war, and endeavoured to develop it in line with both the post-war expansion of the social services and changing concepts of social casework, will be replaced by women of similar life-long dedication when the time comes for them to retire. This is a situation which applies not only to moral welfare work but to teaching, nursing and other forms of social work also, but it is one that must be borne in mind in any realistic consideration of the future of the work.

PART THREE

The Organisation of
Moral Welfare Work

7

THE ADMINISTRATIVE PATTERN

IT has already been shown in Chapter 1 that, apart from the work undertaken by religious communities and, later, the Church Army, most nineteenth century moral welfare work was localised. Many of the early homes were quite small ventures, started by groups of people who were desirous of rescuing their 'fallen' sisters or sheltering friendless girls in their own particular area, and who formed associations of one kind or another to further these schemes. It was not until the closing years of the last century that dioceses began to appoint organising secretaries to co-ordinate the work of local associations, develop new work and integrate these sporadic manifestations of Christian charity into the accepted patterns of church organisation.

As time went on the number of diocesan organisations increased, local associations were linked with them, and through them with each other, and now moral welfare work in all the forty-three Anglican dioceses in Great Britain is organised on some variation of this diocesan and local pattern.[1] Within each diocese associations vary in age and character and both the associations themselves and the nature and size of the areas they cover bear the marks of their *ad hoc* origins. In the two dioceses we surveyed some associations could trace their history beyond the turn of the century, as, for example, a home in the northern diocese which owed its origin to a visit of Ellice Hopkins to that part of the country, others had only recently been started when the survey began.

The origins and histories of the older associations, most of which started work in the early years of the present century, were very similar and broadly in accordance with the pattern outlined above. For example, in one area in the southern diocese the work began in 1908. A shelter for girls, most of whom were in domestic service, was opened by a group concerned about the welfare of young girls entitled 'Girls Aid'. The 'worker' managed the shelter and lived in it; the committee was composed of those who supported the work. Unmarried mothers were received into the home, as were borderline defectives, and in addition to the care of the girls in the shelter, the worker paid regular visits to the local workhouse and infirmary. This 'sheltering home' remained open until 1934, since when an outdoor worker has been employed by the association. Sometimes the home survived longer than this, perhaps changing its function from that of shelter to that of a mother and baby home. In one town in this diocese the local home is still run as a shelter, and, in addition to the superintendent, an outdoor worker who has an office in the home, has been employed by the association since 1950.

The origins of the newer associations were more varied, but they were usually started to meet the need for outdoor work in areas hitherto without their own caseworker. Sometimes this involved quite complex negotiations, as was the case with a recently formed association in the northern diocese, which covers two deaneries with little in common with each other. Moral welfare work began in one of these deaneries during the First World War with the opening of a shelter from which the worker carried on a certain amount of outdoor work—a common enough pattern in those days. Later the shelter was turned into a children's home which is still in existence, but which was felt to be unsuitable for use as the centre for outdoor work in the deanery. When, during the Second World War, Circular 2866 was issued, the relevant local authority appointed a health visitor to specialise in the care of unmarried mothers and their children and the question of the appointment of a moral welfare worker remained in abeyance. With the retirement of this health visitor in 1955, a group of people was called together by the organising secretary to discuss the problems of moral welfare in this and the neighbouring deanery and to consider the appointment of a fully qualified worker. The second deanery was at that time virtually without a moral welfare worker, but money had been put aside by the diocesan board for the purpose of financing a full-time worker there, and with these funds and the offer of rent-free accommodation from the county borough covered by the first deanery, it was possible to make a start. The two neighbouring, but somewhat disparate, areas were linked together in one association, a worker was appointed and work begun. A new challenge, which can scarcely have been anticipated when this 'marriage' took place, is now facing the association since a small, isolated and rather inaccessible industrial settlement in its hitherto predominantly rural hinterland has been designated a new town.

The story of this piece of work not only illustrates the *ad hoc* and almost accidental beginnings of some moral welfare work, but also brings out the role of the organising secretary in promoting new work. In this case quiet observation and long-term preparation enabled her to seize the opportunity when it arose, and without her intervention it is unlikely that the work would have been started. The same is also probably true of the most recently formed of the local associations in this diocese, an association centred on an industrial town with marked individuality and strong local traditions. The northern diocese was, in fact, particularly interesting in that, whereas each town, even each township had its own strongly marked characteristics, its own ways of doing things, its own cherished local traditions and fierce local loyalties, the influence of the diocesan organiser was apparent everywhere in guiding and shaping policy. This may have been due in part to the small size and compact character of the diocese, with its natural centre of communications in the one large city, but it may also have been associated with a strong tradition of diocesan leadership in moral welfare work. It was less apparent in the more widely flung southern diocese which has no natural geographical centre and whose two counties face in opposite directions—one part of the Greater London region, the other belonging unmistakably to the Midlands—but even here the diocesan influence could be felt. It had manifested itself in the creation of a diocesan mother and baby home for particularly difficult cases, the formation of an adoption association and the sponsoring of an interesting experiment on a new housing area, all of which were directly under diocesan auspices. In both dioceses, however, the local character and organisation of the work was, at the time of the survey, still one of its most important characteristics.

Just as moral welfare work conforms to the accepted pattern of ecclesiastical organisation throughout the country in that it is carried on on a diocesan basis, so within each diocese most local associations are linked with the deaneries. These units of ecclesiastical administration may or may not coincide with local government areas. This may not have been of any great consequence in the days before the 'welfare state', but in these days close co-operation with a number of statutory services is essential if the work is to be effective, and the degree to which ecclesiastical and civil units of administration correspond may help or hinder this work quite considerably. This was very noticeable in the northern of the two survey dioceses. As already pointed out, this is a small, geographically compact diocese, but it is both densely populated and socially, economically and administratively diversified. It covers only about one-third of the county in which it is situated, but includes a large city with, of course, county borough status, five other county boroughs, all medium-sized industrial towns except one which is a holiday resort, and one municipal borough, also an industrial town. The remaining areas, which range from quite remote and thinly populated farmlands in the north to thickly populated mining and industrial areas in the south and which are diversified by a number of new housing areas, including two satellite towns, are divided between a number of urban district and rural district councils. A bewildering array of *ad hoc* administrative units—county health divisions, child care areas, divisional educational executives, National Assistance Board areas and petty sessional divisions—none of which appear to coincide with any of the others, add to the complexity of the scene.[2] As, outside the city, the areas covered by moral welfare associations were for the most part based on deaneries, their boundaries were different again. The boundaries of each particular unit had presumably been chosen by the relevant authority as the most convenient for its own purpose, but the whole set-up appeared calculated to ensure the maximum degree of administrative confusion and frustration.

In the areas of one or two local moral welfare associations administrative complexity could hardly have gone further, and the fact that they cut across a number of local authority boundaries added to the worker's difficulty of making personal contacts with officials. This was very marked in the case of an association which consisted of one large deanery and part of another, and which included within its compass not only a county borough of rather more than 100,000 inhabitants, but a municipal borough and three urban districts; nor was the correspondence between civil and ecclesiastical boundaries exact. This association's area was a large area for one worker to cover, and almost more seriously, it appeared virtually impossible for her to develop close liaison with her social work colleagues in the several authorities involved. 'The worker is so overloaded. She has so far to go. It is beyond one human being,' observed a superintendent health visitor excusing what she felt to be lack of co-operation. A close working relationship between the moral welfare worker and the county divisional health and welfare services had been established in part of the area, but even here the situation had become confused, as this local association covered only part of this particular health division, while the remainder of the division, which includes a large satellite town and its environs, was part of the large area covered by one of the city moral welfare workers. In conversation with two officials in this particular division it was evident that, despite their interest in moral welfare work, they were not aware that the city worker operated in part of their area.[3]

In both dioceses there have been considerable movements of population during the post-war period, which has meant that the areas covered by some associations, while appropriate when they were founded, have become unsuitable for present-day conditions. There was some evidence of this in the northern diocese, but it was particularly manifest in the southern of the two counties which make up the southern diocese. This county has received the full impact of London's over-spill. Four new towns have been created there, two small existing towns expanded and two large London County Council housing estates built. Superimposed on an area hitherto predominantly rural or middle-class residential, these developments have created a number of social problems and placed very heavy additional responsibilities on the educational, health and other social services as well as on the Church.

The steps taken by the moral welfare organisations to deal with the situation have varied greatly from one part of the county to another. At the time of the survey it appeared as though in some areas the influx of population had been ignored and the work was being carried on along traditional lines. Thus, at this time, a new town, whose population had increased from 7,000 to 36,000 in thirteen years and was still increasing, was 'covered' by a moral welfare worker whose office was sixteen miles away and for whom this was only one part of her extensive and populous area. It was hardly surprising that, at the time of our visit, officials and social workers in this new town scarcely knew of her existence.[4] The same worker covered an area which in addition to considerable stretches of countryside included twin new towns planned to cater for a population of about 60,000 and several existing towns, including the cathedral city of the diocese where she had her office. In the extreme south of the diocese a large L.C.C. estate, which was accounted a particularly vulnerable area, was visited once or twice a week by a worker from a neighbouring town who had a make-shift office in a church vestry there.

This failure on the part of diocesan and local organisations to adapt themselves to changing needs and conditions, was not, however, repeated everywhere. The development of the fourth of the new towns was followed in 1956 by the appointment of a full-time worker who both lived and had her office there. A still more enterprising venture was the appointment of a parish worker with moral welfare work training and experience to work in close collaboration with two priests in a large new housing area.[5] This work was sponsored by the diocese and made possible by a grant from a large Trust, and illustrates the need for diocesan as well as local planning to meet situations of this kind.

Partly because of the local origins of much of the work, partly because of the ecclesiastical divisions on which for the most part it is based, and partly because of movements of population, areas covered by local associations and workers in both dioceses varied considerably in size and population. For example, in one rural area in the southern diocese a worker coped single-handed with an area covering five deaneries which had a scattered population of about 13,000. In the extreme north of this same diocese two workers shared what was probably the largest area geographically, including a county town and six country deaneries, whereas at the other end of the diocese two workers were responsible for one relatively thickly populated deanery.

Although areas covered by different workers varied in size they were all relatively large, and in some of them public transport was neither convenient or rapid. Hence, the provision or not of a car could make a great deal of difference to the ease and effectiveness with which the worker handled her caseload. Records kept by outdoor workers in the two dioceses for the second week in February, 1961, as well as the experiences of the fieldworker, showed that without a car a whole afternoon could be spent visiting one case.[6] Even with a car it was possible for workers to spend between one-third and half their working time in getting from one place to another.[7] It appeared, too, from the detailed schedules that sometimes, at least, a worker who spent a lot of time travelling would lengthen her day to make up the time lost, sacrificing leisure rather than working time. Workers without cars were sometimes offered assistance with transport by committee members, which might ease the situation, particularly in an emergency, but which was no real substitute for a car at the worker's own disposal.

In large and scattered areas particularly the siting of the office was of considerable importance. The local market town is the natural focus of predominantly rural areas, and journeys to and from an office situated there are generally straightforward even if sometimes long and tedious. Difficulties occur when the worker has to weld together two or more separate districts, the area includes several centres of population and a good case can be made for siting the office in any of them. In this event the worker may resort to the expedient of a sub-office where she will be available once or twice a week. Such accommodation is not always easy to find. The worker in the northern diocese with the large and straggling area already described used a room in a vicarage as a make-shift sub-office for a time, but with the departure of this particular vicar the arrangement broke down. Accommodation was then found in the office of a related voluntary organisation, but no telephone messages could be taken there.

Hardly less important than the position of the office in relation to the area served is its location in the town in which it is situated, its ease of access and its proximity to other social services, and the larger the town the more important this becomes. Some offices in the two dioceses surveyed were well situated, others less so. The office in the northern city was in the business area with the municipal offices, police headquarters, citizens' advice bureau and family casework organisation all within walking distance. In another county borough in the same diocese the office was almost next door to the Town Hall and actually in the same building as the Housing Department. In the southern diocese too, most offices were near the centre of the town in which they were situated or, even if a little distance away, in or near the same building as other health or social services. The workers on the two housing areas had been provided with flats by their respective housing authorities, and although in each case they were some way from the centre of the estate, there were compensations; in one area the flat was on a bus route which passed the largest hospital in the area. The most inaccessible office accommodation in this diocese was that in the moral welfare shelter which was situated at the top of a steep hill and away from other offices in the town.

The premises themselves were found to be diverse in character, age and state of repair and decoration but were nearly all deficient in one or more of these respects. It should be realised, however, that the choice of office accommodation in any particular area may be limited since moral welfare associations, like other voluntary bodies, may have to make do with what can be obtained at a reasonable rent. In some areas, too, standards generally appeared to be low, and the criticisms made here of moral welfare accommodation could be applied with equal cogency to some of the cramped and uninviting local authority offices we visited.

At the time of the survey two outdoor workers were installed in modern flats, pleasant in appearance, anonymous and with excellent toilet and kitchen facilities, but no proper waiting rooms for clients. The work of two other associations was based on local moral welfare homes, an unsatisfactory arrangement, both because of the position of the homes and the lack of convenient places for clients to wait. In another area a house, formerly used as a shelter and now serving two outdoor workers as both home and offices, had serious disadvantages in that waiting space was limited, one worker had to interview in the living or dining room, while any attempts to brighten the room used by the other worker as her office were defeated by the heavy furniture, sepia pictures and dark brown paint. The impression given by the whole house was old-fashioned and out of keeping with the bustling prosperity of the modern town in which it was situated.

One of the remaining workers had a room in a private house and four shared converted private houses with other organisations. The one office in a municipal building was small but had its own waiting room and the building was used by the public on many different errands. Three offices were in property owned by local churches; one of these, a small room in a church hall, was among the worst we saw. Inadequately heated and poorly furnished, it had no storage space and a number of second-hand prams had to be wheeled into the entrance hall each time it was used. The worker admitted that she spent as little of her time as possible there. There were, however, two examples of the conversion of church owned premises into reasonably comfortable offices. The first was that of a recently formed association which had taken over the ground floor of a house formerly occupied by a community of nuns, repainted it in warm colours, laid Marley tiles on the floor and installed efficient heating. The second, the city office, was the first floor of an old church school which had been partitioned off to provide separate offices for three workers and a secretary, and a spacious area for clients to wait. It was always warm and light there and magazines and toys were provided for waiting clients.[8]

For people in trouble and perhaps doubtful as to their reception first impressions are important, and it was regrettable that some offices were difficult to find, with unprepossessing approaches, up cold and sometimes steep stairs and along dark corridors.[9] These were not altogether typical, however, and even where the approach was unprepossessing, a matter outside the powers of the association to rectify, the initial bad impression might be dispelled by the efforts made by the worker or committee to brighten the interviewing room by pictures, ornaments and flowers so that it was always friendly and welcoming.

Every worker had access to a telephone and every worker except one had a typewriter. In one diocese each office was equipped with a locking filing cabinet—an important item of equipment in view of both the confidential nature of the work and the large sums of money passing through the workers' hands. The initial situation in the other diocese was less satisfactory, but improved during the survey period. Secretarial assistance was, however, exceptional. Apart from the two diocesan offices, full-time clerical assistance was only available in the city office where three workers shared a secretary. Two other workers had voluntary help either regularly or occasionally.[10] Almost all the workers told us that they would like such help, but one preferred to handle all the paper work herself, partly on the grounds of maintaining

135

confidence and partly because she thought it helped her keep in touch with every case.

The major responsibility for the conditions under which both caseworkers and residential workers (whose particular problems will be considered later) carry out their work, rests with the local associations, who are usually the employing bodies, and in Chapter 9 we will look at their composition and functioning more closely. First, however, we must consider the diocesan framework within which local associations and workers discharge their respective functions, together with the role of the organising secretary.

8

DIOCESAN ORGANISATION AND ORGANISERS

AS indicated in the preceding chapter, the constitutional framework of moral welfare work throughout the country is closely linked with the diocesan, deanery and parochial organisation of the Church and in each diocese there is a central body, the diocesan board or council with a number of affiliated local committees each responsible for a defined area, usually a deanery or group of deaneries.

The major functions of these diocesan bodies, as defined in their constitutions, appear to be very similar. Thus, although the two survey dioceses differed in many respects, their constitutions resembled each other in both their coverage and phraseology. Both diocesan bodies were responsible for the co-ordination of existing work and the initiation of new developments. In addition, each had a general educational function, described as the promotion of 'thought discussion and action in relation to matters concerned with the place of sex, marriage and the family in Christian life' in one diocese, and the promotion of 'a healthy public opinion on all moral questions' in the other. Both bodies had been given financial responsibilities, in the one case to raise money by 'organising the Women's Offering or similar scheme', and in the other 'to receive and administer funds for the work'. The board of the northern diocese was also specifically commissioned to act as a link between moral welfare workers and social workers employed by other organisations and, within the Church, between the Church of England Moral Welfare Council (later Council for Social Work) and the local committees and workers.

In both dioceses the moral welfare board or council was a committee of the diocesan conference. Individual members were chosen almost exclusively in virtue of their participation in the organisation and activities of the Church, but opportunities existed for certain statutory and other interested bodies to be represented. Local authority representation was specifically required by the constitution of one diocese. In this diocese, too, the work of the diocesan council could be delegated to one or other of its standing committees; these included both a Finance and Executive Committee together with a specially constituted Adoption Committee specifically responsible for this particular work, which in this diocese is undertaken by the Council.

The executive officer of the diocesan organisations throughout the country is the organising secretary. She holds a key position and status *vis-à-vis* both church and social work organisations, and upon her interests, and indeed also upon her limitations, depend to quite a large extent the policy, direction and particular emphasis of moral welfare work in her diocese. Her position thus invited investigation, and for this purpose we asked organisers throughout the country to co-operate by completing a questionnaire about their duties, position and hopes for the future.[1] Replies were received from forty-one out of the forty-three dioceses in England and Wales, and despite the wide range in size and social conditions of these differing dioceses, the replies were broadly similar in their descriptions of the content of the organiser's work, its opportunities and its difficulties.

Included in our questions was one asking organisers to list the chief components of their work. The replies received reiterated the two themes of co-ordination and oversight, while in addition several made specific mention of casework, adoption and educational or propaganda work. Less emphasis was placed on developing the work; this may in part be because the final section of the questionnaire was devoted to future developments or it may accurately reflect the order of priorities held by most organisers.

The great majority of organising secretaries apparently regarded co-ordination as the most important of their functions. Thirty-six out of the forty-one replies received specifically mentioned some form of liaison work and of the five who did not do so one later in her reply quoted a phrase from her terms of appointment, 'to maintain liaison with the local authorities'. In one case the work throughout the diocese was organised from a single centre, which may have obviated the need for liaison work, at least with other moral welfare workers and committees, another organiser was single-handed in a small diocese. The remaining two had only been recently appointed at the time and felt unable to answer this section of the questionnaire adequately. Not all organisers specified what was involved in the liaison work to which they attached so much importance, but it was apparent that it was carried on both within moral welfare work itself and between moral welfare work and other forms of social work both statutory and voluntary. The latter was specifically mentioned by nineteen organisers, and the ways in which they envisaged it ranged from the strictly practical, 'dispensing grant money and accounting for it,' to the very general, 'representing the Church in the social work field'. The organising secretary who so described herself was a member of the county council health and children's case committees, the local probation case committee and the local marriage guidance council. She was also an approved school manager. Nor was she alone in this wide range of local commitments.

The liaison between the diocesan council and board and its associated committees was usually effected by the organising secretary's *ex officio* membership of them. Thirty-six of the forty-one were *ex officio* members of all moral welfare committees in their diocese and only two were not members of any; one stated she was without transport and dare not take on extra work without a car, while the other worked in a diocese where the work was centralised and there were no deanery committees. Of the remaining three, two organising secretaries were *ex officio* members of all committees but one, and one of all but two.

Three replies spoke of liaison with other diocesan boards or committees, for example diocesan boards of education, but only four expressly mentioned liaison between the diocese and the central moral welfare council, although it was implied by others.

It became apparent during the field work, and it was stressed at the various conferences we attended, that an important, if not essential part of the job of the organising secretary is that of leader of the moral welfare workers in her diocese, a person whom any one of them could consult individually at need and round whom they could gather as a group from time to time. At least thirty-three organisers listed this as one of their functions, and replies that did not mention it included several from small dioceses where only one or two workers were employed. The terms used to describe this function are interesting as they had a religious rather than social work connotation. One organiser spoke of 'pastoral care', another of 'spiritual responsibility for the workers and their work'. Eighteen considered general friendship, care and help as part at least of what was involved in their relationship with workers, while several spoke of fellowship and of being a counsellor and friend.

The advantages which accrue to the workers, especially for those living and working in relative isolation, of being able to rely on their diocesan organiser in this way are considerable, but there are obstacles in the way of its realisation. In the more far-flung rural dioceses in which distances are great and communications difficult, it is not easy for the organiser to be in close personal contact with the more remote of her workers, and letters and telephone calls are not wholly adequate substitutes. But a more serious problem than that of geography appeared to be the set up of much diocesan moral welfare work. Although in many dioceses local appointments must be confirmed by the diocesan council, the local committee remains the employing body, and one or two organisers commented on the anomaly of being held responsible by statutory authorities for the standard of work throughout the diocese, yet of having no direct oversight over the workers and of being unable to impose sanctions. The organiser's responsibilities in connection with the maintenance of high standards of work were mentioned or implied in seventeen replies, for although only one actually used the word 'standards', fourteen spoke of advice or consultation over casework and seven mentioned the recruitment and training of new workers. The need for helping workers in their relations with their own local committees or the diocesan body was also mentioned, and a small number remarked that it was sometimes necessary for them to intervene on behalf of their workers with statutory officials or other agencies.

This discussion of the role of the organising secretary *vis-à-vis* the workers in her diocese raises the whole question of casework supervision, the importance of which, for new recruits in particular, is being increasingly stressed by professional social workers and coming to be expected by new workers in their first posts. Not every organising secretary is fitted by temperament or by training to undertake this quite onerous task, however, especially if it has to be added on to an already over-full weekly schedule, and the possibility of appointing senior caseworkers, who will act as casework consultants and supervisors as well as carrying their own case loads, is being considered in some dioceses, while some appointments have been made already.

In addition to her administrative duties and the responsibilities associated with her position as leader of a team of workers, the diocesan organiser may also participate directly in the work itself, that is in casework, adoption work or educational work. There were wide variations between dioceses in this respect, and the situation in any particular diocese appeared to be governed, partly at least, by the organiser's own personal preferences and abilities, but, whereas educational and propaganda work was apparently often regarded as an integral part of the organiser's responsibility, direct participation in casework and the arrangement of adoptions was felt to be additional to it. In some of the smaller dioceses the organiser was appointed as a part-time caseworker, in others her administrative duties were regarded as too onerous to allow her to undertake casework in addition. From the replies received it appeared that fifteen organisers undertook neither casework nor adoption work, although some of these would do relief work in an emergency, four were responsible for adoptions but not for casework, twelve had a case load of their own, ten with an area for which they were responsible, but did not undertake adoptions. This left ten who undertook both casework and adoption work in addition to their duties as organisers, eight with their own areas. Of the eighteen organisers with their own casework areas (eight with and ten without specific responsibilities for adoptions as well as the general run of casework) eight made comments which suggested that they were hindered by their case loads, which might range from eighty to a hundred cases annually, from doing what they regarded as their proper job as organiser, and that this constituted a serious obstacle to the further development of the work.

The limiting effects of shortages of money and trained woman power on both present work and future plans were referred to over and over again in the replies the organisers sent in. The shortage of woman power is, moreover, apparent among the ranks of the organisers themselves. At the time when the 1961 Directory of Moral Welfare Work was printed the organiser's post was vacant in three English dioceses, and from the replies received it would seem that at least five of the forty-one organisers who replied to the questionnaire were approaching retirement. There would also appear to be some difficulty in filling these senior appointments from among the moral welfare workers who have experience in the field, for of the organisers appointed between 1948 and 1960 eight, including five appointed after 1957, were older women trained on the London course and five had no previous experience of moral welfare work. One factor in the situation may be that many workers do not wish to exchange casework, which brings them into contact with people in difficulty, for work which they regard as largely administrative and promotional, while the overall shortage of women with good academic qualifications as well as practical experience shows itself particularly clearly at this level of appointment.

As well as the influence which each organising secretary wields in her own diocese, organisers as a group have done much through their own association, the Association of Organising Secretaries, to make their influence felt throughout moral welfare work as a whole, particularly through their efforts in co-operation with the central council, both to raise standards of work and see that the interests of the workers are safeguarded. A group of relatively senior women, used to high-level negotiations with both diocesan and local authority officials, they represent, more than any other group, the administrative and professional element in moral welfare work. At the other end of the scale, the local committees, whose role we now go on to consider, are the embodiment of the contribution which is made by the ordinary church member.

9

LOCAL ASSOCIATIONS AND COMMITTEES

DIOCESAN boards or councils are, in general, responsible for the co-ordination and extension of moral welfare work in their respective dioceses, but its day-to-day administration is the task of the local associations who are affiliated to them.

At the time the fieldwork started eight local associations were affiliated to the council of the southern diocese, while a sub-committee of the council itself was responsible for the management of the diocesan mother and baby home. Each committee was responsible for all the moral welfare work in its own particular area; for two of them this included the management of a home as well as the employment of one, or sometimes two, workers. The terms of affiliation, as stated in the constitution of the diocesan council were that the constitution of the local committee must be approved by the council and must provide that the majority of its members are members of the Church of England, from which majority the chairman must be chosen. The northern diocesan board had formulated no such explicit rules for affiliation, but we found a very similar pattern of organisation. Ten committees were affiliated to the board, the eleventh, that of the large city, is a sub-committee of it. At the time of the field-work one local committee was responsible for running a mother and baby home together with the outdoor work which, at that time, was attached to it, five were outdoor work committees, two others responsible for mother and baby homes and one for a children's home. Two were boards of managers of recognised approved schools.

We met members of all committees in both dioceses except the managers of one approved school.[1] Our meetings took a variety of forms. Sometimes we were invited to attend routine meetings as observers, normally with an opportunity to ask questions at the end of the meeting; other committees convened a special meeting or reduced other business to a minimum in order that more time might be available for discussion of the issues we wished to raise; still others gathered together a few members, perhaps the officers of the association for more intimate discussion. We had prepared a questionnaire for use at these meetings, but in practice we found it of limited value as the discussions were generally free and informal and ranged widely.

The areas covered by the different committees and the amount of work undertaken varied considerably and so, too, did the complexity of their constitutional structure. Four indoor and four outdoor committees were each wholly responsible for the work of their local associations without delegation to sub-committees. A further three had one or more sub-committees with clearly defined practical responsibilities, two were house committees in charge of the everyday management of the home concerned, while another had two case committees attached to it. These advised on particular cases submitted to them by the workers. The pattern of the remaining committees was for a general committee or council of the association, a large body usually composed of representatives of every parish in the area, to meet at long intervals, while the executive committee, meeting in the intervening months, undertook most of the practical responsibility for the work. In some areas, the executive functions were in turn sub-divided, so that in one area there were three case committees in addition to the executive, while in another the executive acted as case committee and there were separate finance and programme committees.

In many areas, every incumbent in the area covered had the right to sit on the committee, but, fortunately, this right was never exercised simultaneously. Sometimes the incumbent delegated his right to a lay person, elsewhere every parish might send both clerical and lay representatives. Other committees (particularly executive committees) limited such representation. At least in theory the majority of the committees were interdenominational, but we found that in several places the Free Church, or more commonly Roman Catholic, membership had lapsed, while in one or two others the nonconformist members who were serving had been invited on to the committee for reasons which had nothing to do with their denominational allegiance. By the conditions of diocesan affiliation non-Anglicans were precluded from holding office as chairman, and in some cases were barred from other offices as well, but this latter exclusion was not universal and several secretaries and treasurers whom we met were Free Churchmen. Committee constitutions usually also required the majority of members to be Anglicans, and whether required or not, this always was so in fact.

Several committees mentioned that although they warmly welcomed non-Anglicans they found difficulty in appointing them because of lack of personal contact with members of other churches, an indication that the appointment was regarded as a personal matter rather than as an invitation to another branch of the Church to nominate its own representative. A different attitude was, however, evinced in one area where, before a new committee was formed, the diocesan organising secretary and the rector of the town agreed that they must have the backing of all the churches before they could approach the local authority for support. This committee is interdenominational in the fullest sense with active Roman Catholic and Free Church representation, both clerical and lay. In other areas some members whom we met evidently felt that there were unsatisfactory features in the position, the particular points made being that non-Anglicans were denied participation at the diocesan level and not all offices were open to them. It was also felt that Free Church members, in particular, were in a difficult position because they were not specifically empowered to speak on behalf of the nonconformist position, although this was what they were supposed to represent. Underlying these specific discontents was the feeling, expressed by a Presbyterian minister, who, interestingly enough, was acting as chairman on the occasion on which we attended the committee of which he was a member, that the Anglican approach to the Free Churches was simply that of 'asking for money'. 'It is an Anglican society, with the Free Churches merely represented,' he added, and evidently felt that it was not always easy for nonconformists, with their own national organisations and commitments, to support the work on these terms.

Representation of statutory and voluntary social work agencies was provided for by the majority of the committees in one diocese and nearly half of the committees in the other. The local authority health department was the one most frequently represented, but social welfare (where separate from health) and children's departments were also represented on more than one committee, as was the probation service. When we interviewed senior officials in these departments, however, we found a general lack of interest in this form of co operation, although there were exceptions, notably the medical officer of health of a county borough who himself sat on the local moral welfare committee, 'because what Miss X is doing is worthwhile and she bears too much of the burden of it alone'. The absence of cross-representation was occasionally regretted, but for the most part, contacts between officials and workers at the informal level were thought to be more satisfactory.

Voluntary bodies were less frequently represented than the statutory services, but those that were included such social work organisations as the local marriage guidance council and council of social service, together with specifically church societies such as the Mothers' Union and Church of England Men's Society. Sometimes the position as to who was representing what was not altogether straightforward, as in the case of the committee member who was a representative of her parish but who happened to be a marriage guidance counsellor, so that, in the view of the committee, marriage guidance was 'represented'. In another area a probation officer was an active member of a committee and acted as a link with the service, but he served on the committee in his personal capacity as representative of the Church of England Men's Society. Nor were members themselves necessarily clear about the basis of their membership, and in some cases their appointment seemed to have been almost haphazard. 'I came because the organising secretary rang me up'; 'Canon N. rang and asked me'; 'Mrs. So-and-So asked me', were three explanations as to why they were there, all given by members of a committee which, by its constitution, was supposed to be made up of parochial and other representatives.

Some idea of the type of membership that emerged from this procedure can be gained from the following list of those present at six of the committees we visited, which we have chosen as examples:

2 clergymen (one the deanery youth chaplain)
1 layman (chairman of a sub-committee)
4 ladies (including the hon. secretary and treasurer)
The organising secretary
(Outdoor Work Committee)

1 Presbyterian clergyman (acting chairman)
2 Anglican clergymen
1 layman (the treasurer, a banker)
8 ladies (including the hon. secretary)
The organising secretary
The worker
(Outdoor Work Committee)

2 clergymen (one the chairman)
6 ladies (including the hon. secretary)
The organising secretary
2 workers
(Outdoor Work Committee)

3 clergymen (the chairman, the chaplain and one other)
1 layman (the treasurer, who was a banker and a Methodist)
7 ladies (including the hon. secretary, one a local councillor)
The organising secretary
(Committee of a Mother and Baby Home)

2 laymen (the chairman who was the borough treasurer, the other a bank
  manager)
3 Anglican clergymen
1 Methodist minister
1 Roman Catholic priest
4 ladies (one representing the Catholic Women's League)
The superintendent health visitor
A mental health worker
The organising secretary
The worker
(Outdoor Work Committee)

16 present, all ladies, including the organising secretary, who was acting as chairman, the treasurer, (an elderly Presbyterian) and the
  worker.
(Children's Home).

From our observations it appeared that the treasurer, who
might be a local banker or businessman, and quite possibly a
nonconformist, was often the only male member not ordained,
and in some cases the committees appeared to be made up largely
of clergymen and middle-aged married women. One committee
we visited expressed concern at the high proportion of elderly

women serving on moral welfare committees, and, while recognising that they were often people of relevant experience and mature judgment, thought it would be desirable to attract more lay men, including an educationalist. Only four committees visited had evening meetings, however, and it is not often possible for persons employed in full-time educational or other work to attend meetings during the day. We were told that some committees had given considerable thought to the matter and had made real efforts to find a time reasonably convenient for both clergy and laity, married women and people in employment, but this had proved far from easy. On the other hand, it seemed that in one or two cases at least, the time of meeting was traditional and might have remained unaltered, or even unconsidered, for the past 50 years or more.

According to the handbook entitled *The Committee Member* issued by the Church of England Moral Welfare Council in 1955, the functions of a local moral welfare committee are fourfold; the appointment of workers, the guidance of policy, financing the work and the provision of suitable equipment for it. It appeared from our contacts, however, that in the two dioceses surveyed, the third of these functions, that of raising the money necessary to keep the work going, tended to overshadow the rest, and we have devoted a separate chapter to it. This concentration on finance was probably inevitable in view of the difficulties with which most associations were faced. Some whose position was a little easier than the rest, were able to say, with a touch of pride, that their meetings were not entirely devoted to discussions about finance, but for the majority the statement made, only half-jokingly, at one meeting, 'This committee is too busy raising money to have time to think about the work,' seemed to be nearer the truth.

While for most committees finance appeared to overshadow policy-making, the Church of England Moral Welfare Council's handbook gives the latter precedence, and on our visits to local committees we encouraged members to discuss policy issues with us and with each other. As any discussion of policy presupposes some understanding of the nature of the work undertaken, and some assessment of its value, whether or not this is made explicit, we usually began by asking committee members to define or describe moral welfare work as they understood it.

Committees did not find it easy to arrive at general definitions of the work, perhaps because most members were not accustomed to thinking in these terms. In attempting them some members used such euphemistic phrases as 'to guide those in difficulties' or 'help those strayed from the narrow path'; or deal with 'moral lapses of any sort, children, family and so on'; but these moralistic overtones were not evident everywhere. There appeared to be some consensus of opinion that moral welfare work was not synonymous with, and should not be confined to, work with unmarried mothers, but at the same time it might be recognised that, in practice, these cases constituted by far the greater part of the worker's case load and with only one worker to cover a large area, this limitation of scope was well-nigh inevitable. One committee, which thought that helping unmarried mothers was 'essentially moral welfare', were quite definite that this did not mean that as a group unmarried mothers were more 'immoral' than, for example, delinquent boys.

In discussing possible developments in the work the committees in one diocese, following the lead of the organising secretary, were in favour of moral welfare being equated with family casework carried on by and in the name of the Church; other possible developments discussed in one or other diocese were work among men and boys, marriage guidance and mental health. These developments did not appear to be envisaged as immediately practical possibilities, however, and some committees were evidently worried about the repercussions any change in the scope and character of the work might have on local authority grants. The possibility of developing the educational side of moral welfare work received rather more support, but again the impression received was of concern rather than action and there was some uncertainty as to what was implied by the term and involved in the work. The remark made in one committee that, 'while sex instruction should be under our umbrella, we should not necessarily be active in the matter,' probably summarises the views of others also.

Finally, in attempting to elucidate the attitudes of local committees towards the work we asked them to tell us what in their view disinguished it from other social work. The distinguishing characteristics were regarded as twofold, first that the work was on a voluntary as opposed to a statutory basis, and secondly that it had a religious foundation.

The belief was widespread among the committee members with whom we were in contact that statutory workers are limited in the help they can give and bound to be 'more tied by statutory duties' than the moral welfare worker who, we were told, can give long term help and might be able to help other members of the family because her interest is not confined to the client. Remarks were also made to the effect that moral welfare does not stop at satisfying physical needs, 'which is where the state more or less finishes'. Although there was one committee which recognised that statutory workers might go to great lengths to help people, the National Assistance Board being the example given, several committees thought that the statutory services are more impersonal in their approach than voluntary services. The phrase 'bearding a clerk' was used in one committee to convey this impression, while in another committee a member tried to get her meaning across by saying, 'There is more personal feeling [in a moral welfare home] than in a local authority home which is not quite the same.' The confidential nature of moral welfare work was also referred to, while still another point made was the freedom of voluntary organisations to provide for groups which are not the responsibility of any one department. Moral welfare, we were told, 'bridges the gap'—but no specific indication was given of the gaps to be bridged.

Two main points emerged from the committees' discussions of the specifically religious basis of their work. First, 'however good the local authority, it is not its function to do Christian service'. Moral welfare workers, it was said, are able to 'go further', and 'the possibility of the grace of God comes in'. On being challenged, it was readily conceded by most committees that many Christians find their vocation in one or other of the statutory services, but it was pointed out that a moral welfare committee making an appointment can make sure that the worker holds the Christian faith, whereas a statutory authority does not necessarily make this a stipulation. Secondly, it was believed that a moral welfare worker can 'let her faith glow through' and be more definite in the expression of her beliefs than the Christian employed in a statutory service. The legitimacy of bringing religious pressure to bear on people seeking help was not questioned, 'provided *undue* pressure is not used.'

Taken together, we felt that the discussions we held with local moral welfare association committees revealed a certain lack of understanding on the part of many of their members of both the duties and responsibilities of the statutory services, and of the social casework now being undertaken in connection with them. In the case of some members this imperfect knowledge and understanding of what is involved in social work in general coloured their beliefs about the moral welfare work for which they were directly responsible. Some committee members were evidently concerned about their own ignorance, regretted it, and sought to overcome it. A factor which they felt prevented them from acquiring a better understanding of the work is the geographical isolation of committees and committee members from one another; in some parts of the country this is being tackled by day conferences for committee members. Some members also lamented the lack of good informative and propaganda material; this they thought, it was the responsibility of the central council to supply.

Lack of adequate knowledge and understanding on the part of committee members is bound to be reflected not only in the degree of effectiveness of their policy-making but in their role as employers. Relationships between committees and workers are complicated by two modern trends, namely the growing professionalism of social work and the fact that the organisation of moral welfare work is such that the worker moves at the same time in two almost entirely separate situations. On the one hand she is the employee, perhaps the sole employee, of a local association and responsible to them; on the other she is one of a group of workers in the diocese and beyond, with whom she shares the same professional outlook, knowledge and skills.[2] Most committees whom we met seemed to appreciate the standing of the worker with her colleagues, and were aware that she was the possessor of knowledge and skills which they themselves lacked, but it was not always an easy position. A particular issue over which differences in outlook sometimes became apparent was that of the confidential nature of the work. This was specially noticeable in those areas, usually rural areas or small towns, where the old-fashioned custom of the worker giving a synopsis

151

of the history and progress of each case to the monthly meeting of the committee still prevailed. Elsewhere this custom had been dropped; in some areas the worker had regular discussions about her cases with a specially appointed 'case committee' whose members were either professional social workers or other knowledgeable people,[3] while in others a panel of professional people had been established, members of which the worker could consult at need.

The isolation of the worker and the burden of her work were fully recognised by some committees, and it was clear that in certain areas, in particular, individual members were making it their business to give her personal friendship and help, sometimes including such practical assistance as driving her on remote visits. Homes appear to provide numerous opportunities for practical help of all kinds, and perhaps because of this, we found that committees responsible for residential work were, in general, more directly involved in the work and convinced of their usefulness than were the members of outdoor work committees. The temporary closing of a home in one area had, so we were told, 'made a world of difference to local interest in and support of the work'.

It is this local interest and support that the associations and committees described represent. They gave us the general impression that, despite their limitations, they worked hard and gave generously of both time and effort to keep the work going. Nevertheless the set-up had its unsatisfactory features. We met committee members who were uncertain of their function and dissatisfied with the prospect of remaining little more than money-raisers, workers who felt they lacked the support which a more knowledgeable and understanding employing body might have given them and local officials who were uninterested and non-participant, together with an overall lack of any real sense of diocesan direction and strategy. The need for the re-organisation of moral welfare work in such a way as to strengthen diocesan control in the interests of greater efficiency and more uniform standards of work was already being discussed in different parts of the country at the time of the fieldwork, and discussions and experiments have been carried further since. But such re-organisation, however necessary, might possibly involve loss as well as gain, especially in those parts of the country, for example parts of the northern diocese, where committees have come to be associated with local areas each proudly conscious of its separate identity and own way of doing things. The crux of the problem seems to be to find a way of maintaining the enthusiasm, energy and concern of a vigorous local committee while at the same time insuring against uneven and sometimes poor standards of work, seeing that the workers are not left to cope in isolation with unwieldy areas, and keeping the situation sufficiently flexible for new situations to be anticipated and met.

10

DIOCESAN AND LOCAL FINANCE

DURING the survey period the two problems most frequently brought to our notice by officials and committees of diocesan boards and local associations were shortage of workers and shortage of money. Except when a staffing crisis was imminent, it was the latter which appeared to cause more anxiety to the local committee, and it was frequently brought up as a reason for inaction when such matters as salary increases, provision of transport or repairs and decorations to a home were discussed.

It is not easy to give an overall picture of the finances of local associations or compare one association with another, partly because of local variations in account keeping (no two local committees kept their accounts in exactly the same form), but also because of differences in local authority grant-aid procedure, particularly noticeable in the northern diocese with its seven different local authorities, and, additionally, because of the intricacies of the differing financial arrangements made by the two diocesan bodies with their respective local associations. We have, however, endeavoured to set out the sources of income and items of expenditure of the different associations, and where separate from them, committees of management of homes, in such a way as to reveal their relative importance.

Local moral welfare associations in the two dioceses surveyed derived their income from four main sources : —

1. Grants from local authorities, whether paid direct to the association or given in the first instance to the diocesan board or council and distributed by them. Committees responsible for running homes also receive considerable amounts in the

form of maintenance payments from or on behalf of residents.
2. Church sources, including both the diocesan offering, and
contributions made direct to the association by the local
churches, Anglican or non-Anglican.
3. Other voluntary sources including contributions from the
general public, proceeds of special efforts and allocations
from trust funds.
4. Interest from endowments, investments or rents.

Amounts received from these sources are set out in Tables
VIII and IX.

Local authority contributions differed in both amount and
method of payment from one authority to another. In the
northern diocese payments ranged from just under 20% to a little
over 30% of local associations' incomes, and, with slight variations,
both amounts and proportions tended to increase over the
three years of the survey. In the southern diocese, if we leave aside
those associations which were responsible for running homes and
derived a much higher proportion of their income from local
authority grants than did associations undertaking casework only,
the proportions, ranging as they did from 23% to 38% of the
association's income, were somewhat higher.

In the northern diocese, where individual associations tended
to be identified with the county borough where their work was
centred, grants were made direct to the local associations and took
various forms. The majority of the county boroughs made block
grants of varying amounts, the county health committee made
per capita grants in respect of maternity cases handled, while
one local authority, whose monetary contribution to its local
association was negligible, provided free accommodation, lighting
and heating. Grant aid from one of the two counties which make
up the southern diocese was paid direct to the diocesan association, by whom it was allocated to the local associations responsible
for the work in its area, but the grant from the second county was
divided between the two local associations which between them
cover its area, and, by what was apparently a historical anomaly,
was paid to one association direct and to the other through the
diocesan association. The most usual method of assisting moral
welfare homes was that of making *per capita* payments on behalf
of local residents, the amount paid by the authority being fixed

by the management committee of the home, and varying quite considerably from one home to another.[1]

Income from church sources reached the local associations in the survey dioceses through two main channels; firstly the special offerings collected throughout the dioceses usually by and through the women's organisations, and secondly the donations made directly to local associations from individual churches in their area.

Policy with regard to special offerings differed from one diocese to another. In the northern diocese the annual Women's Offering Service, held at the cathedral in October each year was utilised, not only as a means of collecting money but also of stimulating interest. During the preceding fortnight parishes were asked not only to collect but to intercede for the work. A letter was sent by the bishop to all incumbents enclosing duplicated sheets of prayers appropriate for the purpose, and a short statement about the work including an appeal for money and workers appeared in the Diocesan Leaflet for the preceding month. The money to be offered at the service was collected by each deanery in its own way, usually through the Mothers' Union; a suggestion made at a meeting of representatives at which we were present, that the name 'Women's Offering' might be changed was resisted by the majority present on the grounds that, 'Women do the work and make the offering'. Amounts raised in this way, which over the ten years 1952-61 showed an increase from £535 in 1952 to £1,893 in 1961, an increase which, even allowing for the decline in the value of money, was appreciable, were divided between the local associations. A basic amount was allocated to each deanery, but exceptions might be made, for example in order to give extra help to an association just starting work in a particular area, or to another with a large and populous area and heavy commitments.

In the southern diocese the history of the special offering had been different. Named 'Home and Family Offering' in order to stress that it was the responsibility of all church people concerned about family life and not that of women only, it seems to have brought in between £700 and £1,000 a year immediately after the war, but the central collection and service were subsequently given up and deaneries were encouraged to organise their own offerings on which the diocese levied a contribution of £20 a

Diocesan and Local Finance

year to cover the cost of printing and publicity. This was the position during the period of the fieldwork; we have been informed that the matter has been under review since then.

In analysing contributions made direct to local associations from local churches, we endeavoured, where possible, to distinguish contributions from Anglican and those from non-Anglican sources. In the northern diocese, with the notable exception of one association which was started on an inter-denominational basis and has been maintained on that basis since, contributions from non-Anglican churches were limited to small donations from Womens' Fellowships and similar bodies. In the southern diocese also, although there were local exceptions, there was little support from non-Anglican churches.

Without a detailed analysis of the situation in each deanery, or even in each parish, it is impossible to do more than conjecture the reasons for the variations in the support given by local churches to moral welfare work. Prosperity did not seem to be the deciding factor. A wealthy seaside town, including, we were told, the richest parish in the diocese, was a long way behind a nearby industrial area in the total contributions made by local churches, and it appeared that knowledge of and interest in the work counted for more than wealth. In only four of the outdoor work associations[2] in 1958, three in 1959 and two in 1960 did the revenue received from church sources exceed 50% of the total revenue; in three associations in 1958, three in 1959 and one in 1960 it was less than 20%.

Under the heading of 'income from voluntary sources' we grouped together money obtained from annual subscriptions and donations, special efforts and trust funds. The first two of these sources may, to some extent, be regarded as indications of the interest local people take in the work, but it is at least possible that in this respect the distinction between church and non-church sources is less marked than this classification would suggest. Individuals who subscribe to the work may do so because they are keen church people and want to support work carried on in its name, while coffee mornings and jumble sales may be promoted by committee members or church groups.

The two most usual methods of attempting to raise money from the general public were special efforts such as coffee mornings and sales of work and house-to-house collections. In connection with the latter some difficulty was evidently experienced by collectors faced with the task of satisfying the curiosity and allaying the doubts of potential donors. We were told that some people called upon thought that there was no need for voluntary social work in a welfare state; others queried the desirability of giving help to 'naughty girls', especially when married women might be worse off, and in some districts publicity was hampered by the persistence of the feeling that the whole subject was 'not quite nice'. Some committees were helped over these difficulties by leaflets designed for the diocesan offering, which set out the nature of the work, and one committee had acted on its own initiative and drawn up a series of 'Hints for Collectors' giving both useful, practical information and answers to the questions most commonly asked. Other committees had given up house-to-house collecting and were concentrating their energies on the traditional special efforts, 'condemned by high-up bishops' as we were rather defensively told. There were considerable differences both from association to association and from year to year in the amounts obtained from these sources, which is perhaps to be expected as their success depends so often on the enthusiasm and initiative of a few individuals.

Grants from trust funds appear to have been a very present help in time of trouble to various committees and associations, especially those faced with the recurrent crises which seem inseparable from any attempt to maintain a residential institution in an old and dilapidated building, and, in another connection, it was the grant from a Trust which made possible the initiation and maintenance of the experiment in combining social and parish work described in Chapter 14.

As shown by Tables IX and X salaries accounted for more than half the expenditure of all local associations, and varied from over 80% of the expenditure of one association to just over 50% of that of another. These percentage variations were not so much due to differences in the actual amounts paid, for these were not great, as to variations in other items, the one in which differences between associations was greatest being travelling expenditure. By and large both amounts and percentages spent on this item were markedly greater in the southern than in the northern diocese. This is partly a matter of geography, but also partly due to the fact that the majority of workers in this diocese travelled by car while those in the northern diocese made more use of public transport. The amount payable for office accommodation also varied from one association to another, and the tables revealed the very considerable sums which have to be spent by associations responsible for homes to keep old property in a minimum state of repair.

Since the exact amount of the credit or debit balance shown in an association's annual report may depend to some extent on the way in which the account is presented, and since no two associations presented their accounts in the same way, we have not attempted to set the two out in tabular form. There appeared to be wide variations from association to association and year to year. Some associations, particularly those without investments and those involved in heavy expenditure on the upkeep of obsolescent buildings, were evidently finding it difficult to keep going, and it is hard to see how they could have survived at all were it not for the local authority grants. In other words, the continuance of this social work carried out in the name of the Church was dependent on the good will of the political community. Local committees were evidently well aware of this situation, and when discussing possible changes in the character and emphasis of the work, showed how sensitive they were to the repercussions such changes might have on local authority grants. A member of one diocesan body considered that the withdrawal of the statutory grant might be 'no bad thing' if it left moral welfare associations free to develop in any way they thought fit, but this temerity was exceptional, and at the other extreme we encountered a committee who considered that even changing the name from 'moral welfare' to 'church social work' might be 'somewhat dangerous'. While this was, perhaps, being over-cautious it is difficult to see how dependence on local authority grant aid, with its inevitable restricting influence on the character and scope of the work, can be avoided unless and until the Church finds other sources of revenue on which comparable reliance can be placed.

The Organisation of Moral Welfare Work

TABLE VII

Principal Sources of Income of Outdoor Work Associations and Homes—
Northern Diocese
1958, 1959 and 1960

Sources of Income	1958		1959		1960	
	Amount (£)	% of Total Income	Amount (£)	% of Total Income	Amount (£)	% of Total Income
Local Authority Grants						
Association A	740	25·7	809	34·0	787	32·3
,, B	184	23·7	195	28·9	235	29·3
,, C	119	21·2	90	18·1	185	25·8
,, D	150	21·7	171	20·2	170	19·3
,, E	—	—	255	24·5	222	29·8
St Priscilla's	—	—	—	—	—	—
St Perpetua's	525	16·6	525	14·6	425	12·0
St Pelagia's	—	—	25	1·1	25	2·5
St Perelandra's	—	—	—	—	—	—
Church Sources						
Association A	415	14·4	443	18·6	535	22·0
,, B	260	33·5	305	45·2	295	36·7
,, C	307	54·6	331	66·2	355	49·6
,, D	106	15·4	132	15·6	144	16·9
,, E	—	—	446	48·6	335	45·0
St Priscilla's	130	3·5	141	3·7	154	4·0
St Perpetua's	167	5·3	197	5·5	182	5·1
St Pelagia's	259	11·3	243	10·4	186	11·9
St Perelandra's	207	14·6	230	15·6	272	16·9
Other Voluntary Sources						
Association A	1,386	48·1	806	33·9	803	33·0
,, B	189	24·3	93	13·7	118	14·7
,, C	135	24·1	78	15·7	176	24·6
,, D	67	9·7	106	12·5	73	8·6
,, E	—	—	248	26·9	188	25·3
St Priscilla's	391	10·4	815	21·7	882	23·1
St Perpetua's	545	17·2	576	16·0	615	17·4
St Pelagia's	233	10·1	241	10·3	219	21·0
St Perelandra's	294	20·7	310	21·1	209	13·0

TABLE VII *cont.*

Sources of Income	1958		1959		1960	
	Amount (£)	% of Total Income	Amount (£)	% of Total Income	Amount (£)	% of Total Income
Endowments and Interest on Investments						
Association A	321	11·1	299	12·6	300	12·3
„ B	143	18·5	82	12·1	155	19·3
„ C	—	—	—	—	—	—
„ D	366	53·1	438	51·7	467	54·6
„ E	—	—	—	—	—	—
St Priscilla's	—	—	—	—	—	—
St Perpetua's	52	1·6	49	1·4	52	1·5
St Pelagia's	29	1·2	25	1·1	61	5·9
St Perelandra's	75	5·3	76	5·2	103	6·4
Payments by and on behalf of Residents						
St Priscilla's	3,219	85·9	2,801	74·4	2,788	79·9
St Perpetua's	1,868	59·0	2,231	62·1	2,248	63·6
St Pelagia's	1,774	77·2	1,714	73·3	530	50·8
St Perelandra's	825	58·0	825	56·1	1,028	63·7

TABLE VIII

Principal Sources of Income, Local Associations, Southern Diocese 1958, 1959 and 1960

Sources of Income	1958		1959		1960	
	Amount (£)	% of Total Income	Amount (£)	% of Total Income	Amount (£)	% of Total Income
Local Authority Grants						
Association S	200	27·8	300	28·0	250	24·1
„ T	250	33·0	250	32·9	350	36·6
„ U	200	33·3	—	—	—	—
„ V	200	23·3	250	25·2	350	31·9
„ W	255	29·6	300	27·8	300	30·1
„ X	400	29·4	600	38·0	500	31·6
„ Y	887	69·2	1,150	66·0	1,288	84·5
„ Z	1,000	47·8	1,000	36·8	1,000	31·2
Lindisfarne Diocesan Home	—	—	1,034	76.3	2,344	74·7

TABLE VIII *cont.*

Sources of Income	1958 Amount (£)	1958 % of Total Income	1959 Amount (£)	1959 % of Total Income	1960 Amount (£)	1960 % of Total Income
Church Sources						
Association S	330	45·9	482	45·0	491	47·4
" T	419	55·2	458	60·5	475	51·1
" U	46	7·6	49	8·4	—	—
" V	291	33·9	381	38·4	415	37·7
" W	544	63·1	668	62·0	517	51·9
" X	705	52·0	713	45·2	674	42·6
" Y	291	22·8	529	30·4	220	14·4
" Z	313	14·9	298	11·0	320	10·0
Lindisfarne	—	—	—	—	—	—
Other Voluntary Sources						
Association S	164	22·8	272	25·3	263	24·4
" T	62	8·2	28	3·7	81	8·7
" U	354	58·8	529	91·6	—	—
" V	360	42·0	358	36·2	320	29·1
" W	56	6·4	107	10·0	148	14·8
" X	255	18·7	264	16·8	354	22·4
" Y	66	5·1	32	1·8	16	1·1
" Z	205	9·7	263	9·7	285	8·9
Lindisfarne	—	—	85	6·3	80	2·6
Interest on Investments, etc.						
Association S	19	2·8	18	1·7	18	1·8
" T	26	3·5	22	2·9	24	2·6
" U	—	—	—	—	—	—
" V	7	0·8	2	0·2	9	0·8
" W	6	0·7	2	0·2	13	1·3
" X	1	0·1	—	—	—	—
" Y	32	2·5	37	1·8	—	—
" Z	27	1·3	27	1·0	27	0·8
Lindisfarne	—	—	—	—	—	—

Payments by and on behalf of Residents (*associations responsible for Homes only*)

	1958 Amount (£)	1958 % of Total Income	1959 Amount (£)	1959 % of Total Income	1960 Amount (£)	1960 % of Total Income
Association X	6	0·5	Home temporarily closed			
" Y	554	26·3	—	—	1,534	47·9
Lindisfarne	—	—	236	17·4	712	22·7

TABLE IX

Principal Items of Expenditure, Outdoor Work, Northern Diocese 1958, 1959 and 1960

	1958		1959		1960	
	Amount (£)	% of Total Expenditure	Amount (£)	% of Total Expenditure	Amount (£)	% of Total Expenditure
Salaries, Pensions and National Insurance						
Association A (three workers)	1,678	72·4	1,723	76·0	1,817	76·0
,, B	446	71·7	462	59·1	428	67·6
,, C	479	81·3	517	84·6	520	81·7
,, D	437	61·4	474	65·1	512	66·7
,, E*	—	—	505	66·0	464	63·3
Office Rents, Rates, Heating, etc.						
Association A	338	14·6	241	10·6	257	10·8
,, B	61	9·8	55	7·0	66	10·4
,, C		Paid by Local Authority				
,, D	128	18·1	74	10·1	86	11·2
,, E*	—	—	69	9·1	46	6·2
Telephone, Printing, Stationery, etc.						
Association A	133	5·7	123	5·4	115	4·8
,, B	60	11·0	59	7·6	59	9·4
,, C	46	7·9	36	5·9	52	8·2
,, D	57	8·1	74	10·2	78	10·1
,, E	—	—	70	10·3	83	11·3
Travelling Expenses						
Association A	162	7·0	177	7·8	192	8·0
,, B	47	7·5	64	8·2	58	9·2
,, C	62	10·5	56	9·2	60	9·4
,, D	86	12·0	103	14·2	88	11·5
,, E	—	—	107	14·1	137	18·7

*Work started 1959.

TABLE X

*Principal Items of Expenditure, Outdoor Work, Southern Diocese, 1958,
1959 and 1960*

	1958		1959		1960	
	Amount (£)	% of Total Expenditure	Amount (£)	% of Total Expenditure	Amount (£)	% of Total Expenditure
Salaries, Pensions and National Insurance						
Association S	467	59·4	475	50·0	525	56·8
„ T	489	64·6	491	64·2	517	56·7
„ U	484	80·5	391	74·2	— *	—
„ V	480	55·8	517	52·5	547	49·7
„ W	526	53·4	537	53·9	582	57·9
„ X (2 workers)	801	58·8	805	50·6	850	57·6
„ Y (2 workers)	915	59·5	1,046	69·4	1,073	73·2
Office Rents, Rates, Heating, etc.						
Association S	27	3·5	31	3·2	32	3·5
„ T	41	5·4	42	5·5	64	7·1
„ U	35	6·0	31	5·9	— *	—
„ V	58	6·7	82	8·4	86	7·8
„ W	78	8·0	75	7·6	73	7·3
„ X	49	3·5	93	5·8	29	8·7
„ Y	49	3·2	130	8·6	114	7·7
Telephone, Printing, Stationery, etc.						
Association S	59	7·5	56	5·9	109	11·8
„ T	50	6·6	55	7·3	83	9·2
„ U	39	6·5	29	5·6	— *	—
„ V	67	7·8	68	6·9	76	6·9
„ W	87	8·9	76	7·6	78	7·8
„ X	87	6·4	106	6·7	90	6·1
„ Y	94	6·1	70	4·6	89	6·0
Travelling Expenses						
Association S	213	27·1	358	37·7	239	25·8
„ T	154	20·4	157	20·5	213	23·4
„ U	40	6·7	34	6·5	— *	—
„ V	225	26·3	284	28·8	368	33·4
„ W	237	24·0	276	27·7	242	24·1
„ X	206	15·1	550	34·0	399	27·1
„ Y	381	24·8	249	16·5	178	12·0

*Incorporated in association S.

TABLE XI

Principal Items of Expenditure, Residential Work, Northern and
Southern Dioceses*
1958, 1959 and 1960

	1958		1959		1960	
	Amount (£)	% of Total Expenditure	Amount (£)	% of Total Expenditure	Amount (£)	% of Total Expenditure
Salaries, Pensions and National Insurance						
St Priscilla's	1,259	32·9	1,275	31·5	1,261	28·8
St Perpetua's	1,185	36·2	1,140	32·0	1,257	34·1
St Pelagia's	514	28·6	721	34·6	447	30·4
St Perelandra's	545	37·1	599	42·5	597	40·6
†Association Y	173	55·4	153	47·7	—	—
** „ Z	949	39·5	1,111	42·8	1,090	42·3
††Lindisfarne	—	—	582	42·0	1,038	42·0
Household Expenses						
St Priscilla's	1,769	46·3	1,564	38·6	2,159	49·3
St Perpetua's	1,569	47·9	1,627	45·7	1,686	45·8
St Pelagia's	1,137	63·2	1,142	57·7	788	53·6
St Perelandra's	655	44·6	683	48·6	755	51·3
†Association Y	67	21·4	78	24·5	4	6·7
** „ Z	832	34·6	818	31·6	1,255	48·7
††Lindisfarne	—	—	601	43·4	1,231	49·8
Telephone, Printing, Stationery, etc.						
St Priscilla's	80	2·1	86	2·1	102	2·3
St Perpetua's	43	1·3	30	0·9	23	0·6
St Pelagia's	19	1·0	15	0·7	12	0·8
St Perelandra's	36	2·5	42	3·0	40	2·7
†Association Y	45	14·5	41	12·9	42	64·5
** „ Z	89	3·7	115	4·4	109	4·2
††Lindisfarne	—	—	40	2·9	40	1·6

TABLE XI *cont.*

	1958		1959		1960	
	Amount (£)	% of Total Expenditure	Amount (£)	% of Total Expenditure	Amount (£)	% of Total Expenditure
Repairs, Renewals, Maintenance						
St Priscilla's	676	17·7	983	24·3	738	16·9
St Perpetua's	245	7·5	640	18·0	316	8·6
St Pelagra's	115	6·4	188	9·0	184	12·5
St Perelandria's	161	11·0	71	5·0	59	4·0
†Association Y	5	1·8	1	0·4	—	—
** ,, Z	434	18·9	489	18·9	Included in household expenses	
††Lindisfarne	—	—	110	8·0	120	4·9

Notes:

Northern Diocese: St Priscilla's; St Perpetua's; St Pelagia's; St Perelandra's. *Southern Diocese:* Associations Y and Z, and Lindisfarne.

†Until 1958 Association Y ran a mother and baby home as well as undertaking outdoor work. The home was then closed temporarily, the intention being to sell the existing premises and acquire a smaller and more convenient house. This was not accomplished until the autumn of 1959 and the new house was not ready for occupation until after the end of 1960. Expenditure on the "New Home" was kept separately from the general accounts of the association and is not included here.

**This association both runs a shelter and employs an outdoor worker who has her office there, but whose salary and expenses are included in this Table.

††Opened 1959.

PART FOUR

The Scope and Character
of the Work

II

MORAL WELFARE CASEWORK

HAVING considered the background and organisation of moral welfare work we now turn to the work itself, and in this and the two succeeding chapters propose to describe in some detail the outdoor work, residential work and educational work carried out by moral welfare workers in the two dioceses in which the fieldwork was undertaken. The description is based on the observations made and discussions held during the three years of the fieldwork, 1958, 1959 and 1960, and does not take into account changes which may have occurred since.

The two dioceses selected for detailed study were at opposite ends of the country, and differed widely in their economic and social characteristics. Nevertheless, the geographical coverage of the fieldwork was limited, and we realise the danger of drawing general conclusions too readily from localised investigations. The nature of the processes we were investigating and the data we had to go on were also limiting factors. Any assessment of the scope and coverage of a piece of social work must be based on statistics, but the available statistics were found to be variously classified and not always consistent. The ways in which the cases were classified differed from area to area and worker to worker, and cases might be recounted and perhaps classified under different headings as they were transferred from one worker to another or became residents in homes. Hence the figures given, whether totals or proportions, must be regarded as pointers to, rather than accurate assessments of, the extent and coverage of the work.

The data on which qualitative assessments could be based were even more inadequate and liable to misinterpretation than the statistical material. The workers with whom we were in contact were all co-operative and helpful, but their records had been compiled for the worker's own use and not for research purposes. Further, since the time available for writing up cases was limited and workers had little or no secretarial help, case records were often cryptic and incomplete outlines of events rather than records of the casework process. The fieldworker spent some time with each worker, accompanied her on visits and sat in on interviews, but the workers' respect for their clients' desire for privacy, an attitude which we fully appreciated, resulted in her exclusion from certain interviews (notably those with prospective adopters), and may have limited the nature and scope of the discussion when she was present. These limitations may well have distorted our impressions of the nature and depth of the work, so that the picture given here is perhaps somewhat out of focus, but blurred as it may be, certain features stand out and, despite variations from area to area, our findings proved to be coherent and consistent both between areas within each of the two dioceses and between the dioceses themselves.

I

It is to the 'outdoor' or 'case' worker that girls or women in need of any kind of 'moral welfare' help are usually referred in the first instance, even if the reason for referral is residential accommodation, hence the number of new cases these workers deal with gives a fairly accurate idea of the coverage of the work. The numbers of new cases referred in the two dioceses surveyed between 1952 and 1960 are shown in Table XII. Prior to 1952 records are incomplete in one or other of the dioceses.

TABLE XII
New Cases Referred 1952–1960

Diocese	1952	1953	1954	1955	1956	1957	1958	1959	1960
Northern	685	651	620	589	665	626	571	650	640
Southern	1,187*	730	878	901	1,016	1,011	1,015	1,133	1,155

*April–December; prior to 1952 the Southern diocesan year ended on 31st March.

Moral Welfare Casework

From this table it will be seen that, although it is the more populous of the two dioceses, fewer cases were referred to moral welfare workers in the northern than in the southern diocese. Further, whereas in the northern diocese the diocesan total of new referrals remained almost constant over this period,[1] in the southern diocese, although there was a sharp drop in 1953, numbers rose steadily thereafter and the total for 1960 was more than double that for 1953. This was a period during which the population of the latter diocese was expanding rapidly, but a more detailed examination of the distribution of work for the years 1956-60 suggests that, although this may have been one of the factors in the situation, it was not the only one. In both dioceses, the number of referrals in any area, whether considered separately or as a proportion of the diocesan total, appeared to be more closely related to the availability of workers and the degree of confidence they were able to inspire than to population changes, while local authority policy with regard to referrals varied from one area to another. For example, the establishment of a new moral welfare work association in one northern industrial town and the appointment of a full-time caseworker there was followed immediately by a large increase in the number of cases referred. In a neighbouring town, similar in many respects, a long and difficult period when the worker, (who in any case combined indoor and outdoor work), was ill was followed by a period when a new worker took over the residential but not the outdoor work, which had to be dealt with by a part-time worker from another area; there the numbers, never very great, declined. In an area in the southern diocese in which one of the earliest new towns was situated no marked increase in the number of new cases referred to the moral welfare worker followed for some years, possibly because no new worker was appointed to develop the work there.

The distribution of cases between workers was very uneven, particularly in the southern diocese, where the number of new referrals in 1960 varied between 196 and 68; in the northern diocese the range was narrower; the busiest worker had 106 new referrals, while the least number referred to a full-time worker was 69. With the exception of one or two areas changes in the distribution of cases over the period covered by the survey were not marked.

Moral welfare workers classify their cases under four headings,

TABLE XIII
Catagories of New Cases Referred to Outdoor Workers

Category	Northern Diocese*								Southern Diocese							
	1957		1958		1959		1960		1957		1958		1959		1960	
	No.	%	No.	%	No.	%	No.	%	No.	%	No.	%	No.	%	No.	%
Illegitimate children and their Parents	394	66·3	383	70·8	469	72·9	452	74·2	467	46·2	479	47·2	545	48·1	606	52·5
Children and Young People	94	15·8	55	10·2	48	7·5	34	5·6	28	2·8	26	2·6	35	3·1	16	1·4
Matrimonial and Family	19	3·2	55	10·2	71	11·0	78	12·8	133	13·2	149	14·7	133	11·7	101	8·7
Other Personal Problems	87	14·6	48	8·9	55	8·6	45	7·4	383†	37·9	361†	35·6	420†	37·1	432†	37·4
Totals	594	100	541	100	643	100	609	100	1,011	100	1,015	100	1,133	100	1,155	100

* Excluding one area.   † Including applications from prospective adopters and related enquiries.

illegitimate children and their parents, children and young people, matrimonial and family problems, and a remainder category labelled 'other personal problems'. Table XIII shows that cases in which the presenting problem was recorded as that of a woman expecting an illegitimate child predominated in both dioceses, but they formed a much smaller proportion of the total in the southern than in the northern diocese. This may have been partly because the southern diocesan association functions as an adoption agency and enquiries from prospective adopters were classified as 'other personal problems', thus substantially increasing the number and proportion of cases in this category.

Although in both dioceses moral welfare workers handled more cases involving an illegitimate maternity than any other type of case, and it appeared from the available records that there had been little change in this respect since the War, or even before, by no means every mother of an illegitimate child becomes known to a social work agency, nor is moral welfare the only service to offer help. The proportion of illegitimate maternities in any particular area which come to the notice of the Anglican moral welfare workers in that area in any one year is difficult to assess, partly because the mothers sometimes move about the country and may therefore be recorded by more than one worker, and also because the year in which the case is referred may not be the year in which the baby is born. The Midboro' survey quoted by Virginia Wimperis revealed that in 1949 39% of the 278 illegitimate births known to health and social workers were known to moral welfare workers.[2] A survey made in a midland diocese nine years later, in 1958, showed that the official number of illegitimate births in the city and county it covered, taken together, was 886. During the year moral welfare workers in the diocese dealt with 323 new outdoor work cases. The authors of the survey point out that the figures are not strictly comparable, but after taking into account cases receiving help from both city and county departments they conclude, 'It seems likely that nearly half the unmarried mothers in the diocese did not receive any special help from the social services and more than 63% were *not* referred to moral welfare workers'.

The two dioceses included in the present survey did not altogether conform to this pattern. Percentages of illegitimate births referred to Anglican moral welfare workers not only differed markedly from diocese to diocese but within each diocese. The difficulty of obtaining comparable figures for the northern diocese was enhanced by the number of different authorities in its area and the lack of correspondence between civil and ecclesiastical boundaries, but using returns from different areas, we calculated that approximately 38% of the illegitimate births in the diocese were referred to Anglican workers, an overall percentage which conceals wide local divergences. In this diocese there is a large Roman Catholic population, and an active Roman Catholic organisation for the protection of children functions both as an adoption and as a moral welfare agency. Except in one small county borough, where all cases were referred in the first instance to the Anglican worker, who passed on Roman Catholic girls to their own agency, it appeared to be the general practice of health and social workers to refer Roman Catholic girls directly to the Catholic organisation. Thus in this diocese there was a wide divergence between the number of cases referred to all moral welfare workers and the number referred to Anglican workers. In the southern diocese the percentage of cases dealt with to all illegitimate births was much higher, averaging approximately 63% for the three years of the fieldwork, taking the two counties covered by this diocese together.

Details about sources of referral for maternity cases taken by themselves were not available in every area in either diocese, but, in all the areas for which figures were available, the highest proportion of referrals came from statutory sources, the majority from workers in the health services, including almoners, doctors and health visitors. In the southern diocese the way in which sources of referral were classified meant that workers in the health services could not be entirely isolated from other social workers, but in the northern they were responsible for nearly half the referrals in three areas and for nearly two-thirds in the other two. In the first three areas referrals from voluntary social work agencies formed another large group. There were few referrals by clergymen in either diocese; in no area did referrals from this source account for more than 8% of the total number of cases referred, and in some areas there were none at all. It is, of course, impossible to deduce from these figures how far the small number of referrals was due to the fact that few such cases came to the notice of parish clergy, or how far, knowing of them, clergymen chose to offer help themselves without reference to the moral welfare worker.

In trying to estimate the factors likely to influence a health or social worker in her decision as to whether or not to refer a case to a moral welfare worker we were fortunate in obtaining the co-operation of two hospital almoners, one of whom, with permission from her committee, allowed us to study the records of a series of cases of unmarried pregnant women attending the hospital, while the comments of the other, who worked in another hospital in the same area, provided a cross-check on some of the conclusions which emerged.

Over a period of just over twelve months the first almoner handled 104 cases in which the child was conceived out of wedlock; in 68 of these he was born illegitimate. She referred 32 of these latter cases to a moral welfare worker at some stage in the proceedings, about half the girls so referred being Roman Catholics.[8] More detailed study of the cases dealt with over the period showed that, generally speaking, it was the less intelligent, lower class woman who failed to marry before the child's birth, who was most likely to be referred to the moral welfare worker. In contradistinction to the findings of Cyril Greenland, referred to in Chapter 4, age had little effect; neither the very young mother nor the woman over 30 appeared to be referred more or less frequently than those in the middle of the age range, but in this connection the second almoner commented that she would be more likely to refer a young mother to the local children's department than to a moral welfare worker. This almoner also said that she sometimes referred to moral welfare workers older women in their late thirties, a group whom she thought often needed special help because the hurt went deeper. Judging by the first almoner's case records, religious allegiance hardly seemed to enter into the decision; there was a slight indication that if a woman was recorded as non-practising she would not be referred, but this was not necessarily the reason for non-referral. This impression was confirmed by the second almoner who said religious allegiance or lack of it made no difference, but mentioned that a few clients to whom it was suggested they might go to a moral welfare agency refused because they were 'hedging about religion'.

On the positive side there was some indication from the records that moral welfare workers might be asked to help when the parental background was unstable or lacking, sometimes but not always, by arranging residential care. The second almoner, who worked in a general hospital in a settled working class area, said that she found few parents unwilling to help, but if this were so, she would refer the case to a moral welfare worker for residential accommodation. Girls pregnant as a result of a casual or transient relationship were far more likely to be referred than those engaged, 'going steady' or cohabiting and presumably able to look forward to a fairly stable future. Young women in this latter category evidently felt that they had little need of social work help of any kind. Married, widowed or divorced women, even those with complicated marital problems, were not usually referred, perhaps because another social work agency, such as the probation service or marriage guidance council, was considered the more appropriate body to help.

An analysis of cases referred by the first almoner indicated that accommodation and long-term care were the kinds of help most frequently expected from moral welfare workers; they were the only kinds of help mentioned more than twice.[4] According to the second almoner, cases where advice on adoption or on obtaining an affiliation order was needed might be referred, when suitable, to a moral welfare worker, but some of the women preferred to go to other agencies. As this almoner did no home visiting herself, referral might be made to moral welfare workers or possibly to health visitors, should such visiting be necessary. The practice of the first almoner, on the other hand, was to refer those who wanted advice specifically on adoption to a local adoption society and to undertake herself any home visiting that was needed.

This investigation of a group of cases suggested that the women and girls referred to moral welfare workers by at least one almoner were usually those in need of specific help on practical matters, more especially those requiring residential accommodation. They might well be also the girls with less adequate resources in the way of parental support, intelligence or general *savoir faire*. This impression was confirmed in the discussions with local authority health officials, already described in Chapter 5, which indicated that, like the two almoners, many of these officials regarded moral welfare workers as persons able to help unmarried mothers with some form of specialist care or technical advice (such as by providing residential accommodation or advice on obtaining an affiliation order), and to whom complicated cases might be referred.

Both the type of help given and the way in which they handled their cases demonstrated moral welfare workers' competence to give such specialist help and to find ways and means of providing the necessary practical assistance, even when this was not easy to obtain. Personal consideration was shown for each client, and she was given realistic and practical help in dealing with the almost overwhelming legal, financial and social difficulties with which an unmarried pregnant woman may be faced. In such a predicament the relief of finding someone both knowledgeable and sympathetic and able to give some practical help in the situation is in itself beneficial. It did seem to us, however, that there were times when an opportunity for taking the case further presented itself but was missed,[5] perhaps because of pressure of work.

It is one of the claims made by moral welfare workers that, whenever possible, they help the unmarried mother in the context of her family, and this help may develop into a form of family casework. The workers with whom we were in touch undertook a considerable amount of home visiting, and in many cases contacts were made with one or both parents. Such contacts were usually directed primarily to ensuring the welfare of the girl and her baby, but, on occasion, discussions of this kind might lead the parents to confide their own troubles to the worker.[6] It would seem, not only from the cases referred by the almoners with whom we were in contact, but from more general surveys referred to in Chapter 4, that many cases referred to moral welfare workers are girls or women with unstable or incomplete home backgrounds, and on reading through the workers' case records we were struck by the number of such girls. Whether or not the worker attempts intensive casework with the family, and we did not come across much in the way of deliberate exploration of the family background with the object of discovering to what extent the roots of the girl's problems were to be found there, the worker may give much practical help by finding lodgings or arranging other accommodation, and she may also be called upon to use her good offices with relatives and others involved.[7]

In addition to the girl and her family there is the putative father to be considered. The equal responsibility of the two partners is accepted as fundamental by moral welfare workers and we found that in many cases contact was made with the alleged father, but this may be a difficult undertaking, and several workers admitted that the amount they were able to accomplish was very limited. 'They do not think they need help,' said one worker, who confessed that she did not know what help could be given, 'short of conversion,' if a contact was made. She did not want to become known as 'the woman that tells you off for having babies'. She also found that, if approached too soon, the putative father was not to be found when wanted later for money or a medical reference. Views similar to this were taken by some of the workers, but not by all. For example, a worker in another area said, 'In very many cases the man is seen and is always given the option of talking to a man, but rarely chooses to do so. Many are seriously worried at what has happened and are glad to talk about it. Some are in need of medical or psychiatric treatment; in many cases the girl is the more to blame.' This worker had found that contact with a married putative father often led to matrimonial work with his family, and this was endorsed by several others. A private agreement may be arranged to dispense with the necessity of going to court, in which case the money is then often paid through the moral welfare office and a tenuous link may be kept up for years. But it cannot be said that anything very positive is achieved with more than a minority of cases, and figures given in annual reports indicated that in many cases the workers were able to learn little or nothing about the father of the child.

We found that the workers differed in their attitudes towards long-term care in maternity cases. Some felt that it was more helpful for the worker to withdraw, especially if the child had been adopted, others preferred to maintain a friendly contact in case further help were needed. Mothers who received some payment through the moral welfare office, whether a boarding-out grant[8] or money paid under a private agreement, had an incentive to keep in touch with the moral welfare worker, but it was difficult to make an accurate estimate of the overall number of cases who remain in touch with the workers for any length of time. Of the 30 maternity cases in one area who by 1959 had maintained contact for more than two years, 12 were known to receive or make payments through the moral welfare office, another 6 were recorded as being continuously in touch, and a further three were included in the 1952 research project[9] and therefore visited from time to time. In 11 cases more than one illegitimate pregnancy had taken place, and in some of these cases there was little or no contact with the worker between the arrival of the first child and the second pregnancy.

There was no evidence that we could discover that moral welfare workers are committed to any one particular policy with regard to the mother parting with or keeping her child; still less that this was ever made a condition of her receiving help. Workers might express an opinion that they had found by experience that one or other plan, such as residence in a long stay mother-and-baby hostel or the placement of the child in a residential nursery or with a foster mother, was unlikely to prove satisfactory in the long run, but they were united in their belief that the mother should arrive at her own decision, and, at the same time, concerned that the welfare of the child should receive proper consideration. Several workers commented on the change in attitude which took place in an unmarried mother between the first occasion when she walked into the office demanding a home for the period of the confinement and adoption for the child, and the time when she was able to consider a number of possible alternatives with some concern about the child's well-being. On the controversial issue of early adoption placements we found that the general practice was to discourage the mother from making a decision before the baby's birth, and placements direct from hospital were also generally discouraged although this was by no means an inflexible rule. This is a question which will be taken up again in connection with residential care, which, although for convenience considered separately, forms an integral part of moral welfare work with unmarried mothers and their children.

In one of the two dioceses surveyed the diocesan council was registered as an adoption society, but not in the other. Judging by the records three considerations appear to have influenced the registering council to take this action. In the first place it was thought that moral welfare workers, with their intimate knowledge of the unmarried mother's personality and background, were particularly well suited to advise on the placement of the child. It was also believed that the subsequent rehabilitation of the mother would be made easier if the worker could assure her that she had herself met the couple who were adopting the child. Thirdly, it was regarded as important that children who had been, in some sense, in the care of church workers, should be placed in homes where, to quote the council's annual report for 1954, the year of registration, 'it appears likely that they will have a Christian environment and definite Christian teaching of the denomination to which their mother belongs'. In the first eight months of the council's work as an adoption society 47 applications were received from prospective adopters; by 1960 the number of enquiries from prospective adopters had risen to 142. In that year, too, 87 couples were accepted, 74 babies placed, and 82 court orders were made in respect of babies placed by the council.[10]

As constituted at the time of the survey, the adoption case committee was a standing committee of the diocesan council and responsible to it, and, apart from three members whom the committee could itself co-opt, all members were elected annually by the council on the nomination of the Executive. By the terms of its constitution the committee was required to include a clergyman and a medical practitioner; in 1959 its other eight members were all women. Nearly all of them were married (four were clergymen's wives) and several, including a barrister, a social worker and a teacher had qualified in their own profession before marriage. One was the mother of an adopted child.

The main task of the committee was to consider applications from prospective adopters and it retained the right to accept, defer or reject applicants, but the bulk of the work fell to its secretary, at that time the diocesan organising secretary. She was responsible for calling the committee, which had to meet fortnightly to get through the work, and for the preparation of all applications for its consideration, including taking up references and seeing that the legal documents were in order. She also undertook all the initial interviews with prospective adopters and, acting in consultation with both the outdoor worker who made the required home visits to the prospective adopters and the worker presenting the baby, herself 'matched' the baby to the adopters. This procedure not only made considerable inroads into the time, and demands on the resources and skill, of the adoption secretary, who was at the same time carrying a heavy load of responsibility in her capacity as organising secretary of an extensive diocese, it also meant that no one really got to know both parties to the adoption, since responsibility was divided between the adoption secretary, the worker who visited the adopters and the worker responsible for the case work with the mother surrendering the child. Even with this division of responsibility, adoptions meant a considerable amount of extra work for the caseworkers, who not only visited applicants in their own homes and reported on home conditions, but attended committee meetings when required, were present at the placement and carried out at least three visits afterwards. We gathered that, despite the demands made on their time, most workers concerned found considerable satisfaction in this happier side of moral welfare work, but, rewarding as adoption work may be, it is among the most responsible and demanding of all forms of social work, and raises in an acute form the related question of priorities in the allocation of staff time and the advisability of an association entering a new sphere of work, however intrinsically desirable, without adequate additional staff.

II

Since a large proportion of cases referred to moral welfare workers in both the dioceses surveyed were those classified by them as 'illegitimate children and their parents', it has been necessary to devote a considerable amount of attention to their character, origins and the way they are handled, but as was shown in Table XIII, moral welfare workers also deal with a considerable number and variety of other cases which they classify as 'Children and Young People', 'Matrimonial and Family', and 'Other Personal Problems'.

We found that the extent of the work with children and young people and the importance attached to it varied not only from diocese to diocese, but between areas within the dioceses. In a large city in the northern diocese a specialist worker dealt with all referrals of young people under 17; she was responsible to her own case committee and her cases were recorded separately from those of other workers. In this diocese the practice of appointing a specialist 'children's worker' dates back to 1929[11] and the records were sufficiently complete to enable us to compile the following table, which shows the lines along which the work has developed.

TABLE XIV

Categories of Cases Referred to City Children's Worker

New Cases Referred	1932	1937	1942	1947	1952	1957	1958	1959	1960	1961
1. Broken homes or bad home conditions, illegitimate children	18	34	40	57	78	21	13	20	18	15
2. Delinquent children or behaviour difficulties	34	31	34	36	43	29	24	22	12	21
3. Young unmarried mothers	—	—	—	1	9	13	23	25	37	30
4. Victims of sex assault	49	40	41	9	3	—	—	—	1	—
5. General help and advice	8	22	37	19	43	34	33	20	9	24
Total	109	127	152	122	176	97	93	87	77	90

The most noticeable difference between cases dealt with in the late fifties and those handled before the war is the virtual disappearance of the child victim of sexual assault, who now comes within the purview of the local authority children's department, and the increasing preponderance of the young unmarried mother. Over the years the work seems to have become centred on adolescent girls with personal and behaviour difficulties, notably extra-marital pregnancy, that is, it more closely resembles general moral welfare work now than in the past. In view of this, the wisdom of continuing a specialist appointment of this kind might be questioned, for it could be argued that the problems of the unmarried mother under 17 are not very different from those of the girl in the same predicament in her late teens and early twenties dealt with by the other workers, while the children's worker's other cases could be dealt with quite appropriately either by the local authority children's department or by a family case-work agency. The diocesan organising secretary told us, however, that she was convinced that the appointment should be continued, for she believed that there were children and young people in the city who were in urgent need of the kind of help a children's moral welfare worker could give, and who were not getting it from any other source. The interest taken in the work by the local children's department, which makes a substantial annual grant towards the worker's salary, may be regarded as evidence in support of this view. During the three years of the fieldwork the agencies refer-ring the largest number of cases were the children's department (15, 16, 13), and the various health services, together with local voluntary organisations and other social workers. Referrals from clergy and parish workers numbered 6 in 1958, 7 in 1959 and 8 in 1960.

Elsewhere than in this city the number of cases classified under the heading 'Children and Young People' was too small for statistical analysis, but we did make a detailed study of the records of 32 cases, from which it appeared that, in general, they were similar to those dealt with by the city worker. The majority were teenage girls referred because of behaviour problems, often involving sexual misbehaviour. There were some instances of girls requiring emergency accommodation, having wandered from or left home in anger, and a few young children were also referred. Referrals were from a number of different sources including the clergy, other moral welfare workers, voluntary social work agencies and the statutory services including, in cases where the need for accommodation was urgent, the police.

Although with such small numbers it would be rash to generalise, several cases classified as 'Children and Young People', particularly those involving sexual difficulties or where it was believed that the worker could arrange shelter accommoda-tion, seem to have reached the moral welfare worker because of her own specialism; where moral welfare workers from other areas referred the case they probably regarded her as the obvious per-son to contact. With cases from other sources it appeared sometimes to be a matter of chance that the case was referred to moral welfare rather than to the children's department, although

183

in other instances the statutory officials may have encountered a need which they regarded as outside their own terms of reference.

The questionnaire we addressed to probation and children's officers included a query as to whether, and if so, under what circumstances, a child or young person with behaviour difficulties and, although not a court case, in need of some kind of care or protection, would be referred to a 'moral welfare worker. Eight of the twelve probation officers contacted and three of the eight county or area children's officers gave straight negative answers, and even those answers which suggested that there might be circumstances in which referral might take place indicated that this was regarded as a rare occurrence. Several probation officers pointed out that voluntary supervision was part of their job and they would 'help the child themselves', while two mentioned child guidance as a more likely referral than moral welfare. One reply made a point which can easily be overlooked, but which is important, namely that many officers refer cases 'to the person rather than the organisation best fitted to help'.

In sum, it appeared that, judging both by the number of cases dealt with, other than those involving unmarried motherhood, and by our contacts with social workers in related fields, moral welfare casework with children and young people is a small-scale and marginal activity. Similarly, although the help given in matrimonial and family problems is regarded by moral welfare workers as an interesting and important part of their work, in as far as it was not a by-product of casework with unmarried mothers and was recorded separately, almost everywhere in the two dioceses it formed only a small proportion of the worker's case load.

Although the majority of moral welfare workers in the dioceses surveyed were single women, nearly all of them accepted matrimonial work as a matter of course. There were some, however, who felt that it was difficult for a person who had not herself experienced married life to help in difficult and intimate matrimonial problems, and it was noticeable that a clergyman's widow, appointed to a newly created post in one area, soon had a number of matrimonial cases referred to her, and appeared to be particularly successful in this kind of work. This was a town without its own marriage guidance council, which might have influenced the number and type of case referred to the moral welfare worker.

Moral Welfare Casework

The existence of other agencies with a special responsibility for this particular type of work must, of course, be taken into account when assessing the contribution made by moral welfare workers. The probation service has a general overall responsibility for such work and probation officers handle large numbers of matrimonial cases.[12] In the northern diocese there is an active marriage guidance council which receives cases from most parts of the diocese. It dealt with 561 new clients in 1959-60 and 530 in 1960-61, numbers which may be compared with the 71 in 1959 and 78 in 1960 classified by moral welfare workers in the diocese as 'Matrimonial and Family'. In the southern diocese there are three marriage guidance councils, one in the northern and two in its southern half.

As with children and young people, there were considerable differences between local areas in the number of cases referred. This might have been chance (the numbers dealt with were very small), or might have been an indication of good personal contacts between the moral welfare worker and a particular referring agency. For example, in the town where the moral welfare worker's office was in the same building as the local authority housing department, cases were passed on from this department, which the worker believed would not have come her way but for the geographical proximity. In some areas no matrimonial and family cases at all were referred by the clergy, but in general they referred proportionately more of this kind of case than those of unmarried mothers, and a study we made of case records indicated that cases referred by clergy were often serious, while other agencies were more likely to refer the client for some kind of practical help. This suggests that whereas a clergyman might regard the moral welfare worker as an expert in this type of work, other social workers did not so regard her and referred matrimonial and family cases elsewhere.

This conclusion received some confirmation from our contacts with local officials. The probation officers whom we met regarded matrimonial work as their province; if it transpired that a moral welfare worker was already interested in a particular case co-operation would ensure to avoid overlapping; otherwise it took place but rarely. 'Would not think of moral welfare, would refer to marriage guidance' said one probation officer in an interview, amending this in his written reply to the questionnaire to, 'Very rarely unless there is a strong attachment to a certain religious persuasion and it is felt that the moral welfare worker could help from that direction.' Although there appeared to be little inclination on the part of probation officers to seek the co-operation of moral welfare workers, we only heard one comment which suggested that the Church's attitude towards divorce might deter people from seeking help from a church sponsored organisation and thus hinder the extension of moral welfare workers' matrimonial and family work.

Public health officials viewed matrimonial and family problems rather differently from probation officers and child care workers, but, like their colleagues, they gave the impression that they regarded moral welfare as being on the fringe of this kind of work, and, except perhaps in one or two areas, they did not consider its contribution as particularly significant. They were asked if their authority employed its own special workers 'with the time and skill to provide a casework service where there are serious matrimonial and family problems', whether there were voluntary organisations in the area providing such a service, if there was a need for more social workers capable of giving this kind of help, and if so should they be employed by a statutory or voluntary body. Only the two southern counties employed their own family social workers and, as with the care of the unmarried mother, the tendency of the health officials was to rely on the health visitor. Officials of the twelve health authorities with whom we were in contact listed the principal voluntary bodies dealing with matrimonial and family problems as marriage guidance councils, councils of social service and moral welfare associations, marriage guidance being mentioned in six returns compared with moral welfare in four. In reply to the question as to whether in their opinion more social workers were required for this kind of work, six out of twelve medical officers gave generally negative replies, while in three cases no reply was given. The issue was, perhaps, obscured by the fact that in the questionnaire we linked together matrimonial and family (generally interpreted as problem family) problems. The general picture which emerged was that, except perhaps in the two counties which employ their own workers, the health visitor was widely regarded by the medical officers of health concerned as providing a 'basic' family service, which could be supplemented by the work of a variety of voluntary organisations of which moral welfare was sometimes regarded as one.

Despite the small numbers involved, the difficulties of classification and the limitations of the case records, it was possible to divide cases placed by workers in the 'matrimonial and family' category into certain broad groups. One such group consisted of women originally referred because of an illegitimate maternity, but who later returned to the moral welfare worker with other family problems, including those of a growing child, and sometimes remained in contact over a long period.[18] In one area six out of the eight cases recorded in this section in one year involved mothers and their illegitimate children. The help asked for included accommodation, advice about leaving the putative father, and the provision of nursery or foster home care. Families to whom auxiliary boarding out grants were paid might be placed in this category. The known connection of moral welfare work with adoption work brought in a number of 'family' cases, including a category of case which some workers are finding particularly disturbing, namely married couples asking for the adoption of their expected legitimate baby. Moral welfare workers also undertake investigations and other work for the Church of England Children's Society.

A further group of cases were those referred, in the first instance at any rate, for specific practical or material help, such as holidays, clothing, money or accommodation. Some might prove to be in need of more than this, but other families seemed to need only a certain amount of friendly advice, help or support, as for example in the case of a boy, the youngest son of a widow, and neither strong nor particularly intelligent, whose mother was so worried because other boys teased him that she had to stay off work. The moral welfare worker visited and helped him to look for a job, but soon handed the case over to a Church Army captain.

Several workers had 'problem families' referred to them from time to time, perhaps for some kind of practical help, and in all, although numbers were small, the scope of 'matrimonial and family' problems dealt with was wide and their variety great, for many moral welfare workers are known to be willing to help almost any person or family not obviously within the scope of another agency, whether statutory or voluntary.

The difficulty of classification, already encountered in the other three categories became acute in dealing with those cases subsumed under the heading 'Other Personal Problems and Miscellaneous Inquiries'. Broadly speaking, it seemed that any case which could not be classified under any other heading was included in this category, and even a cursory examination of a limited number of case records revealed considerable differences between workers. Some workers made a sharp distinction between 'Inquiries' and 'Other Personal Problems', but others did not; some workers included cases concerned with illegitimacy or children and young people or marital problems under this heading if they were of limited duration or were referred elsewhere for help, while other workers classified them in their respective categories, however brief the contact. In the main, however, the cases placed in this category in the two survey dioceses appeared to be short-term ones, which did not involve more than five or six interviews and, in a minority of cases, contact with two or three other social services. Sometimes intensive help was given for a very limited period, at other times contact was scarcely established.

The largest constellation of problems in this group, even allowing for the differences in classification already mentioned, centred around the problem of illegitimacy. Interviews with putative fathers undertaken on behalf of workers in other areas or on behalf of the National Council for the Unmarried Mother and her Child were normally recorded in this category, and occasionally a worker would record in this group all interviews with the putative fathers of her own clients. A number of problems connected with adoption, such as that of obtaining the final consent of a mother who had moved or of the husband of a married woman, which were referred to moral welfare workers by their colleagues in other areas, were recorded here. Mothers of illegitimate children, not previously known, and needing help in finding accommodation or employment or seeking advice about the eventual adoption of the child might consult the worker and be placed in this category. Again, their known connection with illegitimacy sometimes brought to moral welfare workers applications from prospective foster parents or adopters which might be, but were not invariably recorded under this heading.

More general problems were sometimes encountered, some quite simple, others more complex, and their type varied from area to area, so that one worker was found to be helping old people, another undertaking mental health after-care. All in all, it seemed that work undertaken with cases classified under this heading represented a limited but useful contribution to social work, but, apart from those cases associated with the problem of illegitimacy, there seemed to be no special reason why moral welfare, rather than any other social work agency should be the agency handling them.

III

It was recognised from the first that any attempt to assess the quality of the casework undertaken, or to identify anything in the workers' conduct of their cases which would distinguish the work as having a specifically religious character and end would be a task of extreme difficulty and delicacy, and it was rendered even more difficult by the inadequacy of the case records and the confidential nature of the work, difficulties referred to at the beginning of the chapter. Spiritual counsel or help in religious difficulties would hardly be likely to be given in the presence of an observer, and we regarded ourselves as debarred from making direct enquiries from the client as these might prejudice the casework relationship. In considering the characteristics of the work we had, therefore, to rely on the information that was available about sources of referral (in particular the number of cases referred by clergy), distinguishing features of cases referred, and the general impressions we received of the kind of help given.

It will have become clear already that the number of cases referred by clergymen was small, and we found very little evidence that the clergy regarded moral welfare workers as social workers attached to the church to whom reference might readily be made in cases of difficulty.[14] The great majority of the cases dealt with were referred by one or other of the social service agencies, either statutory or voluntary.

When we came to look at the distinguishing features of the cases dealt with we found no common theme other than some connection with illegitimacy; apart from this, their only similarity seemed to lie in their variety. We thought it possible that among those referred there might be a relatively high proportion of people with known religious affiliations, but, apart from the housing estate where parish and social work were combined,[15] there was no evidence of this. Long-term after care is sometimes cited as one of the particular strengths of voluntary agencies, but although long-term care was given in some cases, they were not usually referred for this reason; cases referred were sometimes outside the scope of any other agency in the area, but this was a haphazard business which did not produce any recognisable pattern; problems of sex and personal relationships predominated in the small group of cases concerning children and young people, but it would probably be hard to find an agency dealing with this age group in which these problems do not play an important part. Nowhere in our casework investigations did we find any clear indication that, apart from its traditional identification with the care of the unmarried mother and her child, moral welfare work could be distinguished from that undertaken by other social work agencies in either avenue of referral or type of case referred.

Since moral welfare is church work, we tried to discern whether specifically religious or moral help and guidance was given in the cases dealt with, and we thought that referral to a clergyman for help of this kind or an attempt to link the client with the life of the local congregation might be regarded as indicative of this. It was recognised that the possibility of such referrals is likely to be restricted by the caseworker's obligation to respect the confidence and wishes of the client, but even allowing for this, there did not seem to be much active co-operation with parish priests. There were cases in which help of this kind had been given but they seemed to be isolated instances. The extent to which referrals were made seemed to depend partly on the degree of pastoral skill and understanding shown by a particular clergyman and the closeness of the worker's acquaintance with him. One worker mentioned that there were some clergymen to whom she could refer cases for prayer, even if there was no more active part they could take.

How far moral welfare workers themselves offered spiritual counsel or help with religious difficulties, and the extent to which such help was effective, could not be assessed. In the vast majority of cases, no mention was made of these matters either in the records or in conversations at which the fieldworker was present. Occasionally a relevant note appeared on a case file, such as

'Mother and daughter, anyway, now attend Church regularly', or, in the case of a family on the housing estate, 'Church-going noticeably dropped off. . . . Now starting to come back to Church.' The field worker's notes on a visit to an unmarried mother who had kept her baby concluded, 'As we were leaving, moral welfare worker said, "Have you had your baby christened yet?" She had not. A very friendly visit.'

From conversations with workers, we gathered that some moral welfare workers were known as church workers and people spoke to them freely about the church and religion. This was particularly true of an elderly worker who had worked for over twenty years in the same town and who was well known to many of the clergy, social workers and other inhabitants. The practice of workers differed in the matter of making their church affiliation known. One said that she told her clients 'otherwise they wouldn't know. They come to me as part of the welfare state'. This worker was a Church Army sister, whose uniform, one would have thought, would identify her, unless it was regarded as a variation of that of the health visitor. Another worker thought that clients came to realise for themselves that the work was sponsored by the Church, while still another believed that, given time, the opportunity would arise for making this known, and instanced a case where she had for years visited the family weekly in the evening. At last they asked why she bothered to go on coming 'and I was able to go on from there'.

The overall impression we brought away from our observations was that the approach of outdoor moral welfare workers to the general run of their cases differed little from that of many social workers employed in the statutory services or by the secular voluntary organisations. Their devotion to their work, concern for and interest in their clients was evident, but this can be paralleled by that of many other sincere and hardworking social workers,[16] and there was little evidence of a specifically religious approach being used. This paucity of evidence cannot be regarded as conclusive, however, and we were told, moreover, that it was in the residential work that the church attachment of moral welfare work was most overt, so any general discussion of this particular issue must be postponed until this type of work has been described.

12

RESIDENTIAL WORK

THE provision of residential accommodation formed the basis of most early moral welfare work, and, although compared with outdoor work its relative importance has declined, it is still regarded as an intrinsic and essential part of the total work undertaken, and we paid a good deal of attention to it.

As with the casework already described, our investigations were limited in a number of respects. In the first place close personal investigation was confined to the eight Church of England moral welfare homes in the two dioceses selected for intensive study. All of these were managed by lay committees and staffed by lay workers. In neither diocese was there a home run by an Anglican community, nor were there any homes for which the Church Army was directly responsible. Five of the eight homes made some provision for unmarried mothers, but two were classed officially not as mother and baby homes but as shelters. In one case this meant, in practice, the occasional admission of an overnight case, but the other provided hostel accommodation for all and sundry. During the course of the survey the committee decided that the home should cease to cater for mothers and babies except in special circumstances, and that in no case should provision be made to take more than one baby at any one time. The remaining homes catering for unmarried mothers and their children were mother and baby homes, one of which specialised in the care of young mothers, usually those under twenty-one. The three additional homes were all in the northern diocese and consisted of a home for girls of school age judged to be in moral danger and needing residential care, and two approved schools, both of which were for senior girls. During the survey period one of the approved schools was compelled to close, largely because of staffing difficulties, accentuated by the unsuitability of the premises for a school run on modern lines.[1] Although both the children's home and the two approved schools were affiliated to the diocesan board, their links with the Home Office and local children's departments were strong, and, while the head of each home attended moral welfare workers' meetings and regarded her work as essentially diocesan work, the homes remained a little apart from the main stream of moral welfare work. For this reason, and because, in effect, our experience of homes other than mother and baby homes was limited to one of each of two categories, we have confined this chapter to the mother and baby homes including the two 'shelters'.

In making our investigations into the care given to unmarried mothers and their children in these homes, we were conscious that neither of us had sufficient medical or nursing knowledge to enable us to make a proper assessment of the standards observed in connection with such matters of health care as the medical supervision of expectant mothers or the hygienic precautions necessary to protect young infants from the risk of infection, and in the main we have limited our observations to what might be described as the 'social work' aspects of residential care. Like the preceding chapter dealing with case work this chapter is mainly descriptive; discussion of the wider issues raised by the continued responsibility of moral welfare associations sponsored by the Church for this and related residential care is postponed to the concluding section of the study.

The limited scope of our investigation made it all the more necessary for its findings to be compared with those of others in the same or related fields before conclusions could be drawn from them. One such enquiry had just been completed when we started the survey. This was an investigation into the staffing of moral welfare homes undertaken by the Church of England Moral Welfare Council by means of a postal questionnaire addressed to the superintendents of the 136 Anglican moral welfare homes listed in the 1958 Directory of Moral Welfare Work and to two outdoor workers who had 'shelter' beds in their own homes. The findings of this postal enquiry are summarised in the Council's journal, *Moral Welfare,* July 1958,[2] and are referred to both in this chapter and later in the study. The second investigation, which was carried out about the same time as our own survey, and whose findings we have been able to compare with our own, was carried out by officials of the Ministry of Health. At the time of the Ministry survey there were approximately 160 mother and baby homes throughout the country. These homes functioned under different auspices; less than 30 were provided by local health authorities while about 130 were managed by voluntary organisations, mostly denominational in character. Officials of the Ministry visited 42 homes, a cross-section of the whole group. This investigation not only covered the aspects of residential care dealt with in this chapter, but also some matters discussed in the previous chapter, together with specific health and medical questions, which, as already stated, we did not attempt to investigate. The findings of this survey have not been published and we are grateful to the Ministry for allowing us to refer to it.[3]

I

Most of the homes we visited began their work during the early years of the present century, and one was founded as long ago as 1884. The majority of these homes have occupied their present premises for a good number of years, and the problems arising from the upkeep and management of buildings inconveniently planned and shabby with age were constantly being encountered by the committees we met. One such building, a pleasing late eighteenth century house, was large and rambling with great areas of wood flooring to be polished and yards of stone passages to be kept clean. Many improvements in fabric and decoration had been effected by the superintendent but these and other inconveniences remained. Another home was inconvenient in a different way, being a tall, narrow town house, with steep stairs and only two or three rooms on each floor. Accommodation for the staff (including the outdoor worker who had an office in the house), committee meetings and waiting clients was quite inadequate. Had a suitable alternative been available at a reasonable price, the committee was prepared to move house, but this had so far proved impossible in a boom town where the price of property was soaring. In marked contrast to these older premises were those of a mother and baby home opened in 1959. This was a spacious bungalow set in a large and lovely garden on the edge of the country. Built between the wars, it was in good repair and conveniently planned; the rooms were light and most of them had been attractively decorated. Apart from the need for running water in the nursery and the provision of a sluice, conditions were excellent.

Even where the premises themselves were far from ideal the staff nearly always made great efforts to brighten the rooms and make them as attractive as possible. Gay tablecloths in the dining-room, flowers in the hall and pretty cot covers in the nursery were found everywhere, but even allowing for difficulties, not all committees appeared sufficiently sensitive to the need for making staff quarters really comfortable and attractive, especially if it is borne in mind that for resident workers the institution they serve is not only their work place but their home for the greater part of the year.

The perennial financial shortages and consequent difficulties of maintaining satisfactory standards, which dog so much voluntary work, were seen more clearly in residential than in outdoor moral welfare work. Heavy overheads, ageing premises and recurrent renewals of second-hand equipment and furniture proved a constant source of anxiety to the committees responsible for the homes, and a disproportionate amount of time and attention had to be devoted to these matters.

All homes were subsidised in one way or another from statutory sources. At the time when they were visited most of the homes were in receipt of block grants from the authority in whose area they were situated in addition to *per capita* payments made on behalf of residents by the local authorities of the areas from which they came.[4] The fees charged by the homes surveyed varied considerably, ranging from £3.3.0 a week before the baby's birth and £4.4.0 afterwards in one home to £7.10.0 in another. This last was exceptionally high for a moral welfare home, but it had been calculated on a realistic assessment of running costs and with the full agreement of the county officials. Although overheads were particularly high in this small home, which was without capital or endowments, it is probable that the lower fees charged in most homes were barely economic. In some they had not been altered for a number of years, during which running costs had greatly increased. A regular review of costs and fees would seem a most important task for every committee, and the impression gained during the survey was that most local authorities would be ready to listen sympathetically to requests to increase grants, provided that the case for doing so were adequately presented. At one committee meeting which we attended, at a time when the financial position of the home in question was causing great concern, it was the local authority representative who first suggested that application be made for larger contributions towards fees, which could then be raised, and it seemed as though committees were sometimes too hesitant in pressing their claims upon statutory bodies. Were the Church not providing residential care the local authorities would themselves have to provide premises and staff, and many officials to whom we spoke stressed the value they attached to the voluntary home and the importance of the Church maintaining this part of its work. Finance did not appear to be their major concern, but the fact remains that it is less costly for an authority to subsidise a voluntary home, even on a very generous scale, than to provide one of its own. One county council in the southern diocese provided its own mother and baby home for a period of about six years, but then closed it down. At the time of the survey it was paying twenty guineas per week, or £1,000 per annum to secure four beds, whether or not they were occupied, in the diocesan home, no doubt judging that it was worth its while to do so.

Financial problems may be serious, but the difficulty of finding suitable residential staff appeared to be causing even more anxiety. When visited in the course of the field work, only three out of the five homes catering for unmarried mothers and their children had their full complement of staff. Of the others, one, which had seldom been fully staffed during the three years since the then superintendent took over, was without a nurse and a permanent house-matron, (a retired worker was temporarily acting in the latter capacity) while the other, which admitted up to fourteen girls and sometimes more, was run by one worker (who was also responsible for outdoor work) and an assistant. In this and in at least one other home, it was doubtful whether, quite apart from temporary shortages, the complement of staff allowed was adequate to ensure reasonable hours and working conditions for both superintendents and assistants.[5] The two smaller homes were both fully staffed with two resident workers and one non-resident helper, and the position was judged to be satisfactory. This review does not, however, adequately convey the real seriousness of the situation. Two homes subsequently underwent acute staffing crises and remained seriously under-staffed for a long time; in one of these the elderly superintendent was for long periods the only resident member of staff, and there is no doubt but that the standard of work and the reputation of the home suffered.

'The aim of church homes,' we were told on more than one occasion, 'is to build a Christian family,' and of this family the superintendent is regarded as the head, responsible for the welfare of each member and both ready and able to give help and counsel in whatever practical, social, moral and spiritual problems are brought to her notice. In addition to this quite onerous respons-ibility she is expected not only to supervise the running of the home, which involves some responsibility for the maintenance of the fabric, but to undertake all the secretarial and general administrative work which is inseparable from the admission and discharge of a continually changing group of residents. Contacts must also be maintained with local health and social workers and with actual and possible supporters of the work as well as with those former residents who wish to keep in touch. We could not fail to be impressed by the way in which short-staffed or even single-handed superintendents tackled these multifarious duties, but under the circumstances prevailing in some homes one or other aspect of the work was bound to suffer, or if standards were maintained the resulting overwork and strain, combined with the stresses and strains peculiar to residential work, might be serious. These strains are not confined to moral welfare homes,[6] but in such homes may be increased by the problems of a single-sex community in which the workers are responsible for the man-agement and care of a group of difficult girls and women many of whom are going through a traumatic experience. Even where premises are satisfactory, and there is an adequate and competent staff who have good relationships with one another, the demands on the patience, self-discipline and charity of superintendents and assistants are continuous and considerable; where these condi-tions are not fulfilled the situation must sometimes become almost intolerable.

Even where staff relationships are good a working community, of whatever kind, has its own problems of status and function, and these are to be found in moral welfare homes as elsewhere. One such problem which was encountered during the course of the survey was that of the relationship between the superintendent and the assistant worker or workers. In some mother and baby homes the assistant worker is a trained nurse, in which case her function is clearly defined, although her responsibilities still have to be worked out in relation to those of the superintendent. In homes where this was not the case her role was less clearly defined and we came across one or two homes where she appeared to be little more than a 'domestic help'.[7] Improvements in the status and extension of the responsibilities of the assistant may be hampered by the shortage of suitably trained women to undertake this form of residential work, but the situation would seem to be a circular one in that as long as the assistant's status remains a low one, her salary and working conditions poor, suitable applicants are unlikely to come forward.

Another problem of staff relationships, which again is not confined to moral welfare work, is that of the respective roles of the outdoor caseworker and the superintendent of the home. We found that superintendents differed in their views on this issue; some were prepared to play an active part in making arrangements for the welfare of the girls after they left the home, while others evidently regarded it as outside their proper sphere. One superintendent told us that she never discussed future plans with residents unless and until they had seen the outdoor worker as she regarded such discussions as part of the latter's job. In her view the role of the indoor worker was to provide 'a happy setting in which the residents' problems could be worked through from outside'.

These divergences of viewpoint may be associated to some extent with the wide range of qualifications and background to be found among those undertaking residential moral welfare work. Of the 380 superintendents and assistants employed in moral welfare homes in England and Wales in 1958 only 89 had a moral welfare qualification and might therefore regard themselves as undertaking a social work job;[8] 60 were trained nurses but had no social work qualification; 21 were Church Army sisters; 4 had taken a Home Office course (presumably one for residential workers); 19 were nursery nurses and 2 had a domestic science qualification. 137 superintendents and assistants were without any qualifications and the returns also mention 48 daily workers, presumably domestic workers without qualifications.[9] It would seem that only a minority of the workers in moral welfare homes have the kind of training likely to prepare them for the social as well as the medical or domestic aspects of their work.

II

In most homes the residents formed a group with considerable differences of age, background and intelligence. Apart from the one home catering for girls under 21, the group was not usually a particularly young one, and might include a number of women in their late twenties and even thirties for whom the home was meeting a real and urgent need. Occupational differences might be as great as those of age, ranging from teacher or nurse to factory girl, and while some girls were above average intelligence, some were sub-normal or nearly so. Sometimes the staff regarded this variety as an unfortunate necessity which made working with the group difficult, but one superintendent whom we met took the opposite view and thought that intermixture brought out the best in each girl and encouraged them to help each other. While there appear to be considerable advantages to be derived from making special arrangements for the very young, and perhaps for the specially difficult, in most homes we visited the mixed group appeared to have settled down surprisingly well together.

While some homes had an official 'first babies only' rule on paper, in practice the decision as to whether or not to admit women expecting a second or subsequent child was invariably left to the superintendent, and, as far as we could gather, no difficulties were encountered.

A stay of six weeks before and six weeks after confinement is said to be common practice in moral welfare homes, but in fact only one of the homes included in the survey followed this rule. The home for young unmarried mothers had a prescribed length of stay of three-and-a-half months, six weeks before and eight weeks after the confinement. Both the 'shelters' were flexible in their requirements and the mother and baby home opened in 1959, which was intended primarily to cope with emergencies and the more difficult type of case, such as the married woman expecting an illegitimate child, had made its own special arrangements with the local authority reserving beds there whereby the normal period of residence before confinement was reduced from six weeks to two. In special circumstances this arrangement could be varied, the decision in such cases being based on the client's need rather than on any question of cost. Although when the system was first put into operation certain adjustments were found to be necessary, when the home was visited in the summer of 1960 arrangements seemed to be working smoothly. Another home, which discharged most cases at the end of six weeks, was prepared to allow girls to remain there until they had found suitable employment; at the time of our visit a mother with a child three months old was in residence.

The question of length of stay is one on which opinions among social workers differ markedly, especially in connection with those cases where the girl had already made up her mind to have the baby adopted before entering the home. Some, perhaps most, of the moral welfare workers whom we encountered considered that in such cases the mother should remain in the home for the normal period of six weeks after the baby's birth in order to give her time to realise the full implication of her decision before the placement was actually made. They believed that in the long run she would not regret caring for her baby for a period even if, in the end, she parted with it. We met other social workers who viewed the situation differently, however; among them were some who considered that moral welfare workers were too prone to accept without further examination the proposition that it was generally desirable for an unmarried mother to remain in a home for six weeks before and six weeks after the confinement. For example, the almoner of one maternity hospital was of the opinion that, 'While plans made in the ante-natal period should be flexible, it is possible for many unmarried mothers to reach a decision before the baby is born, particularly if she is helped by a skilled caseworker.' She considered that if the mother had already made up her mind to part with the child she might be caused considerable distress if forced to keep it for the six week period.

Not only was the required length of stay in a mother and baby home sometimes called in question, but also whether this was the best type of provision for all the cases which found their way there, and during the fieldwork we received the impression that hard-pressed outdoor workers were sometimes tempted to regard admission to a mother and baby home as the obvious answer to the girl's predicament without perhaps giving sufficient consideration to possible alternatives. It is important, therefore, that the type of cases dealt with in mother and baby homes, the purposes these homes are intended to serve, and the extent to which they fulfil these expectations should be kept under review.

From discussions with workers and our own observations it appeared that the majority of residents in the homes visited could be divided into three categories. One group consisted of those who prior to entry had definitely decided to have the child adopted, had to find somewhere to stay until the baby was placed, but hoped on leaving the home to take up life again where they had left off. Secondly, there were those for whom it was virtually impossible to remain in their own homes, perhaps because of the presence of younger children or the inability of the girl's parents to tolerate her pregnancy, so that she was forced to take refuge elsewhere, at least for the time being. In addition to these two groups there were those without a permanent home or living away from home and without parental support.[10] Included in this last category might be found a few married women, whether living with or separated from their husbands, but expecting an illegitimate child. Judging by the two latter categories of cases dealt with, moral welfare mother and baby homes appeared to be providing a temporary refuge to many mothers of illegitimate children whose home circumstances were exceptionally difficult. To such cases, and, in particular, to those who were markedly distressed and disturbed by their situation, the type of care given and degree of understanding shown, might be all important.

Whatever the size of the group or type of resident, the daily routine of the homes visited varied very little from one home to another. The housework, which occupied most of the mornings, was shared by all residents, the expectant mothers generally undertaking the larger share. Although the staff were always available to help, advise and guide them, the mothers were entirely responsible for the care of their babies, and at night either took it in turns to sleep in the night nursery or had their babies with them in their dormitories. Meals were regarded as family gatherings and were shared by the staff; tea and sometimes the evening meal being the only exceptions to this. Girls might give some assistance with the preparation of the meal and always helped to serve, clear away and wash up. The food was usually adequate, if plain, and a mid-morning break and a milk drink at night were usual, in addition to the three or four set meals a day. In every home the needs of the nursery determined the times of meals and, to a great extent, the general routine of the home.

As already pointed out at the beginning of the chapter, the age and character of most of the premises used as mother and baby homes in the two dioceses surveyed was such as to add to the extent and difficulty of the household chores, but although the fieldworker lived in each home in turn for a period of not less than a week, nowhere did we find any evidence to support the belief that unmarried mothers in church homes are condemned to 'the excessive scrubbing of stone floors in the hope that this will wash away their own sins and those of society'.[11] Our own observations accorded much more closely with one of the findings of the Ministry of Health investigation referred to above, namely that, 'In a few instances a definite attempt was made to use the working time as an educational experience which might lead to improvements in the girls' own standards. In general, the tasks done by the girls were not arduous, and where necessary they were adjusted to physical ability.' On the whole we considered underoccupation a more serious problem than overwork.

Apart from housework and baby care there were not usually any organised activities. Mothers had ample occupation, but most of the time of the expectant mothers, apart from that spent on housework and attending clinics, was filled with knitting and watching television or listening to the wireless. This relative idleness appeared to be taken for granted by most superintendents. One thought the ante-natal period was mainly a 'waiting period' when the girls were rather hostile and unresponsive, another, while asserting that she would prefer admittances earlier than a fortnight before confinement, could give no clear indication of the way she thought this period should be used. On the other hand some interested people with whom this point was discussed were more concerned, as for example, a trained nurse at that time in training for moral welfare work, who thought these six weeks of relative idleness were physically bad for expectant mothers, making their labour more difficult, apart from the moral degeneration which might be caused by having little to do but knit and gossip for several weeks.

In some homes thought evidently had been given to the possibility of providing constructive occupation for this mixed and often reluctant group, but nowhere did we think the problem had been really successfully overcome.[12] In one home, a weekly relaxation class taken by a physiotherapist had been organised and, once during the stay of every expectant mother, a talk on childbirth was given by a health visitor. Instruction on mothercraft was also emphasised in more than one home. One superintendent, responsible for young mothers, had tried to organise classes in educational and recreational subjects, for example in handicrafts, but an approach made to the L.E.A. had proved abortive, in spite of the fact that some of the girls were of compulsory school age.[13] In this home, as in several others, the 'chaplain's hour' provided an opportunity for informal teaching on various topics other than the strictly 'religious'.

All homes allowed some free time, usually in the afternoon, when many residents liked to go out shopping or to the cinema. The ease with which they could do so varied with the position of the home. Only one was situated in the country, and two were right on the edge of the town and relied on a fairly infrequent bus service. Another home was fifteen minutes walk from the town centre and at the top of a steep hill. These conditions, and the length of time for which the girls were allowed out, to some extent determined the range and nature of their activities. Only one home issued 'late passes' which allowed residents to remain out until 7.30 p.m. twice a week. This was the small shelter which had many of the elements of a hostel. It may well be thought desirable to restrict the activities of possibly unstable girls and women who are in the last stages of pregnancy, and most residents seemed to accept the restrictions without complaint, but they are quite alien to the experience of most of those who enter mother and baby homes and, in the case of older women, particularly, a more liberal approach might well be appreciated.

Visits from parents were usually welcomed, although some limitations had to be placed on the times of their visits. The attitude of superintendents to visits from the putative father or other boy friends varied; on the whole, such visits were discouraged, though exceptions might be made, and in the small hostel, where the position was rather different, residents were encouraged to bring their boy friends to the home and introduce them to the superintendent, as they would to parents at home.

Although conditions in a mother and baby home are bound to be to some extent artificial, many superintendents emphasised that they were trying to provide something in the nature of family life for the residents. More than this, they were concerned that the life of the home should be that of a Christian family, and in the homes visited the religious emphasis was much more overt than in connection with the outdoor work. With one exception every home had its own small chapel[14] where a short and usually informal service, led by the superintendent, was held each morning; sometimes evening prayers took place there as well. In three homes services were conducted by a clergyman; in one this service was a celebration of Holy Communion in which all who had been confirmed and so desired were invited to participate.

It was assumed that all would attend prayers and participate in the religious life of the home, and in most homes all residents were also expected to attend either the parish church or, alternatively, the church of their own denomination every Sunday.[15] Objections to attending prayers or Sunday services were seldom heard; what, if anything, they meant to young women who, apart from school assemblies and haphazard attendance at Sunday School, may have had little or no experience of Christian worship or teaching until their arrival in the home, is an open question. For some they may have been a real help and comfort; for others simply part of the routine which could be carried out while in the home with apparent conviction, but shed on leaving as easily as the maternity smock. Far more difficult than providing opportunities for religious observance was the task of demonstrating the relevance of religious practice to daily life. The influence of the chaplain may be important in this connection, and all the survey homes had a visiting chaplain who came at least once a week, and usually both took a service and had more or less informal discussions with the group in the home, as well as interviewing individually new arrivals and those due to leave. As far as we could judge, chaplains were accepted by the residents, and in two homes he was obviously well-known to them.[16]

Although the help the chaplain was able to give some unmarried mothers in the moral and spiritual dilemmas which they had to face was appreciated by them, we suspected that for most girls the acid test of the relevance of 'religion' for daily life was the way in which their queries and perplexities were met by members of the staff in intimate daily contact with them. When asked what opportunities were given for spiritual counselling and guidance in religious and ethical difficulties, several superintendents mentioned the chaplain's part and only one or two said they would themselves discuss such questions as they arose. In the life of a community where religion is practised, innumerable opportunities arise for such informal discussions, but our impression was that they were usually limited to matters of fact, such as the differences between Roman Catholics and Protestants. While these may have played a useful part in removing misunderstandings they could only be preparatory to the discussion of personal difficulties at a deeper level. These, by the nature of the case, we could not directly observe. No doubt there were great variations in both the help given and the response made, and one or two letters from those who have been in the homes which we were shown indicated that in a few instances at least, a real interest in religion had been aroused, which might survive after much else had been forgotten. This would be the hope of all workers, and for many the ultimate justification of their work.

13

EDUCATIONAL WORK

MORAL welfare work began as an attempt to rescue outcast girls and women from lives of sin and degradation and compassionate care of the individual has always been at the centre of the work. Nevertheless, it has long been realised that this is only part of the task and, as we have seen already, educational work of all kinds was a major concern of the Church of England Moral Welfare Council from its early days as the Archbishops' Advisory Board onwards. At the diocesan and local level, however, we found considerable variations in the amount and nature of the work done and some uncertainty as to how much it was desirable and possible for a local moral welfare association to undertake. This appeared to be the case whether the term 'educational work' was used to signify work undertaken to help young people achieve fuller knowledge of their own physical development and accompanying emotional needs, together with some understanding of the relevance of Christian teaching to this and related issues, or whether it was used to cover the education of public opinion on policy issues relating to sex, marriage and the family.

In our attempts to find out what actually was being done in the way of educational work in the two dioceses surveyed we first sought to discover the extent to which moral welfare workers themselves participated directly in it, and secondly the share which committees and workers took in sponsoring or assisting efforts which might be made by other organisations both inside and outside the church.

Educational work may be regarded as either a diocesan or local responsibility or both. Two replies received from local workers indicated that in their view the work should be undertaken at the diocesan level by the organising secretary, but this

Educational Work

did not appear to be the general assumption. Moreover, the replies we received to a questionnaire we sent to organising secretaries throughout the country[1] confirmed the impression we gained from the dioceses surveyed that, even if interested, an organising secretary is not usually in the position to give much time and attention to this work herself. Only 18 of the 41 organising secretaries who replied to the questionnaire included educational work among the main components of their work, and a further seven, although they included it in their return gave fewer than ten educational talks in 1958. Rather more than half the total replies received indicated that the organising secretary in question would have liked to see educational work in her diocese developed further, but the number in which aspiration was being translated into actuality appeared to be small. Specific hindrances to the development of the work were stated to be lack of suitable people to undertake it, the size of the problem, lack of money and insufficient guidance from educationalists.

In the two dioceses surveyed we tried to obtain information about the position not only from the organising secretary but from the caseworkers. Discussions with outdoor workers in both dioceses showed that, apart from one or two workers with an exceptional interest in, or a flair for the work, little was being done. Two workers who at that time were undertaking more engagements of this kind than was general, were a married woman in an industrial area and the city children's worker referred to in Chapter 11,[2] a young married woman, who, working at times in co-operation with the Student Christian Movement in schools, was arranging and participating in discussions for school leavers and members of youth clubs.

The reasons volunteered by the workers for their non-participation in educational work were firstly, that their case work, which they regarded as having priority, left them without the time to attempt anything extra; secondly, that they were neither suited nor qualified for the work; and thirdly, that it was already being done by other people. 'Heavy case load, not right to spend time on educational work,' aptly sums up the reaction of one worker, who did, however, make the point that a certain amount of such work could be done informally when interviewing parents. Another, very conscious of the complexity and difficulty of educational work of this kind, was quite clear that only those with a special talent for it should undertake it. 'It is better left undone than done by the wrong person,' she said, and her views were evidently shared by a worker from another area who said, 'Wants doing by experts, otherwise does so much harm.'

The belief that the work needs doing, but by 'experts' rather than by hard-pressed and reluctant caseworkers raises the question as to who these 'experts' should be and under whose auspices they should work. It was recognised by outdoor workers in both dioceses that something was being attempted in the schools, but some, at least, among those interviewed were under the impression that the teaching given was largely biological in emphasis, and pointed out that those giving it might be quite young teachers with little or no experience outside school or college.[3] Hence, it was averred, it was inadequate to meet the needs of young people, 'who certainly need help and guidance wherever they get it from'.

Since guidance on personal and social problems is generally regarded as one of the functions of the Church, we thought it relevant to our investigation to try to learn something of the extent to which teaching, help and guidance on sexual morality and related questions is given to young people through the medium of their parish churches and related youth organisations. We utilised for this purpose the contacts we made with a one-in-four sample of parochial clergy in the northern diocese—forty-nine incumbents in all, further details of which are given in the next chapter. Forty-three of the parishes in this sample had some kind of club or fellowship for young people, although two were in abeyance at the time we made the survey. Although it appeared that in practice the range and variety of membership conditions was such that it was very difficult to make clear-cut distinctions, we classified 33 of these organisations as 'closed' in the sense that, in theory at any rate, membership was restricted to young people connected with the church. It would seem from these replies that the majority of incumbents interviewed regarded the parish youth club as a fellowship which brought the younger members of the congregation together and helped them to grow into the faith and worship of their church. A minority regarded their youth organisations mainly as media for evangelism or as expressions of social concern, but even so, membership might be restricted to some extent, this being dependent on a number of variables such as the availability of suitable helpers and the adequacy of the premises. From this it would seem that such guidance in matters of sex morality and personal relationships as was being given to teen-agers through the youth organisations connected with the parish churches in this sample was largely restricted to young people who were prepared to identify themselves, at least to some extent, with the life and worship of the church. The same naturally applies to the teaching given to confirmation candidates which was mentioned several times in the course of our conversations.

We then tried to obtain from the incumbents what information we could as to the extent to which guidance on matters relating to sex and morals was being given in connection with parish youth organisations either through group discussion or by means of individual counselling. Fourteen of our informants said that group discussions on general topics took place in their youth clubs either regularly or occasionally, but only in six cases did the informant recall occasions on which the group had given specific consideration to the topics in which we were interested, and this with varying effect. The larger number of clergy interviewed considered that their responsibilities for helping young people in these matters could be better discharged by means of personal contacts and individual discussions, but several of them referred to the difficulties they experienced in making contact with the young people, and it appeared that in many instances a real desire to help was frustrated by almost complete failure to achieve effective communication. Only in a minority of parishes did relationships between the clergy and the young people appear to be sufficiently easy for these questions to be tackled seriously and constructively.

The problem, then, was not merely lack of access, but what is perhaps more serious, lack of communication. In part this might have been due to natural reticence on both sides, but it appeared that this could easily be accentuated by social and personal factors. One or two of the older men, working single-handed, evidently felt that the gap between the generations was too great for them to bridge and emphasised their need for a younger colleague to whom the young people would go. 'They are very hard to get near and don't talk to me, no not at all,' confessed one elderly vicar rather sadly. In such parishes too, the incumbent might be so overwhelmed by day-to-day routine administrative work as to lack the time to get down to what he evidently regarded as his 'real job' as a parish priest, and this in itself would include ministering to the aged, sick, and dying, those who had lost their faith and those in spiritual difficulties of all kinds, as well as counselling bewildered youngsters.

Differences in education, outlook and vocabulary were also mentioned in connection with this problem of communication, and one or two of the younger clergy raised the question of the relevance of training given in theological colleges to the situations ordinands were likely to meet. One of our informants, a keen youth worker, strongly criticised the practice of handing over the parish youth work to young and inexperienced curates with no proper youth service training, while another spoke with some heat, and possibly a certain amount of exaggeration, of the young men coming out of theological colleges 'knowing nothing' of the personal and social problems they would encounter.

Lack of time precluded us from making a similar enquiry in the southern diocese, but we received a certain amount of unsought, indirect evidence which suggested that the situation there might be not unlike that in the north. A group of probation officers discussing adolescent problems thought that 'nothing would eradicate these difficulties', but that they might be minimised by an effective youth service. One of them added, 'The normal church organisation does not set out to cope, and never has done, with the teaching of personal relations. In the development of clubs there is hope for the future but leaders must accept responsibility for sex education and its wider implications.' He went on to say 'the clergy in general are not prepared in their training to do so'. The point was made even more directly by an experienced moral welfare worker in another discussion. 'The clergy run away from moral welfare work because they feel unable to cope,' she said.

From all this it would appear that not only clergymen but also lay people who share in the Church's youth work, need and would probably welcome, some assistance in helping and guiding their young people in matters relating to sex and morals, and several of the clergy interviewed evidently felt that 'expert help' was needed. They were not always certain where to look for it, and when asked, only three of them spontaneously thought of moral welfare as a possible source of such help. In one of these cases the local moral welfare worker (a young worker who has since left the diocese) had given a series of talks to young people, while another incumbent had previously worked in Southwark and had known the diocesan lecturer there. Three of the clergy interviewed had sought the help of the local marriage guidance council (one of these added that it had 'never occurred to him' to approach moral welfare), one referred to the help he received from a male probation officer who was a member of his church, four mentioned contacts with doctors, and one the help given to young people at the Lee Abbey Camp. These contacts appeared to be largely fortuitous, however, and to mask rather than to meet the need for better training for both lay and clerical workers with young people, and the desirability of closer co-operation between individuals and organisations, inside and outside the Church, who are concerned about this problem.

Within the Church itself the Church of England Youth Council (one of the constituent Councils of the Board of Education) would appear to occupy a key position in connection with possible developments of this kind, since its associated diocesan committees and officers act both as advisers to the parish clergy and as the church's representatives on secular youth organisations, while its functions include the training of voluntary youth leaders, arranging clergy schools and week-end parties and conferences for young people. An official of the Council, with whom we had an interesting discussion, endorsed what local clergy, probation officers and moral welfare workers had already told us, namely that, in her own words, 'there is a tremendous need and not nearly enough done in training leaders and clergy to help young people'. She made the point, however, that many of the questions raised by adolescents are really very simple and can and should be answered as they arise by 'mature Christian people'. 'There is no need to call in a specialist every time,' she said. 'He has his place and function, but it is vital that lay people, including parents, should also be prepared to share in the work, and be helped by training to do so.' Like a moral welfare worker already quoted, she believed that many young people were longing for firm guidance and standards from adults, 'But,' she added, 'we are not sufficiently courageous in this matter.'

We received the impression from this official that there was close liaison between the work of her Council and that of the

Church of England Moral Welfare Council, but such co-operation did not appear to have been developed to any extent in the two dioceses surveyed, possibly because of local circumstances. One diocese did not employ a full-time youth organiser at the time of the survey. In the other a Diocesan Council for Education had been established in 1955 and it appeared from what we were told by workers and committee members that projects involving both the youth and the moral welfare council were organised from time to time, but action along these lines seemed to be somewhat sporadic and it was difficult to discern any signs of widespread and continuing co-operation. A deanery youth chaplain, who was a member of one of the local moral welfare committees which we attended, said that the link between his work as youth chaplain and moral welfare was 'practically nil'.

Co-operation between moral welfare councils and committees and diocesan boards of education, where it exists, is co-operation within the framework of the institutional church. Another aspect of co-operation which frequently came up for discussion in connection with educational as well as casework was the question of co-operation between moral welfare organisations and local marriage guidance councils. Here the situation appeared to vary from area to area. At the time of the field work the National Marriage Guidance Council was expanding its educational work, but coverage was evidently uneven, and in some rural areas the nearest marriage council might be some distance away. Even where a local marriage guidance council existed it might not be undertaking educational work. Within the areas surveyed this type of work was most highly developed in the northern diocese where a well-established and active marriage guidance council had appointed a highly educated married woman with university and church connections as its educational organiser. She and the city children's worker came in contact with one another in connection with educational projects, and she spoke highly of the latter's work. She considered, however, that, in general, marriage guidance councils possess two assets for this kind of work which are not shared by moral welfare organisations. In the first place, the people undertaking it are married couples, who often work together. They are accustomed to dealing with normal young people in their own family life and 'educational work' is to them an extension of their natural responsibility rather than a specialist activity. Like the Secretary to the Church of England Youth Council she evidently felt that too much emphasis could be placed on expertise, and she regarded the amateur status of marriage guidance education workers as, in some respects at least, their strength rather than their weakness.

The other advantage possessed by marriage guidance councils, according to this marriage guidance worker, was that they have no denominational attachments or allegiances, nor are they identified with religion in general. She considered that the image of the Church which is retained by most young people is often such as to create a barrier which has to be broken down before effective contact can be made, but speakers not identified with the Church do not have to overcome this initial difficulty. A similar point was also made by a member of a deanery committee in the southern diocese when discussing the same question. On the other hand, some keen church people whom we met in the course of the survey expressed concern at the lack of positive Christian teaching which, they believed, characterised the approach of marriage guidance councils. These doubts did not appear to be widespread, and our general impression was that in areas in which local marriage guidance councils were operating and actively engaged in educational work, moral welfare committees and workers were prepared, and in some cases anxious, to co-operate with them. Some moral welfare committee members were closely associated with the marriage guidance movement.[4]

The general picture which emerged from a number of discussions was that, although some moral welfare workers considered that this kind of educational work should be in the hands of 'experts', the 'experts' stressed the important part which should be played by those in close and continuing contact with young people—parents, teachers, youth leaders. Apart from the practical difficulty that no organisation, or even combination of organisations, employing any number of experts, can hope to reach more than a small fraction of the nation's young people, it was felt that such matters, involving as they do intimate personal questions, are, in general, better discussed in the context of a natural social relationship than by bringing in an outsider and thus creating an artificial situation at the start. Direct help from outside experts might be useful on occasions, but for the most part the responsibility of helping and guiding young people in this, as in other aspects of their social maturation, lies with those who are in personal contact with them. The role of the expert is to guide and support the educators, to see that they are equipped for their task, and to help them achieve sufficient confidence to discharge it naturally and unselfconsciously.

Not a great deal was being done by moral welfare workers or associations, either singly or in co-operation with other organisations, to tackle the problem of 'educating the educators'. From time to time interesting experiments had been made in both dioceses, for example, a clergy conference was held in conjunction with the local marriage guidance council in a northern city in 1959, but, useful as these limited efforts were, they were no substitute for a really systematic attempt to develop this side of the work. The same could be said about the second and related aspect of educational work, that is 'the promotion of thought, discussion and action in relation to matters concerning the place of marriage and the family in Christian life'.[5]

In the years immediately preceding and covered by the survey, the Church of England Moral Welfare Council had been both active and enterprising in making investigations, advocating policies and endeavouring to influence public opinion on matters relating to sex, marriage and the family. In connection with some controversial issues, such as the reform of the laws relating to homosexuality, its influence had been considerable, but this activity was not reflected to any marked extent in the two dioceses surveyed, where activity was sporadic and interest evidently varied from area to area. This is not altogether surprising; quite apart from the difficulties of bringing people living in scattered areas together, such matters as the working of the Street Offences Act must be nearly as remote from the day to day experience of the inhabitants of respectable surburban and quiet rural areas as the effects of the South African pass laws, and it must be nearly as hard to arouse interest and concern, especially if there is little positive action which can be taken.

Nevertheless, in spite of difficulties, attempts had been made from time to time in both dioceses to undertake general educational and propaganda work of this kind. Thus, one diocesan council report refers to the playing of a tape recording of an address by Dr. Sherwin Bailey on the Wolfenden Report to a number of meetings. The diocesan board in the other diocese, after giving the matter due consideration, decided that, in as far as they dealt with one aspect only of the problem of prostitution and failed to give due attention to the male client, the proposals made in the Wolfenden Report were unjust. The board approached all local members of Parliament asking them to give this matter their careful attention. What, if any, response was elicited is not stated, nor was the matter referred to in subsequent reports.

From time to time, local committees appear to have been roused to take action over some issue about which they felt particularly concerned, although the likelihood of this happening appeared to vary from committee to committee. One of our most interesting experiences was attendance at a very lively committee meeting in an industrial town. At a previous meeting this committee had decided to protest to the Public Morality Council about a film being shown in the town. The Council replied that it had received no other protest about this particular film, and when this was reported to the committee quite a sharp discussion arose as to whether or not the protest should have been made. Two issues were raised, first, whether it was appropriate for the committee to make representations of this kind, and secondly, whether action should have been taken in this particular case. It was the opinions expressed on the first issue which particularly interested us. Some doubts were expressed about the desirability of the committee 'butting in', but the general consensus of opinion seemed to be summed up by two clergymen representing two widely differing denominations. One of them said that 'What they did [i.e., as a moral welfare association] was to attack evil by doing good', but he was happy that on occasion they should make protests of this kind, 'We have a right to do it because of the general work'. The other summed up the situation by saying, 'As a moral welfare body we are interested in what is likely to increase [moral welfare] work'. In this particular instance the wisdom of the action was perhaps doubtful, but the committee was obviously alert to its wider responsibilities, and ready to take action on its own initiative.

The committee whose meeting we have just described was exceptionally vigorous and independent, and we did not encounter anything quite like it elsewhere. One of the deanery associations in the southern diocese had set up its own education committee

215

but we got the impression that its efforts had not been altogether successful, and the desire was expressed for more help and guidance from 'Headquarters' than had hitherto been received. Our general impression of this aspect of educational work was, in fact, rather similar to our impression of the work with young people. Here and there local enterprise issued in effective action; now and then interesting experiments had been made; one or two workers were devoting their time and attention to the work; but, as far as we could discover, there was no long term or concerted planning, and, all in all, the amount accomplished was relatively small.

14
MORAL WELFARE AS CHURCH WORK

I

APART from the chapter just completed, the study so far has been mainly concerned with moral welfare work as a particular form of social work, but, as we were constantly reminded, it is social work undertaken in the name of the Church, and it must now be considered in this context. At the centre, the Church of England Council for Social Work is a constituent council of the Church Assembly Board for Social Responsibility; at the diocesan level moral welfare boards or councils are formally recognised as part of the administrative machinery of their respective dioceses and moral welfare workers, on taking up their appointments, are licensed or authorised by the diocesan bishop. The connection between local moral welfare work and the work of the parochial clergy is, however, less easy to define, and relationships between moral welfare workers and the clergy would seem to vary from person to person, parish to parish and between one area and another.

In the early stages of the field work we derived most of our information about the relationships between workers and clergy from the workers, and the overall impression we received was that they were not particularly close. This impression was confirmed to some extent by the discovery that, in the two dioceses surveyed, very few cases were referred to moral welfare workers by clergymen, while, on their side, the workers obviously had reservations about enlisting clerical help. One obstacle to closer co-operation appeared to be that the worker's professional obligation to respect the confidence of her client was not always appreciated by the parochial clergy, but we did hear of cases which had been referred to the local vicar for help and of other instances where requests were made to him for information and intercession, with the understanding on both sides that, at that juncture, he would not attempt to intervene in any other way.

While at this stage in the investigation our contacts were mainly with workers, and our information derived from them, we did, on occasion, meet members of the clergy and discuss the work with them. These clergymen were, however, mainly committee members and others with some special connection with, or interest in, moral welfare work. In order to see what the work looked like to those parish clergy with no known association with it, we arranged, with the approval of the northern diocesan bishop, to interview a one-in-four sample of the incumbents listed in the diocesan directory.[1] Of the 51 clergymen thus selected 49 were interviewed; the remaining two were ill during the summer of 1960 when the interviews took place. The interviews were based on a questionnaire, but most of the discussions ranged fairly freely and some varied and interesting views were put forward.

We had been told that almost every parish in the diocese invited a moral welfare speaker to visit the Mothers' Union or some other women's group in connection with the Women's Offering Service, and we made this the starting point of our enquiry into points of contact between the parochial clergy and the local moral welfare workers. Only three incumbents said that they had not had a speaker recently; one was uncertain, seven gave no response and two had none of the usual women's groups. We were not told of moral welfare workers addressing any parochial organisations other than women's groups. We asked incumbents whether their parishes supported the work financially, either through the Women's Offering or by contributing to the local moral welfare organisation, and found that 34 out of the 49 parishes contributed to the Women's Offering with varying degrees of enthusiasm and that eight of these also contributed to the local work. It is possible that, although it was not specifically mentioned, this local support was given by other parishes also.

More significant from our point of view than the question of financial support was the extent and nature of the professional contacts between individual clergymen and moral welfare workers both in general and in connection with the referral of cases. Five of the 49 clergy interviewed were new to the diocese in 1959 or 1960, i.e., the longest they could have been there was twenty months, and their replies were analysed separately. Of the remainder, four were new to their present parish in 1959 or 1960, but not to the diocese. Of the 44 who had been two years or more in the diocese, 19 stated that they had had no contact with their local moral welfare worker, but three had been in touch with the organising secretary, two with the local home, and one had known the worker in his previous parish. Of the five who were new to the diocese, three had already been in contact with a moral welfare worker. In all, 28 clergy (25 who had been in the diocese more than two years and three newcomers) said that they had been in touch with the local worker, 18 within the past year and 10 at some time before this,[2] while 21 (19 who had been in the diocese more than two years and two newcomers) had made no such contact.

All but two of the clergy whose responses were positive had been in touch with the moral welfare worker over a case or cases, and several had met the worker in other connections as well, possibly because she lived in the parish or had an office nearby. The kinds of cases mentioned as having been referred included unmarried mothers, matrimonial and family difficulties, children of separated parents or a widower, young people in moral danger or showing behaviour difficulties and in one case an elderly couple. Our informants were unable to produce exact figures as to the number of cases referred, but most of those who had referred cases said that they had done so on more than one occasion.

In order to test their knowledge and understanding of it, each incumbent in the sample was asked to describe or define the Church's moral welfare work as he saw it. More than a third of those who had been in touch with a worker over cases specifically mentioned work with unmarried mothers. The majority added other types of work, either matrimonial or family problems or educational work of some description. One called moral welfare 'an extension of my work'. The others in this group did not mention work with unmarried mothers, but four spoke of difficulties in sexual and family relationships, and two specifically mentioned work for young people. The largest group (11 out of 28) gave a broader interpretation of the work, describing it in such terms as 'social work with a background of Christian compassion' or 'bringing a Christian influence to bear on many social problems'. Only one person made no response; this was on the grounds that he needed time to think over the question.

Those who had little or no direct contact with moral welfare workers revealed much the same degree of understanding of the nature of the work as those who had. More than half this group referred to the care of the unmarried mother, most of them adding other types of work in much the same way as the first group. Six gave a broad interpretation, one example of this being 'a branch of the Church's social concern, side by side with the spiritual gospel. It takes the form of trained workers ... who help in problems of readjustment of young people and others—those in trouble needing help, unmarried mothers and their babies'. One informant described it in terms of sexual and family relationships, and another as 'work for women and girls' (unspecified). Several mentioned temperance work and evidently linked the work of the Board of Moral Welfare with that of the Church of England Temperance Society, whilst another informant confused moral welfare work with the work of the Vigilance Association. In both groups there were one or two answers which revealed real confusion as to both the nature and scope of the work.

It was not always clear from the replies received whether respondents were describing moral welfare work as they saw it, or whether they were attempting a definition which should embrace all that they felt it ought to include. Thus one clergyman spoke passionately of the Church 'castigating one section of the community when it should begin with the elite' and added, 'Moral welfare concerns us all. The Church condemns unchastity, what about usury?' Those who considered that the scope of the work should be extended either envisaged some kind of social action, for example in educational work, or by means of a closer connection between moral welfare and temperance work, or emphasised the need for the Church to witness in relation to wider social issues, such as 'the influence of T.V. programmes which feature vindictive violence and sex', 'gambling', or the 'spectator complex'.

It was recognised by some incumbents that one of the chief obstacles to both the extension of the work and the development of closer working relationships between clergy and workers is the shortage of workers; one clergyman commented that the real problem was that with its present recources moral welfare could do no more. Only a small minority of the whole sample, 10 out of 49, expressed a strong desire for a closer working contact between themselves and moral welfare workers, but this leaves out of account those who considered that a satisfactory relationship already existed.

One of the questions we were interested in was how far the moral welfare worker acts as a link between the local churches and the social services interpreting the one to the other, and whether she can be regarded as indispensable in the sense that, if she were not available, a social work problem would go by default. We therefore asked the clergymen whom we interviewed to whom, if no moral worker were available, they would turn for help in difficulties which would otherwise have been referred to her. Eleven in each group (i.e., those who already had and those who had not a working contact with their local worker) gave answers which showed that they had been in contact at some time with one or other of the social services, probation, children's departments, health visitors, marriage guidance councils and adoption societies being the services most frequently mentioned. Nine indicated that if no moral welfare worker were available they would handle the case themselves and five stated that they did not know what they would do.

In general it appeared that contacts between the clergymen interviewed and social workers in the secular services, whether statutory or voluntary, were somewhat limited, and from what we were told it would seem that contacts with women church workers other than moral welare workers were also limited. According to the interview records less than half the sample stated definitely that they had worked with a woman parish worker, but in 17 cases no answer was recorded. The greater proportion of the sample were noncommittal on the subject of the usefulness of women workers; only nine were positive in their attitudes, making remarks to the effect that a woman worker might be very useful in their parish.

One of the important questions which arose in the course of the survey was the possibility of the Church making use of social workers apart from the present specialism of moral welfare work. Clearly the parochial clergy would be intimately affected by any scheme which sought to link pastoral and social work more closely in the ministry of the Church. We therefore asked the sample 'Do you think the Church should employ its own social workers? If so, could you, as a parish priest, make use of such a worker? Would you prefer this worker to be based on one parish only or a group of parishes?' In asking these questions, we had in mind the Michelhurst experiment, which is described later in this chapter, but the questions were variously interpreted, some respondents envisaging an extension into the parishes of moral welfare work as it is at present, others thinking in terms of something different and wider in scope.

The large majority of our informants (37 out of 49) made positive responses to this group of related questions, but a good many of them qualified their answers on the grounds that shortage of money or lack of workers would make any such scheme impracticable, and sometimes put forward alternative suggestions. Some in this group were in favour of Christian workers 'permeating' the secular social services, a development which would also avoid the possibility of overlapping with other bodies already in the field, while two clergymen suggested 'a voluntary reserve of lay people'. Nevertheless, even among the doubters, there were one or two who could see a place for such a worker, particularly in a large parish, if the difficulties could be overcome.

Other informants were openly enthusiastic. One incumbent working single-handed in a difficult parish, considered it 'a must rather than something which it would be nice to have'. Another, similarly situated, was equally enthusiastic but emphasised that such a worker should be 'entirely concerned with social welfare. . . . She could help people and then lead them into the fellowship'. The area over which such a worker might operate was also discussed. One incumbent, who said he 'would not advocate one worker to every parish', saw a place for a worker attached to a 'leading parish', whilst another in the central city area raised the issue of parish boundaries, suggesting four such workers for eight parishes, using the analogy of group practice in medicine. Others favoured still larger units, and suggested a deanery or a diocesan team. On the other hand there were those who clung to the idea of the worker operating in a single parish as 'part of a parish team under the vicar', and 'employed locally, not by Headquarters'. Many of the clergy interviewed could give no definite ideas as to the type of work such a worker might undertake, but suggestions included youth work, matrimonial problems, persistent long term cases and old people's welfare as well as some of the work an outdoor moral welfare worker does now. Other informants saw her functioning as a link between the church and the social services, and one clergyman thought that 'the normal day to day things could usefully be done by people in the statutory services . . . but there ought to be some sort of a panel of accredited and trained specialists to put people in touch with particular cases'.

Many of the clergymen in the sample raised the question of training, and among these, and others with whom it was discussed, there was a widespread feeling that training was very important. Usually the kind of training envisaged was left undefined, and the most important requirements were generally considered to be good educational background and a sound religious faith. Several thought that the Josephine Butler House training, or an extension of it would be suitable, and others mentioned courses in psychology, theology and/or pastoralia. There was some difference of opinion between those who felt that the training of both clergy and social workers is at present too academic, and advocated a more practical approach, and those who wanted 'the highest possible training'.

The relationship between social and pastoral work, which appears to be a fundamental to this discussion, was regarded in differing lights by the individual clergymen in this sample. Excluding eight answers which were not directly relevant, we were left with 18 replies to the effect that there is no essential difference between the two, six that they are essentially the same but differ in practice, one that although they overlap they are not necessarily the same, and 16 to the effect that they are both theoretically and practically different. The type of parish for which they were responsible seems to have affected some of the answers given, as, for example, one clergyman who replied, 'There is no difference in this type of parish. In practically every house one visits there is some social problem. No time to pay purely pastoral visits.' Several clergymen used the word 'interlocking' to describe the relationship as they saw it, and one thought that social work was a part of pastoral work. Another added : 'People don't know what the Church stands for. They come in trouble to the Church as social work pure and simple.'

The six answers which indicated that pastoral and social work are essentially the same but in practice have become separated, differed in their explanation of this, one laying it at the door of the State, another at that of 'the people who are after what they can get', yet another attributing it to the divisions of the Church. Those who distinguished between the two also differed in their analysis of the situation. Some related the difference to the problems involved, others to the people helped. An example of the latter was the vicar who said 'Pastoral work is caring for those who belong—spiritual care. By rights one should be going more outside and giving less time to the flock. In this case, pastoral and social work are much nearer'.

Up to this point, the interviews had proceeded on the assumption that the Church should continue actively to participate in social work and witness. Before concluding the interviews, however, we asked two general questions designed to test this assumption : the first, 'What do you think is the Church's responsibility, if any, for social work?', the second, 'Do you think that the Church should have a concern for social problems?' with its corollary, 'What kind of problems?' The answers to these questions varied considerably. Some respondents emphasised that the Church's primary responsibility is to preach the Gospel, and evidently considered that, although concern for people's welfare might arise out of this preaching, it would be and remain a 'by-product of the setting out of the Kingdom of God'. Such 'setting out' has social implications in 'acts of mercy' but the gospel can be lived out in other everyday work as well as in social work. This group were fearful lest the claims of social service might over-ride the Church's call to evangelism, which they regarded as paramount.

Answers along these lines were given by a minority of the sample. The great majority of our informants, while accepting the advent of the welfare state and the consequent changed role of the Church in social service, felt that this role was still important. Opinions differed as to how it should be exercised. Some of the clergy considered that, rather than attempt to establish or maintain its own social work organisations, the Church should encourage its members to enter the statutory services, whether as a matter of economic necessity, since the Church's resources in money and manpower are severely limited, or as the most appropriate response to the present situation. They deprecated any attempt to duplicate the statutory services. Others, although they appreciated this point of view, thought that the Church should provide a service of its own, either by initiating new work, filling in gaps or undertaking special pieces of work such as work with teen-agers, residential work or mental health. The attitude of a large number of the clergymen encountered can be summed up in the comment of one of them which was that 'the Church should both offer its own services and help to staff others'.

A number of reasons were put forward in support of the view that the Church should continue to provide its own social services whether or not it encouraged its members to staff those sponsored by other bodies. Among the most interesting contributions made to the discussion were those which emphasised the role of the Church as an accepting and caring community, a 'fellowship of forgiven sinners' offering an understanding welcome to all, whatever their background, who wished to enter. From what we learnt about the relationships between moral welfare case workers and parish clergymen, and the limited extent to which the workers felt able to offer those whom they were and had been helping the fellowship and support of the local church, it would seem that this image of the Church, sincerely put forward as it was, can only be inadequately reflected by many congregations. We were given some examples of people being helped in this way. In one parish, so we were told, the mother of an illegitimate child had received 'an accepting welcome' and now sings in the church choir; in another, one of the church wardens on hearing that the mother was being received back into the full life of the church, rang up the vicar to offer to be god-father to the child.

For the most part, while the local church congregation may have an important, and possibly even a vital part, to play in the spiritual and social rehabilitation of individuals who have been receiving intensive casework help from a social worker, there is little likelihood of the opportunity for this occurring more than very rarely in any one parish, and the general impression we brought away from this piece of field work was that moral welfare work was regarded by most of the clergymen whom we visited as useful, specialist work, but hardly a matter of vital concern either to himself or his parishioners. This made the Michelhurst experiment, in which an attempt was made to break down this isolation and develop the work in a neighbourhood and parish setting all the more significant, and we now consider it in some detail.

II

Until the late 1940's Michelhurst[3] was a prosperous residential district set among the farmlands of a pleasing southern county, but during the next few years the London County Council's re-housing plans completely changed the character of the area by creating two new estates, one to the north and one to the south of the original village, to accommodate 30,000 of its overspill population. Each estate now has its own churches, public houses and small shops, but the main shopping centre is the old village street, refurbished and expanded. Here, too, are located the district council offices, the maternity and child welfare clinic with day nursery attached, and the police station. Situated on one of the estates is the area housing office, a symbol of the division of powers between the authorities concerned, for London is responsible for the allocation of houses and the collection of rents while the county council and the relevant district councils provide all other public services.

There is a small industrial area near at hand, but unlike the new towns, housing here is not linked to employment, so that most of the skilled and semi-skilled workers who form the bulk of the population travel to and from London or its northern environs daily. Long journeys to work, combined with the shift system, mean that husbands may be away from home for many hours at a stretch, and loneliness is a serious problem, especially for the women, who are also deprived of the company of their mothers and other relatives and friends whom they have left behind in London. It has been claimed that loneliness, rather than infidelity, is the major cause of the estate's many marital problems.

As in other new areas, debt is another serious difficulty. High fares, higher rents than they have been accustomed to, and door-to-door salesmen with tempting hire-purchase offers, have proved financially disastrous to some young couples who may never have run their own home before and are isolated from the older relatives and friends who could give help and guidance. The disproportionate number of young couples in the population, together with the gap in the 40-59 age group, has also led to a shortage of leaders, for although there are older people with the requisite experience in old Michelhurst, on the whole the populations do not mix.

At the time when they were being established the newly created estates presented a complicated ecclesiastical pattern as parts of four different parishes were included in the area, but, even before these complications had been unravelled, two Anglican clergymen were working there, welcoming the families as they moved in and helping to solve the problems the new residents encountered. The fact that they were there from the beginning, working from makeshift premises, meant that people became aware of the existence of the clergyman and were able to make his acquaintance as they arrived. They were, therefore, prepared to turn to him in difficulty and, whether church members or not, came to look upon the church primarily as a worshipping and helping community rather than as a building. In their turn, the clergy became acutely aware of the problems and difficulties of the new residents, and it was from this awareness that the 'experiment' grew.

At this time the diocesan bishop made a practice of holding regular meetings with the clergy working in the new areas to discuss their special problems. In the course of these discussions it became apparent that in any one such area an experienced woman social worker attached to a parish church would find plenty of scope, and in 1953 a church worker was appointed to Michelhurst. She had trained as a Church Army sister, and later as a moral welfare worker at Josephine Butler Memorial House, and subsequently had obtained experience in both residential and outdoor moral welfare work. The appointment was made by the diocese, without any intermediate committee, and a grant of £2,000 was obtained from a large Trust to cover the salary and expenses of the worker for at least four years. In the event, this money was augmented from other sources and the experiment actually lasted for nearly six years.

An essential feature of the experiment was that the worker was to live on the estate so that she would both be available at any time and herself experience some of the social problems with which she was dealing, and, although this was impossible to begin with, at the end of the first year the London County Council allocated her a flat. Her role was to be three-fold. She was to be a member of the parish staff, but both her social work training and the needs of the area would make her more than a parish worker; she was to be a moral welfare worker, but with a more limited area and less limited case load than most moral welfare workers; she was to develop educational and preventive work of a kind most moral welfare workers cannot hope to undertake.

In the early days of her employment the main emphasis was placed on parish work, including sick visiting, Sunday school work, confirmation preparation, girl guides and the organisation and leadership of clubs for children and young people. As time went on, however, she found herself less involved in active leadership and more occupied in training leaders and supporting them when in office. She made many individual contacts through church organisations and, as a parish worker, she could visit homes without it becoming known in the neighbourhood that the family was in distress.

The case work grew slowly. In 1954, the first full year of the experiment, the worker dealt with 34 cases of which three were mothers with illegitimate children, 7 concerned children and young people, 10 were matrimonial and family problems and 14 other personal problems. Referrals came from both social work and church sources. The diocesan organising secretary had explained the nature of the experiment to local social workers and a number of cases, including mental health and other difficult cases, were referred by almoners; at no stage did unmarried mothers dominate the case load. On the church side, one of the clergy compiled a special visiting list of families where he sensed that a problem existed, although he was not always certain as to its nature, and church connections became increasingly important sources of referral as people came to have a better understanding of the kind of problems in which the worker could be of help.

Four years later the total number of cases dealt with had risen to 68, 28 old and 40 new, while the proportion of unmarried mothers referred had risen from 8% to 40% of the new cases. This may have reflected an increase in the population at risk, or it could have meant that by then the worker was better known to other social workers and referral agencies. Although not easy to show statistically, the worker also noticed a change in the character of the family and matrimonial problems she dealt with. On their arrival people were faced with urgent practical difficulties, whereas later the more subtle problems of loneliness and incompatibility became more evident, and there was a marked increase in the type of problem which threatened the stability and harmony of the home.

The third approach to the problems of the estate which the worker was charged to make was that of seeking 'ways and means of doing educational and preventive work'. This branch of her work developed mainly from the connections she established with youth organisations, but partly also from other contacts both with church members and others. It was principally concerned with helping young people, and in some respects could be regarded as an extension of family case work into the younger age group. There were also cases in which the worker was able to help with family problems, the initial approach to the family being made because she had become aware of an adolescent member's particular difficulties. More formal educational work was also undertaken in the shape of youth conferences organised with the co-operation of clergy and interested laymen; in one instance this was for Michelhurst youth; in the other two the invitation came from a parish elsewhere. The general theme of these conferences was 'Vocation' and an attempt was made to discuss both employment and personal relationships and marriage within this wider context. These conferences proved popular and were said to be helpful. Another venture was a parish family holiday party, which included eight unattached boys and girls of the 'Teddy boy' type. The adults said at the end 'they were pleased the youngsters came because they had learned to know and understand them better from being with them'.

At the end of six years the money made available for the work ran out and the experiment was brought to an end. Originally it had been hoped that, with the initial help of a grant from the Trust fund, sufficient money could be raised locally to keep the work going and that in the long run it would become self-supporting. This belief proved to be quite unrealistic and would almost certainly prove so again if the experiment were repeated in another area. By the summer of 1959 the financial position was becoming precarious and it had already been realised by both the sponsors of the scheme and the worker herself that sooner or later the work would have to be reorganised. In order to ease the situation the worker resigned and the case work in Michelhurst was combined with that of a neighbouring deanery whose newly appointed moral welfare worker had expressed interest in work on housing estates. The Michelhurst Committee retained its autonomy as a case committee, but in other respects became a sub-committee of the deanery committee. It was hoped that in the course of time the change would strengthen both associations and that the financial position might improve sufficiently to warrant the appointment of a second deanery worker, either full- or part-time, on a more permanent basis than had previously been possible. Meanwhile the new deanery worker was to live on the Michelhurst estate and spend a day a week working there. Although, when the estate was last visited in March 1960, it was difficult to make any real assessment of how the new arrangement was working, it appeared that the preservation of the aims and methods of the original experiment had not proved possible and that it had, in effect, come to an end.

In both conception and initiation the Michelhurst experiment showed imagination and enterprise, and it represents an interesting attempt to combine parish and social work. Its distinguishing feature was that the social work undertaken was less specialised than most moral welfare work but more closely linked with both church and neighbourhood. The worker lived in the area and knew many local people there, apart from the cases she was actually helping; she worshipped at the local church as a member of the congregation, and she was a member of the parish staff, accepted as a colleague by the clergy and working closely with them.

The importance of the worker's residence on the estate was realised from the beginning. Because she lived there she was known to ordinary people and joined them in doing ordinary things, and she believed that this both helped her to keep a sense of proportion and continually revitalised her enthusiasm and energy. She was available at any hour and at week-ends and worked from an anonymous flat to which people could come at any time without advertising the reason for their visit. Since she was known to different people for different reasons she could visit them in their own homes without the neighbours knowing in which role she was making the visit. Her position was thus in marked contrast to that of the average moral welfare worker as well as to that of the other social workers on the estate, the great majority of whom lived outside the area, although a few had sub-offices there. The Michelhurst worker felt that social workers coming in from outside and with their own roots elsewhere contributed to the general feeling of 'rootlessness' and themselves became infected with the instability prevalent in the area. There was, moreover, a quick turnover of staff among the social workers serving the area; at the end of six years only two of those who had been there when the worker arrived still remained.

Within the wider community of the estate was the worshipping congregation of the local church and the worker's close connection with it was important for the development and working of the experiment. The parish work was useful as a point of contact with people, some of whom might need help. People with problems were introduced to church organisations, partly because of the company and recreation they would enjoy there, but also because it was possible to keep in touch with them in this way, although the worker would not necessarily be welcomed in their homes. On the other hand, it was not uncommon for her to meet people who belonged to a club on a social level and later on to find them coming to her about their personal problems. All this meant that a considerable amount of the casework undertaken was with people who already had some connection with the church, and much of the preventive and educational work grew out of contacts made in the various church organisations. The extent of the need of members of the congregation for social work help came as a surprise to the worker, who felt that it was not entirely due to the special difficulties of life on a new housing estate. She believed that many of the problems brought to her would not have been taken to another social worker and hence the presence of the church social worker was of great benefit to such people.

One of the greatest needs of all new areas is for suitable and competent leaders for clubs and other organisations. At the beginning much of the worker's time was given to leadership and to training leaders. She continued to support and help the committees of these organisations even when she had passed on the active leadership to others, and the congregation and the parish organisations were able to support her and the people she helped in several ways, not only introducing clients to new friends and new interests and enabling her to keep in touch informally, but by practical assistance, such as help with old clothes or groceries for a needy family, baby-sitters to look after the children while a father visited his wife in hospital, and hospitality for children whose parents were temporarily unable to care for them. In these and other ways 'moral welfare' came to be seen as the concern of the whole parish as well as of the expert.

The career of the moral welfare committee itself was another example of this process of education of church members. The committee was formed in 1956, when the experiment had been running for two years and when it was felt that the worker would benefit from the support of a local committee. Apart from the clergymen, no one on the committee had had any previous experience of moral welfare work, and meetings were often devoted to explanations of certain aspects of the work; but members were willing to learn, and on one occasion an application for financial help for a 'thoroughly bad girl' was granted immediately, with the comment, 'Isn't this the kind of person we are trying to help?'

The role of the parish clergy in the experiment was of crucial importance. For the greater part of the time the worker was accepted by them as a colleague, and not only were cases referred to her but there was joint consultation, joint prayer and often joint action. Towards the end of her time at Michelhurst the situation changed, however, owing to changes in the parochial staff. When one of the two priests who were originally involved in the experiment moved elsewhere, two young assistant priests were appointed in quick succession, neither of whom received advance briefing as to the nature and purpose of the experiment, and they were not sufficiently experienced to recognise its value without this prior help. This meant that on this part of the estate the previous good co-operation could not be maintained to anything like the same extent. Later when a new incumbent was appointed to the parish covering the other half of the estate, the bishop took steps to acquaint him with the situation and secure his co-operation, and this co-operation was maintained through-out the remainder of the experiment. Where she was accepted as a colleague the worker's knowledge and experience of social work, both generally and as it related to the specific problems associated with sex, marriage and family life, was seen to supplement the pastoral ministry of the clergy, and one of the clergymen associ-ated with the early stages of the experiment told us that he would prefer a 'moral welfare trained parish worker' to a curate in an area such as this housing estate. He went on to emphasise that such a worker must be properly trained in both moral welfare and pastoralia.

The work was definitely Anglican in framework and emphasis, but the worker said she did not encounter any real difficulties because of this. Some people whom she helped, and who had had no previous church connections, were drawn into the life of the worshipping community; others, when once their need was past, were never heard of again, except perhaps when the vicar made one of his regular parochial visits. Roman Catholics were always referred to their own worker and Free Church members were few in number. The lack of denominational discrimination was sufficiently evident for the county council to grant-aid the work in the usual way. When spiritual guidance and pastoral help seemed to be called for, however, the worker, accepting that her work was church work, regarded this as part of her task in co-operation with the parish clergy and acted accordingly. The ex-periment was thus based on the belief that pastoral and social work could be combined, and for this as well as for other reasons is of general as well as local interest. Its implications will be dis-cussed further in the concluding part of the study.

PART FIVE

The Issues Involved

15

MORAL WELFARE WORK TODAY

IN the first two parts of the study we traced the development of moral welfare work in this country from its beginnings in the middle ages and even earlier to the present time and gave some indication of both the contemporary social setting and parallel developments in other fields of social work. The middle portion of the book was devoted to a detailed description of the work as it is carried on today in two dioceses selected for detailed study. In both historical outline and contemporary portrait we allowed the findings to speak for themselves and, for the most part, refrained from comment or assessment. In these two concluding chapters we endeavour to draw together and evaluate the factual material and consider the light which it throws on issues of policy.

I

For the purposes of the study we defined moral welfare work as the casework, residential work and educational work relating to sex, marriage and the family undertaken in the name and on behalf of the Church of England by diocesan and local associations established for the purpose. As such it claims to be both a collective concern for those in distress and compassionate care for them and also a form of social work with a distinctively Christian approach. It is this double claim which we have been at pains to examine.

In attempting to assess the claim of moral welfare work to be regarded as 'church' work it is necessary to take into account both the recognition and support it receives at all levels of church organisation, and the extent to which the work itself is overtly religious in objective and approach.

The Church Assembly accorded formal recognition to the Church of England Advisory Board for Moral Welfare (later the Moral Welfare Council) in the early thirties, and between 1934 and the incorporation of the Council into the Board for Social Responsibility, a constituent Board of the Assembly, in 1958, it gave not only recognition but grant aid. At the diocesan level, formal recognition and support appear to be fairly general. In 1959, the middle year of the field work, only one diocesan association in the Northern Province and two in the Southern were not in receipt of direct grants from their Boards of Finance. One small diocese made a grant of £50, the remaining grants ranged from £150 to well over £1,000. Almost half the organising secretaries who replied to our questionnaire were either members of, or invited to attend, the Diocesan Conference, and in some dioceses reports on moral welfare work were made to the Conference in rotation with those of other recognised activities.

Official recognition of this kind with its associated grant aid, significant and acceptable as it is, is not, however, necessarily indicative of widespread interest and support at either the parish or the diocesan level. We have already described the efforts we made to assess the extent and reality of this support in the two dioceses selected for study. They included discussions with local committees, and in one diocese with a sample of parish clergy, examination of sources of finance and the information given us by workers. From these investigations we gained the overall impression that, among the laity, active interest in the work was confined to a small minority, mostly women, some of whom came into touch with it quite fortuitously, but whether this was so or not became faithful and enthusiastic supporters. For most of the clergy it was one among their many concerns, a marginal interest about which knowledge and understanding varied considerably. In general, it appeared that, although carried on in the name of the Church, moral welfare work is a piece of specialised work of very little interest to the vast majority of church people.

One factor in this situation is the nature of the work itself. In some quarters, at any rate, it seemed that open discussions of questions relating to sexual deviations were still regarded a little askance, and it was noticeable that several of the clergymen interviewed obviously regarded moral welfare work as a woman's affair, the concern of the Mothers' Union rather than of the congregation as a whole. The substitution in one diocese of the term 'Home and Family' for 'Women's' Offering was an attempt to overcome this attitude, as was the circulation by the bishop of the other diocese of intercessions to be used in parishes throughout the diocese on one or other of the two Sundays preceding the annual Women's Offering.

A characteristic of the work which complicates relationships between clergy and workers, and also makes it difficult to publicise it in a way which will arouse the imaginative sympathy of the ordinary, and frequently rather conventional churchgoer, is that details of cases helped are, and must remain, strictly confidential. Another factor which may serve to reduce the participation and interest of church members in the work is the emphasis now placed on the fact that it is work requiring particular professional knowledge and skills such as are possessed only by trained workers. This has tended to minimise, and in some areas has eliminated altogether the role of the local committee as an advisory body on casework. For the most part the direct contact which committee members have with the work is slight and the ways in which they can help are limited, and this is bound to make it difficult to maintain interest. In this respect we noted a difference between committees responsible for homes, whose members were able to give direct practical assistance, and obviously felt that they were 'doing something', and those responsible for outdoor work whose role appeared to be confined to money raising, and whose only link with the work itself was the caseworker's report.

Another feature of the situation was the limited knowledge and understanding shown by a number of the clergymen whom we met, not only of moral welfare work itself, but also of the extent and character of the modern social services and the nature and scope of present day social work. There were, of course, exceptions, but, by and large, our experience was similar to that of the Birmingham investigator who wrote, 'It was surprising how few of the clergy with whom the question was discussed had a clear grasp of the British social services.'[1] We also found a widespread belief among the clergy that social work, whether statutory or voluntary, is primarily or almost solely, directed towards the relief of material distress. The fact that much of the work is now concerned with the adjustment of faulty relationships hardly seemed to be appreciated. Without better understanding on the part of both clergy and laity of the nature and purpose of moral welfare work and of the social milieu in which it operates, the full support and co-operation of the Church in whose name it is carried out is difficult to envisage.

Even more important than the extent of this support and understanding is the question as to how far the work itself is religious in approach and objective. In his foreword to the 1959 annual report the chairman of the diocesan board of moral welfare in one of the dioceses surveyed first listed the numbers of cases helped during the year, then added : 'The Church has to remember that they are not cases, but people they must try to bring to the knowledge and forgiveness and grace of our Lord.' This quotation could, moreover, be paralleled by similar quotations we noted in diocesan or annual reports from all parts of the country, some of which were accompanied by an overt statement, or carried the hidden implication, that it is here that the difference between church work and social work carried out under secular auspices is to be found. It was repeatedly emphasised that the end of the work done in the name of the Church is not merely material assistance or even social rehabilitation, although these may be assumed to be part of it, it is spiritual redemption.

In practice, as already pointed out in Chapter 11, we found little evidence, either in avenues of referral, types of case referred, character of the relationship established or the type of care or treatment given, of a specifically spiritual or religious approach in the outdoor work of the two dioceses surveyed. Reliable evidence on this particular issue was difficult to obtain, but as far as we were able to observe, the fact that they were employed by the Church and acting in its name appeared to make little difference to the workers' day to day handling of concrete situations or to their relationships with more than perhaps a small number of clients, and this was, in fact, admitted by more than one worker in informal conversation.

With few exceptions the local authority officials whom we met appeared to attach little importance to the religious motivation and connections of moral welfare workers. When asked to state what they considered to be the differences between this work and that of the local authorities, several officials replied to the effect that moral welfare work was work carried out by a voluntary organisation with all that this implied in spontaneity, flexibility and freedom of action, and these aspects of the work received considerably more emphasis in their replies than did its specifically religious character. 'The Church doesn't seem to come into it,' remarked one children's officer, and a county welfare officer in another area said she thought that its church connections made 'no difference' to moral welfare work. Far from being 'put off' by these connections the families concerned 'weren't aware that it was a religious organisation'.[2] This may have been an extreme view, and possibly atypical, but that it was held by at least one local authority worker is significant.

More than one local authority worker whom we met stressed how important it was for a social worker to have a coherent philosophy of life if she was to carry out her work properly, but they denied that it was necessary to work in a church setting to get this across to one's clients. As one children's officer expressed it, 'No social worker can make a real contribution unless she has regard to the spiritual side. One has got to have a faith or philosophy, and it has got to come across, but whether one works in a statutory or church setting does not make much difference to the possibilities of bringing this about.'[3] While respecting this point of view and the conviction behind it, many moral welfare workers would, we think, consider that it leaves out of account what is for them the crux of the situation. What really differentiates a church worker from the individual Christian working in a secular agency, we were told, is not the way in which she handles her cases but the spiritual and moral support she obtains from the sense that she is part of a company commissioned by the Church for a particular form of service, and this more than compensates for the higher salaries and better conditions which could be obtained by transferring to secular employment.[4]

Religious attitudes and objectives were much more overt in the adoption work which we saw than in the general casework, particularly when it came to the choice of prospective adopters. The diocesan adoption agency with which we were in contact regarded practising membership of a Christian church (preferably the Church of England) as an essential condition of acceptance as an adoptive parent for, in the view of those responsible for the

work, the spiritual well-being of the child could only be satisfactorily assured if he were placed with parents 'whose faith is real
enough for them to be worshipping, instructed members of the
Church whose faith they profess'. For a church society this is an
entirely logical point of view and, in as far as the Church in making this stipulation, is acting in what it regards as the best interests
of the child, it would seem to be justified in creating its own
agencies for the purpose. Church adoption societies admit, however, that applications to adopt may provide an opportunity for
promoting the spiritual well-being of the prospective adopters,
which then becomes an end in itself as well as a guarantee of the
religious upbringing of the child;[5] and there is a risk, of which
the associations themselves are aware, that this may be interpreted
as implying that they use the prospect of being given a child as a
bait to induce young couples to become practising members of
their church. Any such intention of using the child as 'a carrot for
the soul of the adopters' was strongly disclaimed by both workers
and committee members of church adoption societies whom we
met. They described it as a misinterpretation of the situation, and
said that care was taken to make the line taken by the association
clear to· prospective adopters, especially those whose acceptance
was deferred on the grounds of inadequate evidence of practising
churchmanship. It is a situation in which much depends on the
pastoral as well as the social care given to prospective adopters
both during the probationary period and afterwards.

It was in the residential work that the religious character of
moral welfare work was most apparent. The appointment of chaplains, the setting apart of rooms for use as chapels, the daily prayers
and set times of worship were all outward signs of this, and the
superintendents whom we met were evidently concerned that
residents in their homes should enjoy opportunities for participating in the life of a Christian community and absorbing its
ideals and ethos. The extent to which this is meaningful to more
than a handful of residents was, we considered, doubtful. The
majority probably accept it as part of the artificial situation in
which their unwanted maternity has landed them, and it is even
possible that for some residents the very existence of the chapel
and the unfamiliar ritual merely serve to enhance the remoteness
of the situation from everyday life and reduce the likelihood of the
devotional practices of the mother and baby home being kept up

on return to the outside world. We were told, however, that there were a minority of residents whose whole manner of life was changed as the result of the spiritual help they received in a moral welfare home, and in the eyes of the superintendent this made up for the indifference of the rest.

A fundamental issue raised by this discussion of the effectiveness of the religious influence exercised by moral welfare workers is whether, effective or not, it is right to exercise such influence at all, since this can be said to involve taking advantage of the situation in which the client finds herself to force upon her religious teaching and practice which she neither wants nor appreciates, and is thus an infringement of her freedom. In undertaking moral welfare work the Church of England is catering mainly for nominal rather than active members and many of those seeking the help of a moral welfare worker, or taking refuge in a home, are either indifferent or hostile to religious beliefs and practices. For the most part they do not desire 'moral' guidance or spiritual help and, it is argued, 'they should not have to pay the price of a pseudo-conversion for the help they receive'.[6]

We found nothing to suggest that the residents in the homes we visited were being forced to accept Christian convictions they did not share as a price of receiving help, and in that crude sense the charge of 'religious blackmail' may be regarded as being slightly out of date and misdirected, at least in the case of Anglican homes run by lay committees and staff.[7] But this cannot be accepted as the end of the matter. Christian beliefs may not be forced upon a resident in a home, but she cannot escape their impact, and she is expected to conform to certain practices whether or not she shares the faith of which they are an expression. In this sense she is subject to pressure, and many workers (both indoor and outdoor) evidently considered that in a residential setting it was permissible to emphasise the specifically religious character of the work in ways which would be regarded as out of place in the outdoor worker's office.

Some outdoor workers always discuss with their clients the religious observances expected in the homes to which it is suggested they should go, and we consider that this practice should be generally followed. In theory it gives the girl a chance to refuse the vacancy if she objects to the home's religious emphasis, but as long as there is a shortage of mother and baby and similar homes, and that the majority of those available are under the auspices of one or other of the Christian churches, the choice is unreal and there is a strong inducement to accept help 'with religion thrown in'. The fact that there is no effective alternative places church homes in a privileged position, of which we feel members of staff should always be aware when dealing with girls who are unwilling to conform to the accepted pattern. As long as the Church has a monopoly or near monopoly of any kind of social work, those responsible for it are under a moral obligation to respect the spiritual freedom as well as what they regard as the spiritual welfare of those for whom the service is provided. The only certain way of avoiding any possibility of unmarried mothers and other girls and women in need of residential care being forced to accept vacancies in church homes, where they would be exposed to religious influences which they might conceivably resent, would be for local authorities or secular voluntary agencies to provide an adequate number of homes of this kind, with no provision for spiritual counselling or religious observance other than that commonly found in a National Health Service hospital. In that sense the onus to provide a genuine choice rests with the critics, but so far they have been in no hurry to take up the challenge.

While it was in the outdoor work that the religious emphasis was least apparent, it was the outdoor workers who were most conscious of themselves as social workers and anxious to be accepted as such. This is a phenomenon which has been apparent since the 1920's. During this period, moreover, social workers in general have laid increasing stress on their professional status, and in some branches of casework professional recognition has been limited to persons with certain accepted qualifications and training. The situation is, however, complex in that, while certain social work professions, notably almoning and psychiatric social work, have been able to restrict their membership to those whom they regard as fully-trained social workers, that is workers with a university and professional training, the same is by no means true of child care and probation,[8] while the starting of two year non-university courses for both child care officers and social workers in local authority health and welfare departments makes the definition of a qualified social worker even more difficult. The Younghusband committee postulated three grades of social worker—welfare assistant (in-trained), general social worker (two years general training) and professional social worker (university degree, diploma or certificate in social studies followed by a professional training lasting about a year), but in practice these distinctions have not proved to be wholly tenable. The Home Office Children's Department and the Child Care Officers' Association give full professional recognition to non-graduates who have received a two year child care training, while probation officers who have entered the profession late in life and have been given a one year training by the Probation Training Board take their place with their more fully trained colleagues.

The formal acceptance by other social workers' associations of moral welfare workers as professional colleagues is shown by the fact that the Moral Welfare Workers' Association is represented on the Standing Conference of Organisations of Social Workers. Nevertheless, as we have already pointed out in Chapter 6, comparatively few moral welfare workers have managed to combine a social science degree or certificate with their moral welfare qualification, let alone take a recognised course in applied social studies or similar professional course. The training given at Josephine Butler House is comparable in length with that of the extra-university Younghusband and child care courses and, regarded as an educational experience, probably compares well with them, but the time devoted to theology and related subjects, valuable as this may be as a preparation for church work, inevitably reduces the amount of time available for social work training. At the time of the investigation the time and attention given to the latter was considerably less than that given on the Younghusband courses. The London course has hitherto been of such short duration that, despite the high quality of the training given, it can hardly rank as the equivalent of other extra-university social work training courses. In all, the general standard of training accepted as appropriate for moral welfare workers has, up to the present, been lower than that in other social work professions, and if, in certain professions, such as child care or probation, the number of wholly untrained officers, as well as those with in-service training, is still considerable, the nucleus of workers with professional casework training found in these professions makes it more possible to arrange for the adequate supervision of the less well-trained worker. This supervision is far more difficult to arrange in connection with moral welfare work, not only because of the shortage of fully trained workers, but because the administrative pattern of the work in many dioceses means that the worker may be working single-handed, responsible to her own local committee and without the day to day support of a senior worker.

We found during the fieldwork that the moral welfare worker's status as a social worker was usually taken for granted by local authority officials and workers; sometimes personal contacts were close,[9] and even those officials who were somewhat critical or negative in their attitude towards moral welfare work as a whole frequently spoke warmly of their particular local worker. One or two officials even confessed that their ideas about the work had been radically changed by the coming of a new worker.[10] While attitudes and opinions varied, we found that the extent to which the local moral welfare worker was respected and trusted by other social workers, and accepted as one of them, largely depended on whether or not they regarded her as being 'trained' and as having a 'casework' approach. This appeared to be assessed almost entirely by the quality of her casework and the extent to which she was prepared to co-operate with other workers and not by the length and character of her training, which might not even be known. A moral welfare worker who was noticeably respected and liked by other social workers in the area in which she worked was a clergyman's widow who had taken the London course.

A criticism sometimes made of moral welfare workers by their colleagues in related work is that they are 'judgmental' in their approach to their clients, and some local authority officials appeared to regard this as one of the main differences between their own attitude and that of the moral welfare workers they encountered. One official replying to our questionnaire asserted baldly, 'Moral welfare workers tend to form moral judgments of clients more than child care officers,' and this was reiterated in interview with the additional comment, 'It is so easy for Christian people to be dogmatic. The local authority must be all things to all men.' Another official considered that, 'the very fact of working for a religious organisation suggests to a client, "You have sinned" '. But not all officials saw the situation as simply as this, as may be illustrated by the following carefully thought out statement by a probation officer :

There may not be any difference in approach, but the client expects there to be one. She expects there to be more condemnation from the worker coupled with a bias towards religion. It is necessary to break down the client's prejudices in the early stages and this calls for good interviewing technique. To dispel incorrect views held by the client without, in so doing, lowering the moral standards expected requires consummate skill. The specially trained younger moral welfare worker can do this, the older, more rigid type cannot, and indeed is unlikely to see the necessity of doing so.[11]

In certain instances the criticism made by the local authority workers that the moral welfare workers are rigid or 'moralistic' in their approach may have been associated with their knowledge and experience of a particular worker, but we felt that it was sometimes the outcome of a stereotype which confused judgment with condemnation and assumed that belief in the seriousness of sin as it affects the eternal destiny of man necessarily involves a hard and punishing attitude towards the sinner in need of help. Nothing approaching this kind of attitude was shown by any of the workers with whom we were in contact. 'The attitude of the worker is very accepting. Terribly complicated situations involving illegitimate children of married people, divorces, etc. are taken as they come,' noted the fieldworker at the end of her stay in one area, and that was the general impression that we retained. There were wide variations in belief, outlook and approach among the moral welfare workers we encountered, but, at its best, their attitude towards their cases combined realism with compassion and adherence to church teaching and standards with the capacity to accept patiently, tolerantly and at times with a pleasant sense of humour, the most daunting manifestations of human waywardness—'forgiving one another . . . even as Christ forgave you'. Nor did workers appear to be averse to the idea of enlisting psychiatric help for their clients when this seemed appropriate and was available, and, given the opportunity, for example at conferences or refresher courses, they were ready and often eager to learn from people with psychiatric or sociological training.

If, on the one hand, the more forward-looking moral welfare workers are attaching increasing importance to the acquirement of deeper knowledge of human motivation and behaviour, on the other, many social workers practising in different settings are evidently concerned about the ethical implications of the personal and social problems they encounter and the caseworker's approach to them.[12] Since much of the theory and practice of present day social casework is based upon the presuppositions of psychology and psychiatry,[13] a particularly important issue is that of the relationship between these presuppositions and the Christian doctrine of man. The question as to whether and by what means the two can be linked so as to bring about on the one hand a deeper realisation of the value and importance of the concept of moral responsibility and, on the other, a more compassionate understanding of the complexities of human motivation and behaviour is already receiving some attention but merits more.[14] The responsibility of the Church in this situation is discussed in the next and last chapter of this study.

II

Moral welfare work began as an attempt to rescue from a life of sin and shame women and girls who were regarded as outcasts by contemporary society. It was the prostitutes and girls drifting into prostitution, together with 'betrayed and friendless' girls, often domestic servants, who were the objects of the zeal of the street 'missionaries' and the care of the 'self-devoted women' who founded and staffed the early penitentiaries. Later the emphasis gradually shifted from 'rescue' to 'prevention', from women already on the streets to children and young people 'in moral danger'. During the inter-war years, children's homes were opened, specialist children's workers appointed, and instead of patrolling the streets or visiting common lodging houses, the workers made arrangements with the appropriate authorities for shelters to be used as places of safety and considered the possibilities of educational work. Meanwhile, unmarried mothers and their children continued to receive both casework help and, where appropriate, residential care, and during and after the Second World War this became an increasingly important part of the work. Moral welfare work has thus always dealt with the constellation of problems associated with irregular sex relationships, but the emphasis has changed from time to time.

One aspect of these changes has been that the efforts to reclaim the prostitute, once so prominent a feature of moral welfare work, have declined almost to vanishing point, at least as far as the work organised by moral welfare associations is concerned.[15] This decline appears to be due in part to the changes in the character of prostitution itself, already described in Chapter 4, which make it less likely that prostitutes will seek, or even accept if offered, the help of a welfare agency, and in part to the fact that women police have replaced the voluntary street patrols of former days. At the time of the passing of the Street Offences Act, police everywhere were encouraged, when cautioning a girl, to offer her the help of a welfare agency, but the effectiveness of this may be judged from a comment made in the 1960 Annual Report on Establishment and Crime for a large northern city, which reads, 'Since the Act came into force a total of 249 cautions have been administered to 173 women . . . all were invited to be put in touch with a moral welfare organisation, but only 10 expressed their willingness to seek such advice. None, however, took advantage of the invitation.' Nor is this situation peculiar either to this city or to moral welfare organisations. The principal probation officer of one of the counties in the southern diocese, who was questioned on the subject replied, 'The police have been offered co-operation but there have been no requests for help.'

Whatever the justification for the virtual abandonment of the earlier direct approach to the prostitute, prostitution still stands as a reproach to the conscience and imagination of Christian people. Still, as in the days of Josephine Butler, it is a problem which requires for its solution far more than individual help to one party to the transaction, and to-day, as in her day, it is not only the problem itself which presents a challenge, but the unjust laws passed in attempt to mitigate it. This was recognised by the Church of England Moral Welfare Council and its staff, whose efforts to enlighten public opinion on this and kindred subjects have already been described in Chapter 3. Unsuccessful as they were in the particular instance of the Street Offences Act, these efforts were the expression of Christian concern, and had some impact on public opinion, although this might have been greater had the interest and activity at the centre been reflected more widely by the diocesan and local associations.

At the present time it is the work undertaken on behalf of unmarried mothers and their children that is central to moral welfare work and the greater number of cases reaching the workers are referred to them because of the special problem of illegitimacy. Although this is not generally dealt with in isolation, and the help given both to the parents of unmarried mothers and the putative fathers (where they can be effectively contacted) and if they are married men perhaps also to their families, may be of considerable value, it is doubtful if in itself it justifies the claim often made that moral welfare work in effect constitutes a family casework service under the auspices of the Church of England.[16] We found, moreover, that however cases were classified, and, whether illegitimacy was the presenting problem or one among other factors in the situation, all but comparatively few of the cases dealt with by the workers in the two dioceses surveyed were associated in some way with it. The number of matrimonial cases referred to moral welfare workers was small, especially compared with the numbers of such cases helped by probation officers and (where they existed) by marriage guidance councils. Moreover, the extent to which such cases were referred seemed to depend on the personal qualities of the worker and the existence or otherwise of other casework agencies rather than on the declared interest of moral welfare associations in this kind of work. This was also the case with problem families. The social workers in other fields whom we met regarded the moral welfare worker's activities in connection with both matrimonial and family problems and children and young people as marginal. This latter type of work has been declining since the war, and much of the work that remains could probably be dealt with by an enterprising children's department, especially now that local authorities have been given additional powers and duties in connection with preventive work by Section 1 of the Children and Young Persons Act, 1963.

Judging by what we saw, it seemed that moral welfare work to-day is a specialised activity dealing with a particular group of people in a particular situation rather than general casework under the auspices of a particular institution. The reasons for the present specialism are largely historical, but it was suggested to us that there are good theological reasons to justify the Church's continuing concern for unmarried parents and their children. According to this argument, the Church is committed to saying that, since man is made in the image of God, all human relationships in some sense exemplify His nature and purpose, but of none is this more true than the highest of all personal relationships, that between a man and a woman. Hence conduct that in any way degrades that relationship, whether inside or outside the civil law, condemned or condoned by a particular social group, or whatever the exonerating circumstances, cannot be lightly regarded by the Church. Not only is such conduct socially deviant or inexpedient, it is sinful. But the very seriousness with which the Church regards such behaviour lays upon its representatives a special responsibility for seeking out the sinner and offering not only social rehabilitation but newness of life.[17]

Whether or not this be accepted by church people and workers as the ultimate justification for the Church's participation in social work with unmarried parents and their families, in the world outside unmarried parenthood is increasingly regarded as a psychological and social rather than a moral problem. We have already quoted the view put forward by the Younghusband committee that the difficulties facing unmarried mothers are not essentially different from those of other 'unsupported' mothers and it is 'neither desirable nor necessary to single them out to any greater extent than circumstances make inevitable'.[18] Although in line with the current permissive attitude towards sexual and other deviations from accepted standards, this assumption that the problems encountered by unmarried mothers are similar to those faced by widows and deserted wives is, we think, by itself inadequate and needs to be balanced by other considerations such as those set out in the analysis of the situation in the Report of the Commission set up by the Bishop of Manchester to survey the moral welfare work undertaken in that diocese. This Report contends that, although it would be a great advantage if the care of unmarried mothers, along with similar work with other unsupported mothers could be provided on a general family casework basis, 'the needs of unmarried mothers should not be seen as being the same as those of unsupported mothers in all respects'. Their social needs may be similar but, it is argued, 'their emotional needs are, on the whole, very different from those of deserted or widowed mothers'. Unlike the widow or deserted wife, who is likely to be an object of sympathy, the unmarried mother may feel that she is being judged and perhaps condemned by her family and local community, and she has not known the security of married life nor the steadying experience of creating a home or bringing up children within its framework. Her own home background may have been difficult or unsatisfactory, her relationship with the child's father may have been transient and ended unhappily, while her own future and that of her child is uncertain and fraught with anxiety. It is possible, too, that apart from the condemnation of others she may herself have feelings of guilt or remorse which she needs, but finds it difficult, to express. Hence, while in many cases practical help and advice together with the appropriate social care is all that may be required, there are others who need 'the deeper kind of moral and spiritual help at the level of relationships if they are to work through their emotional insecurity and make a responsible and objective decision about the future of their babies.'[19]

All this, we consider, should be taken into account when weighing up the advantages and disadvantages likely to accrue from the more widespread assumption of statutory responsibility for the care of the unmarried mother and her child, which we regard as a probable consequence of the expansion in the scope of the statutory social services, particularly the child care services, now envisaged. If the needs of the unmarried mother are to be fully met the casework service provided for her must be of good quality, the responsibility of workers with real understanding of her needs and the time and resources to meet them adequately. Whatever the auspices under which the unmarried mother receives social help, and whether or not she is dealt with by a specialist agency, or alternatively, as one of several categories of persons in need of somewhat similar help, it is essential that casework of this kind and quality be made available for her. In view of the continuing shortage of social caseworkers it may well be difficult to find the workers able to provide this, and taking everything into account, it would be unfortunate if, in the changes and developments likely to occur in many areas, the specialised knowledge and skill accumulated by moral welfare workers as the result of their long experience in this field were allowed to be wasted. In some areas, where existing moral welfare work is recognised as being of a satisfactory standard, the local authority may continue to use the association on an agency basis for some time to come; in others the work may perhaps be incorporated into that of a local authority family welfare service, if and when such a service is brought into being. The Church must accept, however, that there are areas where the standard and mode of operation of existing moral welfare work is such that it cannot be expected to survive, and it would seem advisable for resources to be concentrated elsewhere, possibly in areas or situations of special need, or perhaps where there are opportunities for pioneer experimental work.

Whatever the future prospects for casework, local authority officials whom we interviewed showed no anxiety to substitute their own residential accommodation for unmarried mothers for that now provided by the Church,[20] and several of them gave it as their opinion that the Church should not only maintain mother and baby homes, but extend their care to other groups, such as difficult adolescent girls. This would appear to be contrary to existing trends in moral welfare work, for although residential work still absorbs a large share of the total resources of both money and woman power,[21] the number of homes provided by Church of England moral welfare associations decreased by 37 between 1950 and 1960. In 1961 there were still 130 homes listed in the Church

TABLE XV

Numbers and Types of Moral Welfare Homes, 1950 and 1960

Group I — Homes listed in 1950 directory, not listed 1960.
Group II — Homes listed in 1960 directory and not open in 1950.
Group IV — Homes unchanged 1950–1960.

	Group I	Group II		Group IV
Shelters	26	3		42
Mother and Baby Homes	6	1		33
Mother and Baby Hostels	3	2		1
Maternity Homes	2	—		11
Training Homes	6	1		6
Medical Home	1	—		—
Children's Home	—	—		9
TOTAL	44	7	Total loss=37	

The Issues Involved

TABLE XV—*cont.*

Group III — Homes which have changed their function between 1950 and 1960.

Type of Home in 1950	Shelter	Mother and Baby Homes	Mother and Baby Hostel	A/n Hostel	Maternity	Training	Children's	Total
Shelters	—	1	—	2	—	1	2	6
Mother and Baby Hostel	—	1	—	—	—	—	—	1
Maternity Homes	—	2	1	1	—	—	—	4
Training Home	—	—	—	—	—	—	1	1
Children's Homes	1	—	—	—	1	1	—	3

Total gain or loss:

	Loss	Gain	Total loss or gain
Shelters	6	1	−5
Maternity Homes	4	1	−3
Mother & Baby Hostel	1	1	0
Children's Homes	3	3	0
Training Homes	1	2	+1
A/n Hostels	0	3	+3
Mother & Baby Homes	0	4	+4

of England Directory of Moral Welfare Work, 110 of these being concerned directly with the care of the unmarried mother. During the same ten year period there were considerable changes in the character of the work undertaken; the number of shelters, which were often small and uneconomical to run, declined, but there was a slight increase in the number of mother and baby homes and ante-natal hostels. (Table XV). These changes may be indicative both of the swing away from residential care found in all forms of social work, and of the tendency for moral welfare work to become increasingly a specialist service catering for unmarried mothers and their children.

Reviewing the position it seemed to us that a re-examination of the purpose and aims of moral welfare homes was urgently needed. The local authority officials who pressed for an extension of residential accommodation appeared to be motivated, to some extent, at least, by their own difficultes in obtaining staff and the belief that the Church, and only the Church, could attract workers of the right calibre with sufficient sense of vocation to devote themselves to this exacting work. Our own investigations lent no colour to this belief. Rather did we consider that the maintenance of the standards of existing church work was sometimes threatened by staffing shortages and difficulties, which in church as well as local authority setting may well increase with the increased marriage rate, for residential work is more difficult to combine with married life than outdoor work, unless the husband is also prepared to participate in it.

During the course of the survey we were frequently both moved and impressed by the devotion of the residential workers. Working as they did for long hours under difficult conditions, often with inadequate assistance and equipment, the demands made on their energy, skill and devotion were heavy, sometimes we felt too heavy, so that in the long run the quality of the work was bound to suffer. In particular, there was insufficient time for staff to give residents all the individual care, counselling and help which they might need. Under these circumstances church homes may be able to offer little more than shelter, and whatever the justification for this in the past, when the only alternative was the workhouse, it is hardly sufficient for the Church's continued retention of such work to-day. It is the duty of the local authority, not of the Church, to provide Part III accommodation,[22] and if some church homes are providing little more than this it can be argued that their continuing existence is enabling local authorities to avoid shouldering responsibilities which are rightly their's. Serious consideration should, we think, be given to the possibility of concentrating the work in such a way as to ensure that work sponsored by the Church reaches, and is known to reach, a high standard in such matters as the ratio of staff to residents, and proper equipment, while at the same time exemplifying Christian values in a special way. This may seem unrealistic in view of the present pressure on places, but if admissions were scrutinised, greater flexibility with regard to length of stay was introduced and the possibilities of other methods of care explored, it might not seem so ambitious.

There are other ways, too, in which the existing system could be rationalised. One advantage which the Church possesses compared with many local authorities is the diocesan pattern of organisation, for the diocese is usually large enough to be an economic unit; at present the benefits which could accrue from this are largely nullified by the independent administration of most homes by their own local committees. At one conference we attended the suggestion was made that in each diocese a specialist committee should be appointed to be responsible for all the indoor work. This could be responsible for planning and might introduce such economies as bulk buying. Where considered desirable, small house committees might be retained to maintain local interest and keep in touch with the day to day work, but questions of long term policy should be in the hands of the diocesan committee, a matter which is part of the larger question of diocesan reorganisation now being considered in many parts of the country.

Whatever the difficulties and inadequacies of residential work it makes its own welcome and useful contribution to the social services as at present organised. It is doubtful if the same can be said of the contribution made by diocesan and local moral welfare organisations to education in matters relating to sex, marriage and the family. Although they appear to regard this as a most important area of work, and nearly all associations, as well as the diocesan bodies, include the development of educational work among the aims and objects stated in their constitutions, we found in practice that, with one or two notable exceptions, little effective work was being undertaken. Where such work was being carried out it was almost always the result of the activities of individuals with a particular interest in and talent for it. By and large educational work did not seem to be built into the structure of moral welfare work as at present organised; workers were generally reluctant to undertake it, and committees either did not feel any real responsibility for promoting it or had been largely unsuccessful in their efforts to do so.

The situation in the two dioceses surveyed seems to be repeated elsewhere. From the diocesan organisers' replies to our questionnaire, we found that only nine out of the 41 dioceses covered had a diocesan moral welfare education committee and three of these were inactive either temporarily or permanently. In five dioceses an education committee of this kind was either in the process of formation or envisaged, while six other dioceses had some equivalent body which sometimes acted in conjunction with a diocesan youth or adult education committee. Where such a committee existed it might be very active, as appeared to be the case in Southwark, but this was not necessarily so. Some organising secretaries were interested in the expansion of educational work, but few of them could spare the time to do much about it.

During the inter-war period pioneer work in what was then known as 'sex education' was carried out by moral welfare workers who saw it as an essential complement to the rehabilitation of young people whose difficulties might well be due, in part at least, to faulty and inadequate knowledge. To-day much, although not all, of the diffidence which at that time prevented the sane and open discussion of these topics has disappeared; sex education is undertaken in many schools, and other organisations, for example, marriage guidance councils, are developing educational work. In view of these developments and of the present and potential shortage of caseworkers, it may be questioned whether there is a valid reason for the continued utilisation of the resources of diocesan and local moral welfare organisations for this work. Having pioneered in this difficult field should not they hand over the responsibility to some other organisation or organisations whether inside or outside the Church?

The question is rendered more urgent by the fact that, particularly since the emphasis is now on 'educating the educators' rather than on direct participation, it is important that whatever contribution is made by the Church should be of high quality. Neither reluctant and often overburdened caseworkers, nor organising secretaries, already distracted by the range and variety of their commitments, are in a position to undertake educational work of the requisite quality.[28] This means that, if moral welfare associations are to continue to engage in educational work, such work must be properly planned and provided for, possibly by the appointment of a specialist worker or workers on a full or part-time basis under the auspices of a specially chosen and knowledgeable committee. Any development of this kind would involve heavy financial commitments, but there is another and in our view stronger reason, why it may be inappropriate for the diocesan or local moral welfare association to undertake full responsibility for it. Moral welfare work is essentially 'problem centred', concerned with the pathology of the family rather than its normal functioning, but 'education in personal relationships', by whomsoever undertaken, should surely be positive in outlook and regarded as part of the normal spiritual, moral and social education of the whole man. The Church of England Board of Education, like the Board for Social Responsibility, a constituent Board of the Church Assembly, has given, and is giving, some attention to this aspect of education, and in dioceses where there is an active Diocesan Board of Education with a functioning Youth Committee, the work might become a joint responsibility or even taken over altogether; elsewhere other patterns of co-operation might be found to be more appropriate. What is not appropriate is for moral welfare associations to pay lip-service to the idea of 'educational' work while not seriously engaging in it.

In this chapter we have been summarising and discussing the various aspects of moral welfare work covered by our study. The net result of our investigations has been to show that over the years the range and variety of the work has narrowed, and, although the number of cases dealt with may have increased, its relative importance has declined in comparison with the rapid development of other social services, notably the local authority child care service and the voluntary marriage guidance councils. While these services have noticeably expanded, moral welfare has, by comparison, remained relatively static and has, to some extent, been left on one side in current developments in social work. In the eyes of the beholder it often has a slightly old-fashioned look, and one probation officer compared it with the probation work of fifteen years ago. It is, nevertheless, a form of social work with a strong and, in many respects, a fine tradition which has a stabilising as well as a conservative effect. In the rapidly changing conditions of the latter half of the twentieth century, however, tradition by itself is not enough, and, if the work is to be more than a historical survival, it must show itself capable of adaptation and growth to meet new needs and new situations.

16

POLICY ISSUES

A L T H O U G H the scope of this study has been limited in some respects, its basis being a detailed investigation of Anglican moral welfare work in two selected dioceses, it will, we hope, have become apparent to the reader, as it did to us at an early stage in the investigation, that underlying the collection and interpretation of the factual material were basic questions of principle and policy. Fundamental to all the issues discussed in the study is the question as to what is the social function of the Church in a 'welfare' state, and, arising from this, whether, under modern conditions, there are valid reasons for its continued corporate engagement in social work. Because this question is at the heart of the study we raised it in the Introduction; having completed the investigation we must now discuss it further.

Throughout the history of the Christian Church it has been accepted that the task of caring for the bodies and souls of men is inseparable from that of preaching the gospel, and, as the Bishop of Middleton has argued,

fundamentally the justification of the Church's engagement in social work springs from the compassion of our Lord, exemplified in deed and word. The mission of Christ's body the Church can never be reduced to a spoken word, even a word of saving revelation. . . . The New Testament is explicit that the *diakonia* is inseparable from *kerugma* and all the centuries of Church history give evidence of the support of the Christian faith to this fact.[1]

The first disciples were commissioned by Christ himself not only to preach saying, 'The Kingdom of God is at hand', but also, in proof thereof, to 'heal the sick, cleanse the lepers, raise the dead, cast out devils'. This command does not apply only to works of mercy undertaken by individuals, but to the whole Church which, if it is to be true to its Lord, must be a caring as well as a witnessing community, and caring is, indeed, part of the witness. The Church may allocate different tasks to different members, and skilled social care, like the skilled exposition of the Gospel, will, of necessity, be the function of the trained minority, but it is no less an institutional activity because of this. Moreover, as the Body of Christ, the Church is called upon to minister not only to its own members, but to the world outside, not only to those 'deserving' of help, but to outcasts and sinners, those rejected by society as well as those secure in the sympathy of their fellow men. Throughout the Church's history both individuals acting on their own initiative in obedience to what they believed to be their Lord's command, and organised bodies of Christians, have carried on this ministry of compassion, of which the 'preventive and rescue' work described at the beginning of this book is but one small example.

It would seem, then, that the Church's responsibility for social care 'stems from her very title deeds',[2] and cannot lightly be surrendered. The mode in which this responsibility is discharged will, however, always be dependent to some extent on the social setting in which the Church is currently operating. In modern Britain a new situation has been created as the result of the coming into being of the 'welfare state', in the context of which it is now generally accepted that the material and social well-being of the individual citizen is the responsibility of the political community and, in the absence of specific reasons to the contrary, the right and proper way to discharge this responsibility is directly through the organs of central and local government. In this situation, unless a voluntary social service can show that it is discharging a function or meeting a need which cannot be discharged equally efficiently, or met equally effectively by a statutory body, its present position is vulnerable, its future in jeopardy.

From this point of view the Church is one voluntary body among others, and the present position seems to be that for various reasons, mainly historical, one of the principal contributions of the Church of England to social welfare is the provision of a service which operates mainly, though not wholly, for the benefit of unmarried mothers and their children.[3] It is a useful piece of work, and fills a gap in the social services which hitherto the local authorities have not shown themselves eager to occupy, even when given the opportunity of doing so.[4] But, as already pointed out, the scope of the local authority health and child care services is being enlarged and their emphasis is changing, and, slow as it may be in coming, the assumption by the statutory authorities of full responsibility for the social as well as the health care of unmarried mothers and their children is probably inevitable in the long run. The extent to which the authorities will continue to use voluntary bodies as their agents may vary in this as in other fields of work, but the overall long-term effect of current developments in social policy is likely to lessen both the need and the opportunity for the Church to make its own corporate contribution in this particular form of social service. If this prediction proves correct, and the Church accepts the situation, it will from the community's point of view have fulfilled what is widely recognised as one of the classic roles of the voluntary organisation, that of drawing attention to a hitherto unrecognised need, filling a gap in existing services as long as this exists, but of being ready to withdraw as soon as adequate statutory provision is available.

From the point of view of the statutory authority, and perhaps even of the community at large, this may be a satisfactory conclusion, but from the Church's own standpoint it cannot be regarded as the end of the matter. It raises the two related questions; whether even if such abnegation may be appropriate in certain circumstances it is necessarily always the right course of action, and whether, even in a society in which the secular social services are both diverse and extensive, there is scope and opportunity for the Church to discover and develop new ways of expressing its perennial concern to serve men and women in their need.

Even if it be accepted that in a welfare state the main function of a voluntary organisation is to prepare the way for and make up deficiencies in the statutory social services, it can be argued that, since new needs are continuously arising and hitherto unnoticed ones being recognised there will always be gaps waiting to be filled. It can be postulated, further, that there are always likely to be some situations in which voluntary organisations with their greater flexibility and freedom to undertake small-scale and sometimes unpopular pieces of work, are to be preferred to the statutory services. It does not necessarily follow, however, that it will be appropriate for such work to be undertaken directly by the

Church. There are certain forms of voluntary social service for which known religious impartiality and independence would seem to be prerequisite, for example, citizens' advice bureaux, councils of social service, and community associations on a neighbourhood basis, and throughout the country groups of people of varying religious and political affiliations and of none, have come together and by their goodwill and enterprise have established secular organisations undertaking a wide range of such useful services. There are many opportunities for voluntary social service in connection with such ventures, and where this work is undertaken by a Christian layman, as an expression of concern for his fellow men, then, like the work of a professional social worker carrying out what he regards as his Christian vocation in a statutory setting, it is part of the total ministry of the Church and should be recognised as such. It should also be accepted that there may well be circumstances in which the local Church will give better service to the community by supporting some form of co-ordinated effort, such as the work of an old people's welfare council, than by initiating its own independent piece of social work. This is particularly important at the present time when the need for greater co-ordination in social service and the dangers of overlapping and unnecessary multiplication of agencies are constantly being stressed.

Another factor to be taken into account when considering how far, if at all, the Church should seek to retain, create or develop its own social services in present day Britain is that of its other commitments, both evangelistic and social, at home and overseas. An editorial in *Moral Welfare,* commenting on possible future developments in Church social work in connection with the proposals made in the Younghusband Report, stressed this point. 'It would be idealistic,' this Editorial stated, 'in view of the shortage of workers and conflicting claims on available money, to envisage duplicate services allowing a client a choice between voluntary and statutory services in all, or even many, departments; if we had workers to spare for a luxury service like that, we ought to share them liberally with the underdeveloped countries abroad.'[5] Certain, although by no means all, of the clergy whom we interviewed argued along somewhat similar lines, pointing out that since the resources of the Church in money and personnel are limited, it cannot hope to provide an adequate service of its own, and some

263

incumbents even went further, saying that in any case it would be wrong to attempt to duplicate existing statutory services.

The conclusions reached from the discussion so far appear to be almost wholly negative, but these conclusions, although valid within limits, are based on incomplete premises for they leave out of account a very important consideration which must now be examined. It may be claimed that, whatever may be the case with secular voluntary organisations, those sponsored by the Church are not simply social work institutions, but discharge pastoral or related functions which cannot be disregarded, and which might well be lost should the work be passed on to a secular body and that this alters the whole situation. The Younghusband Committee, when considering the role of voluntary organisations in relation to the developing responsibilities of health and welfare departments, admitted that such a claim for special consideration might be allowed,[6] but in order to substantiate this claim and deserve this recognition, the organisation concerned should be able to show that these pastoral and religious functions really form an integral part of the work undertaken. Where this is not so, there is a strong case for accepting the fact that, having prepared the way, the Church should pass over the responsibility to the public authority with its larger resources in money and personnel.

We have already considered in some detail the question as to whether, and if so how far, moral welfare work carried out in the name of the Church can be distinguished from related social work undertaken under other auspices whether in the type of person helped or the kind of help given. We reached the conclusion that the reasons for the present specialism are largely historical, and that the special features of the situation which in the last century led the Church to undertake work with a particular category of social outcasts, as 'fallen women' then were, have largely disappeared, while the compassion for them which moved the pioneers in this field has become more generally diffused throughout society and is being expressed by means of widespread statutory social care. It may well be, however, that the Church will always find opportunities for giving special care to those individuals and groups whose conduct comes within the mistily defined sphere of what is 'unlawful' but not necessarily criminal,[7] for example, prostitutes, homosexuals, alcoholics and potential suicides, to which list some would undoubtedly add unmarried parents and their children. In the social care of these categories of people, and others like them, moral and spiritual issues lie very close to the surface, and spiritual as well as psychological help may be needed to effect a cure. There may also be certain situations in which the Church believes that it has a specific witness to give, or standards to uphold, and its care is, therefore, different in kind from that given by any other body, its counselling based on different premises. We have already given one example of this in the adoption work carried out in one of the dioceses surveyed. During the course of the fieldwork we also encountered a few church people who would have liked to have reversed the present policy of co-operation with the National Marriage Guidance Council, and for the Church of England to establish its own marriage guidance service firmly rooted in Anglican teaching as to the nature of Christian marriage. There are bound to be differences of opinion between church people as to when and under what circumstances it is desirable for the Church to create its own organisations for social service whether or not there are other voluntary organisations or statutory agencies operating in the same field. In general, it would seem right that, on the one hand, this line should only be followed when the religious organisation concerned knows clearly what its distinctive contribution is and why it must make it, and, on the other, that in its role of servant the Church should not demarcate the boundaries of its work too clearly, but should be ready to serve where and in what capacity its help is most needed.

Whether or not the Church continues to provide social services of its own, Christian participation in those undertaken under other auspices need not and should not be regarded as a second best. In the words of Bishop Barry, 'The Church has to find its way into a new partnership with the statutory services, and that is not merely accepting the inevitable, it is embracing an open opportunity.'[8] Not a few of the clergymen with whom the matter was discussed thought that one of the most important contributions the Church had to make to the present social situation was that of encouraging its members to enter the statutory social services. In part this was regarded as a matter of expediency, but it was also seen as providing positive opportunities which both individual Christians and the Church as a corporate body should welcome and follow up. These incumbents urged that not merely is there a place for Christian social workers in the statutory services, it is their duty to be found there, bringing to the work their Christian insights and convictions. They stressed that those in positions of authority in the Church should foster such vocations, 'training its members to put themselves at the disposal of the community in different capacities', as one clergyman phrased it. This raises the question of training, for from these premises it could be argued that the Church's main responsibility may lie not so much in providing specific services as in training for service of all kinds.

An analogy frequently drawn in these discussions was with education, and it was suggested that just as the Church provides training colleges for those who will teach in state schools as well as for those who intend to teach in Church schools, so it should provide comparable facilities for social workers. Candidates accepted for moral welfare training usually enter with the intention of working for the Church, but, as we showed in Chapter 6, they may change their minds and eventually take up work in a statutory service or with a secular voluntary agency. This is surely something to be welcomed, perhaps even on occasion encouraged, and it may also be hoped that in future it may become possible for students entering social work with a real sense of Christian vocation (and others too if they so wish) to be accepted at an institution sponsored by the Church for part of, or additionally to, their training, regardless of the field in which they intend to work. The student in training for social work encounters, sometimes in an acutely personal way, vexed moral and spiritual problems, and fuller provision by the Church for the better theological education and spiritual nourishment of the men and women called to this exacting form of Christian service would meet a real need.

The Church's responsibility does not end with the students' departure from the training institution, nor even with the provision of refresher courses and conferences, valuable as these are. It includes, or should include, concern for and the pastoral care of Christians at work in the field of social service,[9] and behind this, if it is to be adequate, must be a fuller understanding and clearer exposition of the relationship between Christian doctrine and the problems of men and women in present day society. In the last chapter we suggested that many social workers are seeking a deeper philosophical understanding of the moral issues they are

266

continually encountering in their day to day contacts with their clients. In these encounters regard for the value of the individual may seem at odds with the worthlessness of his acts; the claims of human freedom have to be balanced against the rightful demands of society; belief in personal responsibility matched against the overwhelming odds stacked against a person with inadequate physical and mental endowments and subjected to the pressures of a harmful environment. The impact of these and similar conundrums may lead social workers, although being essentially pragmatic they do not often admit it, into deep philosophical waters.[10] Whatever attitude they adopt they cannot avoid giving an answer to these deeper questions, for even non-interference and a 'non-judgmental attitude' imply a decision *not* to interfere and *not* to be judgmental.

This is an area in which the Christian Church should have much to contribute, but only if it deepens and clarifies those aspects of theological thinking which are most closely related to the problems of personal and social relationship characteristic of the mid-twentieth century, together with the issues of social policy which confront the builders and administrators of the welfare state. As Bishop Barry has reminded us, while it may be accepted that Church and welfare state work together, the concept of 'welfare' itself presents Christians with a new challenge. 'In particular the Church must keep on asking the prior question "What is welfare?" It must always be keeping alive the protest that man is the citizen of another city, and the heir of an eternal destiny and that, therefore, no earthly policy can claim his total allegiance or satisfy the needs of his whole being. Otherwise it will be failing in its own witness and no less in its essential contribution to the health and welfare of the community.'[11]

The task is primarily an intellectual one, that of moral theologians working in conjunction with Christian sociologists. There are indications that here and there beginnings have been made with it; but much still remains to be done.[12] Primarily intellectual as the task may be, however, it is not wholly so, for the relevance of Christian teaching to social situations is not something that can simply be thought out, it must be experienced and lived. One of the advantages of the Church's corporate involvement in social work is that it provides opportunities for such experience, and enables Church leaders and workers to engage seriously in discussions with social workers and administrators about problems with which both parties are concerned and policies they are trying to operate. Hence it can be argued that it would be appropriate for the Church to maintain some corporate social work undertakings of its own, not simply because this would be true to its own beliefs, but also in order to hold a 'bridgehead' in the world of social work, without which its witness for social righteousness would be less convincing and easy to sustain. Moreover, if such corporate undertakings were well done they could become a demonstration that the Church is in very truth a caring community, that the knowledge and skills of modern social work can be the vehicles of such caring, and that adherence to Christian teaching and standards is not necessarily opposed to advances in social science but can welcome and utilise them.

It is obvious that to be effective both as a demonstration and as an end in itself social work undertaken corporately by the Church would have to be of a really high standard, and this brings the discussion back to the resources in money and personnel which can be regarded as being available for current and future developments in church social work. Financially, as we have shown in Chapter 10, present day moral welfare work is very heavily dependent on grants from statutory services and it is unlikely that any development of the work into other fields would be eligible for such substantial assistance, at least initially. In the long run, however, the more serious problem is probably the shortage of trained women (and indeed men) coming forward for church social work. In Chapter 6 we drew attention to the comparatively small number of young women prepared to train as moral welfare workers. It is possible that if the scope of the work were widened or altered more would be attracted to it, but earlier marriages and the intense competition from allied professions such as child care make it unlikely that numbers will increase to any large extent. The average age of workers already in the field is high and their spread over the country so thin as to be detrimental to the quality of the work. In this situation, the contribution made by the training of older women on the London Course has been invaluable, and plans have already been made to transfer it to J. B. House and lengthen it to a year to make its scope and standards more akin to those of courses provided for older persons in other kinds of social work. Another possibility is that of providing some form of local or regional training for women unable to leave home for long at a time.

Women recruited and trained in this latter way might be valuable assistants, either paid or voluntary, to the more fully trained workers and this might be a way of seeing that trained workers' time and skill are used to the best advantage. Other practical measures which could be undertaken for the same end are the provision of more adequate office equipment, transport and secretarial help. It is false economy and misuse of both skill and money to employ a qualified worker and allow her to waste her time waiting for buses and doing routine jobs which could well be undertaken by a clerk or voluntary worker.

Measures of this kind are, however, in a sense only palliative, and quite apart from the developments in social policy already discussed, the present situation and future prognosis with regard to recruitment and training mean that sooner or later the choice will have to be made between attempting to continue to maintain minimal national coverage as at present[13] and concentrating the Church's resources, particularly those of its trained social workers, on providing an intensive high quality service with a specifically Christian emphasis in areas and situations where the need is greatest.

But if the Church is unable to draw on large numbers of trained specialist workers, it has in the parish congregations potential reserves of good will such as few other bodies can so easily muster. Except in isolated instances not much appears to have been done to make the most of these resources, but given the appropriate lead the local church may well act as a 'caring community', as appears to have been to some extent the case at Michelhurst during the period of the 'experiment'.[14] At the present time, the Church's growing understanding of the nature and importance of the ministry of the laity is matched in the field of social work by an increasing emphasis on the need for 'community' as distinct from 'institutional' care for the aged, the physically and mentally handicapped, children whose homes are broken or inadequate and other unfortunates, misfits and deviants. This demands understanding help from the local community as well as from professional social workers, and it is perhaps significant that, as we have already pointed out[15] the Home Office Circular drawing the attention of local authorities to the extension of their powers to promote the welfare of children contained in Section 1 of the Children and Young Persons Act, 1963,[16] should include a paragraph (15) dealing specifically with 'Liaison with Churches'. This paragraph suggests that the passing of the Act 'should widen the scope for fruitful co-operation with the clergy and congregations of the various denominations in work contributing to the welfare of children', and it is, perhaps, not too much to hope that, in this and in other spheres of service, there may be scope for new developments, some similar to, others perhaps very different from, those already taking place.

In the last resort the part played by the Church in social work will be conditioned by its own strength and weakness, not least at the diocesan and parish levels, and this is likely to be a relevant factor in determining the character of the work to be undertaken in any particular locality, especially if projects similar to that at Michelhurst are considered. This combination of parish and social work on a neighbourhood basis might prove to be particularly valuable not only in other new housing areas but also in the difficult inner areas of the large cities.

At this point, however, it is necessary to draw attention to one difficulty which was raised whenever we discussed with moral welfare workers the possibility of any developments which would combine parish and social work. This is the present low status of parish workers, who, whatever their qualifications and length of experience, remain technically junior to the youngest curate, and who are without security of tenure since it is open to the parish priest to dispense with their services at any time, should he so desire. This is a position likely to be unacceptable to most women with social work training and their own professional standing and skills. The moral welfare worker, whatever her financial disadvantages compared with her colleagues in the statutory services, (although not in comparison with other women church workers), is employed by an independent committee and has a recognised professional status which enables her to meet both clergy and local officials on an equal footing, and workers would react sharply against any proposal which, by identifying them with parish workers, would jeopardise this independent status. The experience of the worker at Michelhurst showed how essential it is to the success of work of this kind that the clergy understand and respect both the role and status of the social worker which must be preserved not only for the sake of the worker, but for the sake of the work.

Another strength which moral welfare work at present enjoys and which should be preserved if this is at all possible, is its tradition of interdenominational co-operation. We have shown that, although not universal, and in some respects imperfect, this is widespread, and it would be a pity if it were lost, either through the closer combination of parish and social work, or as the result of diocesan reorganisation which, in the course of reducing the status and autonomy of the local committee, emphasised the distinctively Anglican character of the work. We do not believe that this is inevitable, but it is something which should be carefully watched in any reorganisation which is carried out. It is clear from the difficulties encountered by the Birmingham Social Responsibility Project that full Christian co-operation in social service is far from easy, but when attained it would seem to be abundantly worthwhile.

In a rapidly changing situation the future pattern of social work cannot be predicted in detail, and any suggestions we have had to make as to the responses which could or should be made by the Church to possible future needs and conditions can only be very tentative, especially if the limitations of our study are borne in mind. At a time when the scope of the statutory social services, already wide, is still expanding, the importance of the fullest possible Christian participation in such services cannot be overstressed, and we have already emphasised that we think that this should be regarded as much part of the lay ministry of the Church as employment in Church sponsored organisations. This does not necessarily involve the Church's disengagement from all corporate effort, for despite the expansion of the statutory services there is still valuable work to be done both in fields where the Church is already at work, and in new directions also. Thus the need for residential provision for certain categories of people requiring special care is almost certain to continue for many years to come, even if the Church's virtual monopoly of the residential care of unmarried mothers and their children is brought to an end. At the time of writing, at least one diocese (Manchester) appears to be experimenting with the creation of a general family casework service under Church auspices, a service which is intended ultimately to embrace the existing work for unmarried mothers and their children,[17] and although this project raises certain questions such as that of duplication of effort, it is an interesting one, and may prove to be a valid contribution for the Church to make in certain areas. In others there may be possibilities of developing neighbourhood work based either on a single parish or perhaps more profitably on a group of parishes. Projects of this kind could link casework with group and community work and utilise the goodwill and enterprise of church members as well as the knowledge and skill of trained workers. There would be difficulties to encounter and problems to solve, as was shown at Michelhurst, but also opportunities for constructive and interesting work.

These are possible lines of development; there may well be others. Whatever work is undertaken by the Church, however, it should be of sufficiently high quality to stand comparison with similar work undertaken by secular organisations, and also related to the particular witness the Church has to give on personal and social issues. This witness itself needs constant re-examination—one of the tasks which the Church Assembly Board for Social Reponsibility has inherited from its predecessor, the Church of England Moral Welfare Council. The Church to-day is called upon to think out and to communicate by both words and action its contribution to a post-Christian society where not only is there great perplexity over a wide range of moral issues, but standards of enlightenment and belief in the value and liberty of the individual human being cannot be guaranteed. It cannot contract out of these obligations, if for no other reason than that silence itself will be interpreted as policy and it will be presumed that the Church has nothing to say. Nor is it sufficient to concentrate on remedial activities however valuable these may be in themselves. To be both faithful and effective its witness must be intellectual as well as practical, by word as well as by deed, creative as well as compassionate.

NOTES

INTRODUCTION

[1]As early as 1952 Miss C. S. Blackburn, then Warden of the Josephine Butler Memorial House had pleaded for 'a dispassionate review of the existing pattern of our work . . . and a clear re-thinking of the essential nature of the work itself and of conditions today in which this work must be done'. 'Strategy and Priorities in Moral Welfare Work.' *Moral Welfare: a Quarterly Review*, October 1952, p. 4.

[2]Proposals along these lines were made by D. V. Donnison and Mary Stewart on behalf of the Fabian Society (*The Child and the Social Services*, Fabian Research Pamphlet, 1958), and by the Council for Children's Welfare and the Fisher Group who published a very similar pamphlet (*Families With Problems*) also in 1958.

[3]For example, a health visitor whom we interviewed used the term a 'moral welfare case' to designate a case in which there was some doubt as to the legitimacy of the child, irrespective of whether or not she had any intention of referring it to a church 'moral welfare worker'. In another context, a clergyman told us, 'If there had been moral welfare work run by the corporation we should not have thought of appointing our own worker.'

[4]Two alternatives suggested in 1949 were 'Church of England Council for Voluntary Action', and 'Church of England Council for Social and Family Welfare Work'. Address given at the High Leigh Conference, 21st March, 1949, by Miss E. M. Steel, then General Secretary, Church of England Moral Welfare Council.

1. RESCUE AND REFORM

[1]W. E. H. Lecky (*History of European Morals*, Longmans, Green & Co., 1869), states, 'We find no trace for several centuries of Christian foundling hospitals. This form of charity grew up gradually in the early part of the middle ages. It is said that one existed at Treves in the sixth century and at Angers in the seventh century and it is certain that one existed in Milan in the eighth century.' Reprint 1913, Vol. II, p. 32.

[2]Quoted by Mary Hopkirk *Nobody Wanted Sam*, John Murray, 1949, p. 12.

273

Notes to Chapter 1, pages 9—15

[3]Ivy Pinchbeck, 'Social Attitudes towards Illegitimacy', *British Journal of Sociology*, Vol. 5, 1954, p. 8.

[4]Jean S. Heywood, *Children in Care*, Routledge and Kegan Paul, 1959, p. 8.

[5]Ibid., pp. 3-4. For example there is presumptive evidence for the presence of children and poor scholars in the records of at least one hospital in the register of Edmund Lacey, Bishop of Exeter (from the will of William Fylham, D.D., Chancellor of Exeter Cathedral, made October 1435 at Exeter).

[6]Examples of the length to which this practice could go are given in Dorothy Marshall, *The English Poor in the 18th century*, Routledge, 1926, pp. 210 ff.

[7]18 Eliz. C.3. S2. Quoted in the Report of the Commissioners for inquiring into the Administration and Practical Operation of the Poor Law, 1834. Reprint H.M.S.O., 1905, p. 165.

[8]Cf. Report of the Poor Law Commissioners, p. 165.

[9]For examples of the working of these provisions and the abuses to which they gave rise see Marshall, op. cit., pp. 216 ff. and Report of the Poor Law Commissioners, pp. 166 ff.

[10]Report of the Poor Law Commissioners, p. 168.

[11]Marshall, op. cit., p. 95.

[12]Ibid.

[13]Quoted in R. H. Nicholls and F. A. Wray, *The History of the Foundling Hospital*, O.U.P., 1935, pp. 13-14.

[14]Ibid., pp. 61-62.

[15]J. Massie, *Observations Relating to the Foundling Hospital Shewing the Ill Consequences of giving Public Support thereto*, London, 1758.

[16]John Brownlow, *Memoranda or Chronicles of the Foundling Hospital*. Quoted in Nicholls and Wray, op. cit., p. 14.

[17]A footnote to an anniversary sermon preached at the Magdalen Hospital in 1759 reads, 'out of an hundred girls now in the Magdalen House above a seventh part have not yet seen their fifteenth year, several are under fourteen and one-third of the whole have been betrayed before that age'. Quoted in H. F. B. Compston, *The Magdalen Hospital*, S.P.C.K., 1917, p. 171.

[18]John H. Hutchins, *Jonas Hanway, 1712-1786*, S.P.C.K., 1940, p. 109.

[19]Extract from the Constitution quoted in Compston, op. cit., p. 42. In order to prevent embarrassment to any of the inmates, ladies visiting the hospital were required to give their names beforehand, so that any penitent could withdraw should she so wish and so avoid meeting any of her former acquaintances.

[20]The extracts are taken from a description of the charity in Meyler's *Original Bath Guide*, 1831, pp. 90-92. Compare this account with the objectives of the Durham County Penitentiary, opened in 1857, which, according to a conveyance of property dated September that year, were to provide 'An Asylum for females who, having deviated from the paths of

virtue, are desirous of being restored by religious instruction and the formation of moral habits to a reputable condition in Society'.

[21]Evidence of Mr. Nolan. Quoted in the Report, p. 166.

[22]Report, p. 177.

[23]Ibid., p. 346.

[24]Ibid., p. 347.

[25]Thomas Mackay, *A History of the English Poor Law*, King, Re-issue 1904, Vol. III, p. 316.

[26]Cf. the defensive tone of Anthony Trollope's preface to his novel, *The Vicar of Bullhampton* (1870). The hero of this novel seeks to befriend a young woman of his parish who had been 'betrayed' and deserted by her lover and had taken up an immoral life.

[27]Edward, C. Trenholme, *Rescue Work*, S.P.C.K., 1927.

[28]Kathleen Heasman *Evangelicals in Action*, Bles, 1962, pp. 150-151. This book gives an interesting and comprehensive account of the many and wide-ranging activities undertaken by evangelicals whether Anglican or non-conformist in their ecclesiastical allegiance.

[29]Cf. the disillusioned comment of Rev. Arthur Brinckman in his Preface to *Notes on Rescue Work* (G. J. Palmer, 1885). 'Lately there has been much interest awakened in the various efforts made for the promotion and preservation of purity, and for the rescue and reformation of those who have fallen. The consequence is that numbers of persons have suddenly begun this grave and difficult work, only to make a mess of it and then drop it.'

[30]Annual Report C.P.A., 1876-77.

[31]C.P.A. Annual Report, 1858-59.

[32]Report of Reformatory and Refuge Union, 1858.

[33]Ibid., 1859.

[34]Ibid., 1859.

[35]Ibid., 1866.

[36]Ibid., 1873.

[37]S. M. Ferguson and M. Fitzgerald, *Studies in the Social Services*, H.M.S.O., 1954, p. 80.

[38]Heasman, op. cit., pp. 156-157.

[39]Annual Report, Female Mission to the Fallen, 1867

[40]Henry Mayhew, *London Labour and the London Poor*, edited by Peter Quennell, Kimber, 1950, Vol. 4, p. 32. Lecky, op. cit. p. 284 quotes a pamphlet *On The Repression of Prostitution*, published by a certain Dr. Vintras which stated that in 1864, 49,370 prostitutes were known to the police in England and Wales, but adds 'this is certainly much below the entire number'.

[41]Ellice Hopkins, *Power of Womanhood*, Wells, Gardner, Darton & Co., 1899.

[42]Quoted in C. Terrot, *The Maiden Tribute—a Study of the White Slave Traffic in the Nineteenth Century*, Muller, 1959, p. 96.

[43]This comes out in the Report of the Church Penitentiary Association for 1862-3. 'Some withhold support because the Association exerts but little influence upon the stream of vice and wickedness flowing through the country, because the effects of the removal of some 500 a year out of the

numbers who throng the streets of the Metropolis alone can scarcely be appreciated. But it is to be remembered that the Mission of the Association is to rescue individual souls; and if, out of the number who annually leave the Penitentiaries, between 200 and 300 are permanently rescued, who can dare to say that little is done?'

⁴⁴The story of this campaign has been re-told by E. Moberly Bell in her recent biography of Josephine Butler: *Josephine Butler, Flame of Fire*, Constable & Co. Ltd., 1962.

⁴⁵In order to prove his point, Stead, with the assistance of Rebecca Jarrett, an ex-prostitute and brothel keeper, converted by the Salvation Army and later helped by Josephine Butler, bought a child from her mother, placed her in a brothel (under careful protection) for a night and transferred her to Paris, where she was cared for by the Salvation Army. Both Stead and Rebecca Jarrett were subsequently tried and imprisoned for abduction.

⁴⁶A generation later this belief was savagely attacked by Mrs. Christabel Pankhurst in her book, *The Great Scourge and How to End It*, David Nutt, 1913. The 'Great Scourge' was venereal disease which Mrs. Pankhurst asserted was contracted by 75%-80% of the men in the population. She believed it could only be ended by 'Votes For Women', which would give to women more self reliance and a stronger economic position, and 'chastity (by which she meant the same moral standard as women) for men'.

⁴⁷This latter view comes out in Mrs. Gaskell's novel *Ruth* and Anthony Trollope's *The Vicar of Bullhampton*, both already mentioned. An interesting analysis of the latter book is to be found in A. O. J. Cockshut *Anthony Trollope, A critical study*, Collins, 1955, pp. 116-120.

⁴⁸What undertaking this mission meant to a delicately brought up Victorian spinster may be gleaned from the fact that before Ellice Hopkins could make a start it was necessary for Hinton to 'teach her medically all he thought she ought to know, a knowledge fraught with deepest sorrow to both'. Rosa M. Barrett *Ellice Hopkins*, Wells, Gardner, Darton & Co. Ltd., 1907, p. 85.

⁴⁹The story of this movement is told in an article by D. Sherwin Bailey, 'The White Cross League' *Moral Welfare*, April 1952.

⁵⁰Among her writings was a book on this theme already cited, *The Power of Womanhood*, which was primarily addressed to mothers.

⁵¹Quoted in R. M. Barrett, op. cit., p. 107, from *Preventive Work and the Care of our Girls*, Hatchards, 1881.

⁵²Barrett, op. cit., p. 105. The oldest surviving moral welfare home in the northern diocese surveyed was probably founded as the direct result of a visit to the area by Ellice Hopkins.

⁵³E. Moberly Bell, op. cit., p. 74.

⁵⁴Brinckman, op. cit., p. 34. 'Thanks to the unwise conduct of many of the lady agitators for the repeal of the C.D. Acts' and the 'fanatical and ignorant agitation that had been fermented and carried on among ladies both married and single', Mr. Brinckman was 'not surprised at numbers of husbands being very much against their wives having anything to do with any effort to mitigate what is called the Social Evil'.

[55]Ellice Hopkins. Quoted Barrett, op. cit., p. 45.

[56]Brinckman, op. cit., and Rev. Arthur Madison, *Hints on Rescue Work*, Reformatory and Refuge Union, 1894.

[57]Madge Unsworth, *Maiden Tribute*, Salvation Army Publicity and Supplies, 1949, p. 37.

[58]Moral welfare work has been part of the official policy of the Salvation Army since 1877 when Major Catherine Reynolds began outdoor work in Whitechapal. Mrs. Cadman opened a training home in Newcastle three years later. Heasman, op. cit., p. 154.

[59]From the time of the opening of the first Church Army Training Centre for Women in 1887 certain nights were 'partly spent in seeking and rescuing the fallen mostly near Charing Cross', and a small shelter was opened in Tichborne Street in 1888. This shelter was part of the house of one of the lady workers. *A Thread of Gold*, the story of another Fifty Years War. Resumé of the Women's Work of the Church Army issued to commemorate the Fiftieth Year of that Work. Church Army, 1937, pp. 7, 15 and 18 ff.

[60]The Minority Report of the Royal Commission on the Poor Law, 1905-9, suggested (p. 788) that they required 'official inspection and supervision especially from the standpoint of the welfare of the infant. At present they concentrate their attention almost entirely upon the mother and her future welfare'.

[61]P. 5.

[62]Ibid., p. 61.

[63]E.g., Emma Smith, *A Cornish Waif's Story*, ed. A. L. Rowse. Odham's Press, 1954.

[64]As with the speaker in a Convocation debate who described rescue homes as places where 'such girls could not only be kept by God's grace, but could also be rendered more efficient for domestic service'. *Chronicles of Convocation*, 10th February, 1885.

[65]'Whoever takes up this work should do so in the fear of God and in all humility should ever pray for more and more love for God and souls', counsels Brinckman in his Preface to *Notes on Rescue Work*. With characteristic sense and directness he adds, 'Never forget that of all efforts to help souls this work requires in those that attempt to carry it on, some knowledge of the world combined with plenty of tact and common sense.

[66]'So we go on from one woman to another, speaking, pleading, praying and doing our utmost through the dark nights to win souls from a life of bondage and shame to one of peace and purity.' Extract from the Annual Report of the Church Army 1888-89 quoted in *A Thread of Gold*, p. 18.

[67]Brinckman warned workers not to put texts or religious pictures on the walls of the shelters to which girls were taken straight from the streets lest they went away the next morning in a sulk and told their companions 'that there was too much religion for them'. Op. cit., p. 61.

[68]E. Moberly Bell, op. cit., pp. 107-8.

[69]Phrasing taken from the C.P.A. Petition. The evidence presented by Ellice Hopkins to this committee was later produced as a pamphlet, *A Plea*

for the Wider Action of the Church of England in the Prevention of the Degradation of Women, Hatchards, 1879.

[70]Chronicles of Convocation, 10th February, 1885.

[71]These moves may have resulted in part from the growing faith in diocesan initiative and demand for diocesan action which manifested itself in various ways during the closing decades of the century. K. S. Inglis, *Churches and the Working Classes in Victorian England*, Routledge & Kegan Paul Ltd., 1963, pp. 31-34.

[72]These developments are discussed in more detail in Chapter 2.

[73]A. J. S. Maddison, op. cit., p. 6.

[74]Bishop of Newcastle, Preface to Maddison, op. cit.

[75]J. E. Higson, *The Story of a Beginning. An account of Pioneer Work for Moral Welfare*, S.P.C.K., 1955, p. 3.

[76]A syllabus for St. Monica's dated 1912 includes a special course on Prostitution, and another on 'Methods of Rescue Work' which included the general management of homes, classification, children's work, work amongst educated girls, care of the illegitimate child, co-operation with societies allied to rescue work. 'One lecture [is] to be given each week on the Devotional and Theoretical aspects of the work, four hours each day being allowed for study.'

[77]Higson, op. cit., p. 7.

2. MORAL WELFARE WORK BETWEEN THE WARS

[1]Charles Loch Mowat. *Britain between the Wars 1918-1940*, Methuen, 1955, p. 202.

[2]C. L. Mowat points out that within a year of the Armistice three-quarters of a million women had been dismissed and the 1921 Census (England and Wales) showed a decrease in the proportion of women in gainful occupations, 32·3% in 1921 compared with 34·1% in 1911. Those that remained in employment after the war were mostly in the traditional employments of domestic service, textiles, clothing trades, shop assistants, clerks and teachers. Op. cit., pp. 23-24.

[3]The ratio of females to males in England and Wales in 1911 was 1,068 to 1,000. By 1921 it had risen to 1,096 to 1,000 and was still 1,088 to 1,000 in 1931.

[4]Mowat, op. cit., p. 212. This issue is discussed in the COPEC Commission Report, Vol. IV, 'The Relation of the Sexes', 1924, pp. 93-94.

[5]Among those to spread this knowledge was Dr. Marie Stopes, whose writings and lectures received wide publicity during the early twenties.

[6]The dangers consequent on a continuing fall in the birth-rate as they were envisaged at that time are discussed at length in Problems of Population and Parenthood—the Second Report and Chief Evidence taken by the National Birth-rate Commission, 1918-20.

[7]Two such homes opened about this time were Simpson Hill Maternity Home, Heywood, 1916 and 'Ernismore', a mother and baby home at Eccles, 1919, both in the Manchester diocese.

[8]Lettice Fisher tells this story in a pamphlet published by the Council in

1946, *Twenty-One years and After 1918-1946, the Story of the National Council for the Unmarried Mother and her Child.* Much of the above account is taken from this pamphlet.

[9]By 30th April, 1939, 17,405 cases had been handled. Fisher, op. cit., p. 8.

[10]M. Kornitzer, *Child Adoption in the Modern World*, Putnam, 1952, p. 61.

[11]Royal Commission on Venereal Diseases. Final Report of the Commissioners, Cd. 8189, 1916.

[12]W. M. Frazer, *A History of English Public Health 1834-1939* Balliere, Tindall and Cox, 1950, p. 343.

[13]Sir Arthur Newsholme, *Health Problems in an Organised Society,* King, 1927, p. 169.

[14]Quoted in *Sixty years of Moral Welfare,* The Diamond Jubilee Report of the Southwark Diocese Moral Welfare Association, 1958, p. 8.

[15]This resolution is quoted in the Minutes of the Archbishops' Advisory Board, June 1924. The Board's secretary was asked to write to the Bishop of Manchester (William Temple—the presiding genius of the Conference) asking him what was being done to implement it. The reply was that the whole question was being considered by an inter-denominational Committee, and the Board seems to have taken no further action. In this, as in other aspects of the Conference's proceedings there would seem to be some substance in Maurice B. Reckitt's overall criticism of COPEC. 'The ambition was noble, but the question was whether the necessary theological, metaphysical and sociological foundations had been provided or even envisaged.' *Maurice to Temple*, Faber, 1947, p. 172.

[16]Lambeth Conference Report, 1920.

[17]'You are the only lady I know whose handling of this most difficult and repugnant subject does not alarm and distress me' wrote the then Bishop of Durham (Dr. Hensley Henson) to Miss J. E. Higson in 1921 in connection with a drawing room meeting she was proposing to address, and this attitude was probably by no means untypical even among the relatively sympathetic and enlightened. Higson, op. cit., p. 27.

[18]COPEC Report, Vol. IV, The Relation of the Sexes, Longmans, Green & Co., 1924, p. 26.

[19]Ibid. p. 116. No mention is made of the White Cross League here or elsewhere in the Report. It is interesting to note that it is assumed that such work 'does not call for specialised training and knowledge but only for resolute and high minded friendliness whereby the redeeming grace of God is revealed to the sinner'.

[20]The Report of the Committee on the Life and Witness of the Christian Community to the 1930 Conference was even more enthusiastic, 'Great change has come over this whole enterprise in recent years. It is no longer lowering, lugubrious, negative. It is positive, hopeful and adventurous.' p. 93.

[21]The Committee was presided over by Lord Henry Cavendish Bentinck, M.P. No indication is given of the auspices under which it was set up,

but judging by its membership it appears to have been inter-denominational. Miss Morris of Southwark was one of the members.

[22]Op. cit., p. 104.

[23]Op. cit., p. 19.

[24]Many homes were run by religious orders whose members are of course unpaid.

[25]Out of sixty homes only six superintendents' salaries reached £50 a year in addition to their keep, the remainder varied from £25 to £40. Working matrons 'who bear the brunt of the inefficiency or laziness of the girls and work hard themselves' received between £15 and £30, op. cit., p. 59.

[26]Op. cit., p. 25.

[27]The Committee devoted some thought to the special needs of mentally subnormal girls who were not certifiable as feeble-minded but needed special care. Report, pp. 35-39. This concern was prevalent at the time and was shown in the evidence given to the National Birthrate Commission, 1918-20 by Mrs. Bramwell Booth and others, and the discussion of this problem as reported in this Commission's Report, Problems of Population and Parenthood.

[28]*Rescue Work, an Enquiry and Criticism*, p. 63, cf. a letter dated 3.12.17 sent by Miss Higson and Miss Parker of St. Monica's to the Magdalen Home, Liverpool (now closed), on receiving a complaint that older girls were not being sent there for training. 'We feel there is an imperative need for reformation in our two-year Homes throughout the country. The terms "Magdalen", "Penitentiary", "Institution", etc., should be done away with. We desire to see the girls live as ordinary and natural a life as possible ... having educational classes and generally learning what will fit them for a useful after life.

[It is] a great responsibility [to ask] the girls to give two years of the best part of their lives to spend under conditions which fail to adequately supply the many needs of the physical and mental side of their nature as well as the spiritual ...'

[29]Cmd. 2561, p. 79.

[30]*Sixty Years of Moral Welfare*, Southwark Diocesan Moral Welfare Association, 1958, p. 9.

[31]This can be seen by reading Rev. Edward C. Trenholme, *Rescue Work*, published by the Church Penitentiary Association in 1927. Its terminology and ideas are those of the nineteenth century rather than the twentieth, and it might have been written a generation earlier than another book published a year later, 1928, by the Faith Press, *Christian Guidance of the Social Instincts* by J. M. Cole and F. C. Bacon, which may be said to represent the newer outlook. A typical sentence of Trenholme's reads, 'The chief means employed for the thorough restoration of penitents rescued from unchastity is a voluntary sojourn in a two-year training home specially set apart for such inmates,' p. 90.

[32]Trenholme, op. cit., p. 52.

[33]Miss Morris in *Rescue Work: an Enquiry and Criticism*, pp. 69-70 Miss Cole makes the same point: 'All rescue work,' she wrote, 'is at heart

an offer of friendship'—'capable friendship, wise by the study of conditions which make for good and evil, competent with the ability and machinery for varied help, and personal, since the personal touch with individuals is the only way by which ideals can be presented and example shown.' Cole and Bacon, op. cit., p. 62.

[34]The above quotations are all taken from Cole and Bacon, op. cit., Ch. V.

[35]*Sixty Years of Moral Welfare*, p. 7.

[36]Cole and Bacon, op. cit., p. 97. The first home for very young unmarried mothers (Stretton House, Southwark) was opened at about this time.

[37]Home Office Report of the Departmental Committee on Sexual Offences against Young Persons. Cmd 2561.

[38]Op. cit., p. 75. Cf. Report of the Liverpool Diocesan Association, 1929, in which similar views are expressed.

[39]Home Office Report of the Departmental Committee on the Treatment of Young Offenders. Cmd 2831. 1927.

[40]Report, pp. 118 f.

[41]Children and Young Persons Act, 1933. Sections 61, 62 and 63.

[42]The phrases quoted are from Lady Davidson. Minutes of the Board, February 1934.

[43]Limitations of time and space have precluded us from including developments overseas in this brief historical summary, interesting as they are.

[44]She died in 1936 and the story of her life and influence is told in a biography by M.C.S.M., *Edith Davidson of Lambeth*, John Murray, 1938.

[45]Copied from the minutes of the meeting held in February 1918. Unless otherwise stated the information on which this part of the chapter is based was obtained from the Board's Minutes from November 1917 onwards.

[46]A brief but vivid account of moral welfare work as it was at that time, including the role of the Advisory Board, is given by Miss Lila Retallack, then General Secretary to the Board, in an article entitled 'Moral Welfare Work, a Central Responsibility', *The Church Assembly News*, November 1934.

[47]This matter is reverted to several times in the pages which follow.

[48]The last two quotations in this sentence are from the Board's minute book, the first from Higson, op. cit., p. 18. The two accounts of the episode differ slightly.

[49]Above, pp. 29-30.

[50]Higson, op. cit., p. 27.

[51]Mrs. Randall Davidson, quoted in Higson, op. cit., p. 22.

[52]Higson, op. cit., p. 38.

[53]Ibid., p. 49.

[54]Ibid., p. 49.

[55]Cf. the observation of the Committee appointed to consider and report upon problems of Marriage and Sexual Morality, Lambeth Conference, 1920, 'Sad ignorance and apathy exist among Church people concerning preventive and rescue work.... The clergy themselves oftentimes

manifest a strange ignorance of social conditions and a lack of sympathy with efforts being made.'

[56]Canon T. W. Pym, Chairman of the Propaganda Committee in a paper read to the Annual Conference of Principals and Vice-Principals of Theological Colleges at Oxford, January 1924. Quoted in Higson, op. cit.
[57]Handsworth College, Birmingham. Higson, op. cit., p. 65.
[58]Minutes, June 1930.
[59]Minutes, November 1952.
[60]Quoted in Higson, op. cit., p. 55.
[61]Minutes, 23rd January, 1919.
[62]The difficulty of getting men to serve on the Advisory Board is rather ironical in view of a recommendation from a Conference of Organising Secretaries in the Northern Province held in 1917, that 'there should be no homes where the Government is in the hands of men only'. One of the first tasks laid on the new secretary to the Board was 'to find out if any such Homes in fact existed where there was a committee of only men, or where a women's committee met separately on sufferance with practically no powers'. Minutes, November 1917.
[63]Higson, op. cit., Ch. 5.
[64]Sherwin Bailey, op. cit.

3. DEVELOPMENTS DURING AND AFTER THE SECOND WORLD WAR

[1]This is brought out in the classic study by Professor R. M. Titmuss, *Problems of Social Policy*, H.M.S.O., 1950, and its companion volume, S. M. Ferguson and H. Fitzgerald, *Studies in the Social Services*, H.M.S.O., 1954.
[2]Ferguson and Fitzgerald, op. cit., Table I, p. 89. By 1947 numbers had declined to 46,603, i.e., 12.5 per 1,000.
[3]Ibid., p. 100. The writers estimate that about 50% of the beds in moral welfare homes were closed temporarily or permanently. Cf. the removal of civilian patients from hospitals to make room for service or air raid casualties, which occurred at the same time and caused a great deal of unnecessary distress. Titmuss estimated that on the outbreak of war about 140,000 hospital beds were emptied of their patients. Op. cit., p. 183.
[4]Ferguson and Fitzgerald, op. cit., pp. 103 and 104.
[5]Ibid., p. 104.
[6]Dr. Ethel Cassie, Senior Assistant Medical Officer for Birmingham, 'The Care of Illegitimate Children', *Public Health*, the Journal of the Society of Medical Officers of Health, February, 1944, pp. 54-55.
[7]Religious organisations of various kinds and all denominations. Dr. Cassie's remarks quoted above also referred to voluntary homes in general, not necessarily those under the auspices of the Church of England.
[8]*Planning*. No. 255, 13th September, 1946. 'The Unmarried Mother', p. 9.
[9]*Planning*. Op. cit., p. 10.
[10]The letter (unpublished) is dated 4th October, 1946. Writer's italics.

[11]Op. cit., para. 3.

[12]Circular, para. 4.

[13]Ferguson and Fitzgerald, op. cit., p. 128.

[14]'The Problem Presses', *Social Work*, January, 1944.

[15]The Interim Report was published in the *Quarterly Leaflet*, January 1945, the Final Report was published separately later in the same year by the Press and Publications Board of the Church Assembly under the title *Training for Moral Welfare Work*.

[16]Miss Retallack as quoted in Higson, op. cit., p. 137.

[17]'The Problem Presses', loc. cit.

[18]Appointed May 1944, reported April 1945. The Report was published by the Press and Publications Board of the Church Assembly in 1945, with the title *Training for Service*.

[19]Ibid., par. 25, p. 13.

[20]*Training for Service*, Section on Moral Welfare, par. 1, p. 3.

[21]For an account of the aims and practice of the training given at J.B.M.H. two or three years later see Chrystobel Blackburn, 'Commentary on Training for Moral Welfare Work To-day', The Quarterly Review of the Church of England Moral Welfare Council. January 1951, pp. 8-13.

[22]Council Minutes, 14th November, 1947. She suggested that, 'dislike of the term "moral welfare" and all that it implied was more important'. This point is discussed later in the study.

[23]Cf. Almoners, £220 for newly qualified assistants rising to £500-£600 for a head almoner in a large training hospital. Personnel Management (women), £200-£600 (approximately); Probation Officers (women), £240-£320 and consolidation allowance of £48 a year; Senior Probation Officer £50 a year extra. Information from Appendix I, *Report on the Employment and Training of Social Workers*, Carnegie U.K. Trust, 1947.

[24]Cf. The observation of the Archbishops' Committee on Training for Women in the Work of the Church. 'The Church has a right to ask those who serve it to live frugally and accept the discipline of self-sacrifice, but it should not require them to stultify and cramp their personalities and to be so continuously embarrassed by their finances that they cannot work to the best of the ability with which God has endowed them. It will not be possible and indeed desirable for the Church to offer salaries equal to those in the statutory service. Its rates of remuneration, however, must have some recognisable relation to those obtainable in other spheres.' *Training for Service*, 1945, p. 8.

[25]Final Report of the Committee on Procedure in Matrimonial Causes, Cmd 7024, 1947, par. 19, p. 8, (Denning Committee). Report of the Departmental Committee on grants for the Development of Marriage Guidance, Cmd 7566, 1948, par. 19, p. 14. The two other organisations named were the Catholic Marriage Advisory Council and the Family Welfare Association which had recently initiated the 'Family Discussion Bureaux'. Local authorities were encouraged to assist local councils.

[26]The first General Secretary was a Methodist, the present one is a member of the Society of Friends.

[27]As revised in 1952 the statement on this issue reads, 'Children are a

natural fulfilment of marriage and enrich the relationship between husband and wife; nevertheless scientific contraception when used according to conscience within marriage can contribute to the health of the whole family.'

[28]The Church of England Moral Welfare Council's Annual Report for 1947 states that during the year the Education Committee was authorised to invite diocesan bishops and organising secretaries to report on the situation, and, in particular, on any obstacles which seemed to stand in the way of full and harmonious co-operation. The replies showed that in a very high proportion of cases Anglicans were not only actively engaged, but were often taking a lead in marriage guidance. Only in a few cases had doctrinal difficulties been met and led to misgivings.

[29]Lambeth Conference, 1948. Encyclical Letter from the Bishops together with the Resolutions and Reports, p. 100. The meeting of the Moral Welfare Council, November 1948, noted rather sourly that no specific mention of moral welfare work was made in this Committee's report nor in the Conference Resolution (Resolution 93) which endorsed it.

[30]Council Minutes, February 1947. Cf. Resolution 93 of the Lambeth Conference, 1948, which stated specifically that, 'The Church has a primary duty in the pastoral care of those who are married or about to be married' and to this end, 'regular and systematic instruction on the meaning and responsibilities of marriage and particular preparation of engaged persons should be regarded as a normal pastoral duty in every parish, and all parish priests should be equipped for these tasks'.

[31]Gilbert L. Russell, Marriage Guidance and Moral Welfare, The Quarterly Review of the Church of England Moral Welfare Council, January 1950, pp. 8 and 9.

[32]G. R. Dunstan, 'The Clergy and Marriage Counselling', *Moral Welfare*, a Quarterly Review, October 1960, p. 112. ('*Moral Welfare*' was the title given to the Quarterly Review of the Council from January 1951 until it ceased publication in October 1963 and reappeared as *Crucible* in January 1964. *Crucible* is the journal of the Church Assembly Board for Social Responsibility.)

[33]G. R. Dunstan, ibid.

[34]Chapter 13.

[35]For example, in preparation for the Lambeth Conference, 1948, the Council set up a group (known as the Fulham Group) to consider certain important matters relating to sex, marriage and the family and prepare a report which could be presented to the Conference. The report, which was not made public, dealt with:

    a. The Natural Law in Relation to Sex, Marriage and the Family.

    b. Christian Sex Education.

    c. The Church and Planned Parenthood.

[36]The Report was published in 1958 by the S.P.C.K.

[37]Dr. F. W. Dillistone, then Dean of Liverpool.

[38]Cf. the reaction of Peter Wildeblood who came across the pamphlet while awaiting trial in connection with a homosexual offence. 'This pamphlet . . . surprised me too. I had always thought of the Church as the last stronghold of prejudice and never found an occasion for praising it for

its courage in controversial matters; yet here, from Church House, came an attack on the law which was as broad-minded, clear-headed and brilliantly argued as one could wish.' *Against the Law*, Pelican Books, 1955, p. 68.

[39]*Sexual Offenders and Social Punishment*, Evidence submitted on behalf of the Church of England Moral Welfare Council to the Departmental Committee on Homosexual Offences and Prostitution. Compiled and edited by D. Sherwin Bailey, and published for the Moral Welfare Council by the Church Information Board, 1956.

[40]Ibid., p. 58.

[41]Report of the Committee on Homosexual Offences and Prostitution, Cmnd 247.

[42]Annual Report of the Church of England Moral Welfare Council, 1957.

[43]The process is described in an article by Graham Buston, 'Whipped Through Parliament', *Moral Welfare*, October 1959, pp. 113-118.

[44]Report, Chapter II.

[45]Since the passing of the Suicide Act, 1961, suicide is no longer a crime.

[46]Three other Councils as well as the Moral Welfare Council were represented on the advisory group which prepared *The Family in Contemporary Society*, S.P.C.K., 1958.

[47]Moral Welfare Council, Annual Report, 1956.

4. SOCIAL CONDITIONS AND ATTITUDES

[1]The Albemarle Committee pointed out that the average weekly wage for young people between 15 and 20 in 1938 was: boys 26/-; girls 24/-; most of this money being handed over to parents and only a few shillings being retained for discretionary spending. In mid-1958 boys earned an average of £5 12s. and girls £5 6s., about £3 of which was available for discretionary spending. Ministry of Education, The Youth Service in England and Wales, Cmnd 929, 1960, para. 89-92. Cf. Central Advisory Council for Education, England, 15-18, H.M.S.O., 1959 (Crowther Committee Report) paras. 69-70. This points out that while the average weekly earnings of adult men had risen to 372% of the 1938 figure and adult women to 412%, those of boys and girls had risen to 429% and 469% respectively. Even allowing for changes in the value of money this rise is considerable.

[2]A birth is regarded by the Registrar General as having been premaritally conceived if it takes place less than nine months after marriage. Prior to 1952 the duration was 8½ months. 'Maternity' refers to the act of giving birth whether one or two children are born, or the children are born alive or dead.

[3]Ferguson and Fitzgerald, op. cit., pp. 90-92. The authors suggest that the number of children transferred from the legitimate to the illegitimate category as the result of wartime contingencies was in the region of 100,000.

[4]Registrar General's Statistical Reivew, 1960, Part III, Tables XXVI and XXVII. In the paragraph preceding Table XXVII the Registrar General explains the exact connotation of the phrase 'at risk'.

[5]Report of the Ministry of Health for the year 1960, Part II, Cmnd 1550, p. 124.

[6]Registrar General's Statistical Review, 1960, Part II, Tables AA and II.

[7]Virginia Wimperis, after reviewing the evidence contained in a number of local studies, concluded that 'it seems reasonable to assume that, at least in the cities, one in every two or three illegitimate births are to women co-habiting in a more or less permanent relationship'. *The Unmarried Mother and her Child*, Allen & Unwin, 1960, pp 68-69. Cf. the conclusion of a Ministry of Health Study by E. R. Bransby and Rachel A. Elliott 'Probably some 30-40% of the mothers of illegitimate children are co-habiting'. *Monthly Bulletin of the Ministry of Health and Public Health Laboratory Service*, directed by the M.R.C. February 1959, p. 20.

[8]Her conclusions are most fully set out in *Out of Wedlock*, McGraw Hill Book Company Inc., 1954.

[9]Ibid., pp. 36 and 37.

[10]Donald Gough, 'Work with Unmarried Mothers', *The Almoner*, March 1961, pp. 490-91.

[11]Wimperis, op. cit., p. 97. Author's italics.

[12]Leontine R. Young, 'Personality Problems in Unmarried Mothers', *The Family* (Journal of the Family Welfare Association of America), Vol. 16, No. 18, December 1945, p. 297.

[13]By analysing the occupations of 328 Aberdeen women who bore their first illegitimate child between 1949 and 1952, together with those of 1,750 women who had their first legitimate maternity in 1952-3 Miss Thompson found that the incidence of illegitimacy rose from 2% in the professional and technical groups to 19% among catering and cleaning workers; that of pre-nuptial conceptions from 9% in the professional groups to 40% among fish workers. 59% of unmarried women were in unskilled jobs or in the catering, cleaning or fish trades, compared with 38% who married after conception and 22% of those who married before conception. Barbara Thompson, 'Social Study of Illegitimate Maternities', *British Journal of Social and Preventive Medicine*, April 1956.

[14]The incidence of broken homes was 40% in the unmarried group, 23% in the pre-nuptial conception group and 18% among those who conceived after marriage. The most common cause of breakdown was the death of one or more parents.

[15]E. W. Anderson, J. C. Kenna and M. W. Hamilton 'A Study of Extra-marital Conception in Adolescence'. *Psychiatria et Neurologia*, Vol. 139, No. 6, 1960, p. 357.

[16]Cyril Greenland, 'Unmarried Parenthood, Ecological Aspects', *Lancet*, 19th January, 1957, pp. 148-151.

[17]The total number of illegitimate maternities in England and Wales during this same year was 32,503.

[18]Cyril Greenland, 'Unmarried Parenthood: I Unmarried Mothers', *The Medical Officer*, Vol. XCIX, January-June 1958, p. 271.

[19]Ibid., *The Medical Officer*, p. 272.

[20]The original study, which gave the initial impetus to this investigation was published in *Moral Welfare*, January 1954. Celia M. Joy, 'Illegiti-

mate Children and their Parents—A Survey of Case Work for the Year 1952'. An interim report of the 'follow up' survey was published in *Moral Welfare*, January 1957, 'What Happens Afterwards'; the final report in *Moral Welfare* July 1960, 'A Final Study of Unmarried Mothers and their Children'.

[21]Cf. E. E. McDonald, 'Follow up of Illegitimate Children', *The Medical Officer*, 14th December, 1956.

[22]Cyril Greenland, *Unmarried Parenthood*, op. cit.

[23]*The Almoner*, May 1961, p. 71.

[24]Contraceptives did not appear to have been used at any time by the girls in the Manchester survey, but 'several of the boys appear to have used them'. Anderson, *et. al.*, 'A Study of Extra-marital Conception in Adolescence', *Psychiatria et Neurologia*, Vol. 159, No. 6, 1960.

[25]There was an increase of 12% in the number of new cases diagnosed at clinics between 1958 and 1959. Between 1959 and 1960 numbers increased from 31,344 to 33,770, an increase of 8½%. *On the State of Public Health*, 1959, Cmnd 1550, p. 59. For more detailed discussions see R. D. Catterall, 'The Advance of the Venereal Diseases', *The Lancet*, 20th July, 1963.

[26]The effects of this are to some extent discounted by the Committee of the British Medical Association on the Problem of Venereal Disease particularly among Young People. The report of this Committee points out that the resistance referred to is only relative and other effective antibiotics are now available. *Venereal Disease and Young People*. A British Medical Association Report, March 1964.

[27]Cmnd 207, pp. 69-70.

[28]Cmnd 1550, p. 60.

[29]This represents only a proportion of persons treated, since an unknown number receive treatment from general practitioners.

[30]B.M.A. op cit., Table III, p. 22. Since the numbers quoted are numbers treated in clinics, the increase could be due, in part at least, to an increased use of the facilities provided by the clinics.

[31]In a study made by the British Co-operative Clinical group in 1956 relating to 7,151 patients with gonorrhoea, 19% of the women patients admitted to being prostitutes, 36% of the men said that their infection came from prostitutes. Catherall, op. cit., p. 104.

[32]Report, par. 230.

[33]Edited by C. H. Rolph and published for the British Social Biology Council, Secker and Warburg, 1955.

[34]Ibid., p. xiii. Quoted in the Wolfenden Report, par. 223.

[35]U.N. Department of Social and Economic Affairs, New York, 1959, p. 14.

[36]This came out in the series of letters to *The Times* published in the autumn of 1961, under the heading, 'A Nation in Danger'.

[37]Griselda Rowntree, 'New Facts on Teen-age Marriage', *New Society*, 4th November, 1962.

[38]*Registrar General's Statistical Review*, 1959, Part III, p. 7.

[39]Ministry of Education, *15-18*, 1959, p. 38.

[40]*The Youth Service in England and Wales* (Albemarle Report), Cmnd 929, 1960, p. 17.

[41]Paul Johnson, 'Are Virgins Obsolete?', *New Statesman*, 4th January, 1963.

[42]V. A. Demant, *An Exposition of Christian Sex Ethics*, Hodder and Stoughton, 1963, Ch. 6.

[43]Edmund Leach, 'Sins or Rules?' *New Society*, 4th April, 1963. Cf. Ray Gosling 'The Tough and the Tender', ibid., 4th April, 1963.

[44]G. M. Carstairs *This Island Now*, (B.B.C. Reith Lectures, 1962), Hogarth Press Ltd., 1963, pp. 50-51.

[45]E.g. in H. A. Williams' essay entitled 'Psychological Objections', in the collection of essays *Objections to Christian Belief* by A. R. Vidler, *et al.*, Constable, 1963.

[46]E.g. E. Mascall, *Up and Down in Adria*, Faith Press Ltd., Chapter II.

[47]A notable, if controversial, group effort of this kind is *Towards a Quaker View of Sex*, (Ed. A. Heron), Friends' Home Service Committee, 1963. The group responsible for this pamphlet 'gathered in 1957 to re-examine through thought and prayer this most difficult of problems'.

[48]T. R. Milford, 'Talking of Sex', *Frontier*, Autumn, 1963. This article was also the product of group discussion.

[49]John A. T. Robinson, *Honest to God*, S.C.M. Press, 1963, p. 116.

5. CONCURRENT DEVELOPMENTS IN SOCIAL WORK AND POLICY

[1]P. 56 above.

[2]Report, par. 196, p. 44.

[3]Ibid., par. 422, p. 116.

[4]The Development of Community Care. Plans for the Health and Welfare Services in the Local Authorities in England and Wales, Cmnd 1973, par. 40, p. 12.

[5]Above pp. 43-4.

[6]Children and Young Persons Act, 1933, s. 61; Children and Young Persons (Amendment) Act, 1952, s. 1.

[7]Section 2.

[8]An official from another authority expressed himself in very similar terms. 'If, after investigation, it is considered that it would not be in the girl's or the parents' interest to take court action, these cases would be referred to a moral welfare worker. The deciding factors in the case are the character of the girl, of the parents, of the home background, together with the assessment of the co-operation likely to be forthcoming from the girl and her parents.'

[9]*Report of the Working Party on Social Workers in the Local Authority Health and Welfare Services*, paras. 424 and 425, p. 117. Cf. Margaret Wynn, *Fatherless Families, a Study for the Council for Children's Welfare*, Michael Joseph, 1964. This question is taken up again in Part V of this study.

¹⁰D. V. Donnison and Mary Stewart, op. cit. Cf. Report of the Committee on Children and Young Persons (Ingleby Committee Report), Cmnd 1191, 1960, par. 37, p. 16.

¹¹One health official told us, 'If I could implement the full complement of health visitors I could fulfil my obligations in the field of problem family work.' Another said, 'The work is well done by the health visitors,' and added, 'if more social workers were necessary we consider that they should be employed by a voluntary body.'

¹²The two counties in the southern diocese surveyed employed their own 'family' workers. In one of the counties these workers were employed by the local health authority; in the other a 'family welfare officer' worked in the office of the Clerk to the Council and dealt with 'problem families' including the evicted families in the county's 'half-way houses'. None of the county boroughs in the northern diocese employed their own workers of this kind, nor did the county council.

¹³This was noted by the Ingleby committee who commented that 'it was apparent from some of the evidence we received and its existence is common knowledge'. Report, par. 37.

¹⁴The various types of co-ordinating machinery and their methods of working are described in some detail in the Younghusband Report, Chapter 12.

¹⁵Donnison and Stewart, op. cit., p. 6.

¹⁶Donnison and Stewart, op. cit., pp. 7-8. Cf. Council for Children's Welfare and Fisher group. *Families with Problems, a New Approach*, April 1958. These two pamphlets are summarised and criticised in an article by Margaret I. Roxburgh 'A Statutory Family Service, the Question Posed', *Social Work*, July 1958, pp. 184ff.

¹⁷Home Office Circular No. 204/1963, par. 7. The relevant date was 1st October, 1963.

¹⁸Ibid., par. 13.

¹⁹Ibid., par. 15. The specific suggestion made is that 'it might make for easier communication with church members if your authority were to invite local churches or, where they exist local councils of churches, to nominate representatives for purposes of consultation who have knowledge of the statutory social services and of church members willing and able to help'.

²⁰Sylvia Watson 'Manpower in the Child Care Service', *Social Work* January 1964, p. 16.

6. THE RECRUITMENT AND TRAINING OF WORKERS

¹As the length of training varied from four terms to three years, this included some, but not all, of the students who started training in 1946, and some, but not all, of the students who started training in 1957 and 1958.

²It is 21 for the comparable social work professions of almoning, probation and child care, but a 'young' 21-year-old may be advised to postpone professional training for a year or two. In that case she may try and obtain

a trainee job in her chosen profession, or undertake some kind of related work to cover the waiting period.

[3]For example, candidates for the course leading to the Certificate in Social Science at Liverpool University are required to have obtained at least two 'A' level passes or an equivalent educational qualification if they are under 23 but this is not insisted on for older candidates. There is an entrance examination for all candidates other than graduates.

[4]Report, par. 890, p. 252.

[5]Not all those coming forward are new recruits to the health and welfare services; a large number are untrained serving officers recommended for training by their respective authorities.

[6]Chrystobel Blackburn 'Commentary on Training for Moral Welfare Work Today', *The Quarterly Review of the Church of England Moral Welfare Council*, January 1951, pp. 8 and 9.

[7]Details of this course are given in the Report of the Departmental Committee on the Probation Service, (Chairman, Mr. R. P. Morison), Cmnd 1650, 1962, par. 308, p. 118. The London course has now been discontinued. At the time of writing, a course for older women, of approximately one year's duration, was being planned at J. B. House.

[8]An enquiry carried out by the Church of England Council for Social Work into the position with regard to pensions in 1963 revealed that of the 387 respondents, who included all categories of moral welfare workers, 66 were over 60, 176 between 50 and 60, 98 between 40 and 50, 33 between 30 and 40 and only 14 under 30. This response may be rather overweighted by older women who would be more likely to be interested in the position with regard to pensions than the younger ones.

7. THE ADMINISTRATIVE PATTERN

[1]In the tiny diocese of Sodor and Man the diocesan organiser is sole case worker and there are no subdivisions.

[2]In the autumn of 1962 the Local Government Boundaries Commission began its investigations in the area, but at the time of writing its findings were not yet available.

[3]At the time of writing this situation was under review, and it appeared likely that a new worker would be appointed to work in the satellite town.

[4]This situation has now been completely changed. A moral welfare worker now has an office in the town's Family Centre.

[5]This piece of work is described in more detail in Chapter 14.

[6]Cf. Report of the Working Party on Social Workers in the Local Authority Health and Welfare Services (Younghusband Committee Report) par. 402, p. 111, which contrasts a home teacher to the blind with a car who spent 10% of her time travelling and averaged about 30 visits to blind people and two to three to social centres weekly with a visitor to the deaf in the same area who travelled by public transport or on foot and spent 47% of his time travelling with a weekly average of six visits to deaf people and two to three to social centres.

[7]In the week for which records were kept two of the 14 workers spent more than half their working time travelling, another spent one-third of her time in this way.

[8]Unfortunately in both these otherwise good premises toilet facilities were poor, while in other premises heating was inadequate.

[9]One office visited was entered through a wine merchant's yard. Another, which was over a bank, was approached by a side entrance up a steep flight of stairs and down a long passage. The waiting space was part of a narrow passage decorated in the almost inevitable dark brown paint and with a coloured glass window. The office itself was a large light room, brightly decorated, pleasant and welcoming.

[10]Cf. the position with regard to field workers attached to local authority health and welfare departments. Report of the Working Party on Social Workers, par. 399, pp. 110-111.

8. DIOCESAN ORGANISATION AND ORGANISERS

[11]The findings of these questionnaires, on which this part of the chapter is based, were presented in more detail to the Association of Organising Secretaries in October 1960.

9. LOCAL ASSOCIATIONS AND COMMITTEES

[1]Owing to their constitutional set-up and statutory responsibilities the boards of managers of the two approved schools have been excluded from this description of moral welfare committees.

[2]A trained social worker employed by a small local authority may find herself in a somewhat similar position and faced with similar difficulties.

[3]In 1959 the two case committees attached to the moral welfare committee responsible for work in a large city were composed as follows: *Children's Work Case Committee:* A member of staff from each of the following; a family casework organisation, a voluntary child welfare association, the local authority children's department, the education welfare department and the city police—together with a headmaster and a headmistress, a woman doctor, two other members and the organising secretary.

Outdoor Work Case Committee: A member of staff from each of a family casework organisation, a voluntary child welfare association, and a local authority public health department, together with a representative of the Standing Conference of Womens Organisations, three other members and the organising secretary.

There were no denominational restrictions on the membership of these two case committees and, at the time of the field work, the chairman of one of them was a member of the Society of Friends.

10. DIOCESAN AND LOCAL FINANCE

[1]This particular issue is discussed in more detail in Chapter 12, Residential Work.

[2]In associations responsible for residential work proportions are affected by residents' payments.

11. MORAL WELFARE CASEWORK

[1]In 1961 there were 713 referrals to outdoor workers, in 1962 the numbers rose sharply to 886.

[2]Wimperis, op. cit., pp. 52-53.

[3]Cf. Alison Reid, ' "To See or Not to See" Part II—The Maternity Almoner', *The Almoner*, September 1963. It appears from this study that in 30 out of 72 cases in which the birth was illegitimate and in which action was taken after the first interview, contact was made with a moral welfare worker.

[4]In 14 of the 32 cases where the baby was born illegitimate and the case referred to a moral welfare worker, the referral was for residential accommodation either by itself or in connection with advice on other matters, usually unspecified. A further seven were referred for long term care and the remainder for general advice and other unspecified reasons.

[5]After spending a fortnight in one area the field worker recorded her general impressions in these terms, 'Maybe owing to this [pressure of work], there was an emphasis on practical arrangements. No very deep relationship was established in any case [observed]. I sometimes felt that the client wanted to talk more, at other times that she almost resented the routine enquiries.'

[6]For example, the field worker was present at one home visit when discussions about arrangements for the girl and her baby led to a long conversation with the mother about the difficulties she had with her daughter, who was adopted and whom she was rejecting.

[7]One such case concerned a girl in her early twenties whose mother had left home with another man when she was a child. She was placed in a foster home, her parents obtained a divorce and after some years her father also lost interest in her. The foster mother was herself an unstable woman, who on hearing of the girl's pregnancy refused to have her back, although she was willing to take the baby. The girl went to a home in another area and on her discharge every effort was made by the local moral welfare worker there to find her lodgings, but the attempts failed. By this time the foster mother had consented to have her back, and after much consideration she agreed to return. Meanwhile, a suggestion had been made that a friend of the foster mother's should adopt the baby and the moral welfare worker visited this couple. In the end the girl settled down at the foster mother's with the baby, and the foster mother increasingly took responsibility for its care.

[8]Both Dr. Barnado's and the Church of England Children's Society sponsor schemes whereby weekly grants are paid to the mother or foster

parents of an illegitimate child whose mother is doing all she can to support him, but cannot manage the payments herself. The grants are usually made through a regional or local agency which keeps in touch with mother, child and foster parents and reports back to the organisation making the grant at regular intervals.

[9]Referred to in Chapter 4.

[10]Owing to the time lag between the prospective adopter's first enquiry and their placement on the waiting list, and the further time lag, which may be considerable, before a suitable child becomes available, some of the 87 couples accepted might be from among the 142 enquirers, but others may have made their initial enquiry the previous year. Similarly some of the court orders might relate to the 74 babies placed during the year, others to babies placed the previous year.

[11]A number of similar appointments were made in other dioceses during this period, but for the most part they have been discontinued.

[12]In 1960 probation officers in England and Wales dealt with 25,892 matrimonial conciliation cases in which it was necessary to see both parties, 15,657 of which were direct applications. In a further 17,506 cases only one party was seen, 12,086 of these being direct applications. Report of the Departmental Committee on the Probation Service, Cmnd 1650, March 1962, p. 51.

[13]In the area where a special children's worker is employed, one of the outdoor workers for the same area, on leaving her job, handed over twenty such cases, originally referred because of an illegitimate pregnancy or child, to the children's worker as 'Family' cases. This illustrates the difficulty of classifying cases; since these were referred to the children's worker they were presumably regarded primarily as cases involving children or young people. In this instance they were recorded as new referrals, because they were transferred to another worker. In the ordinary way, one worker would continue to deal with such families. It is possible that the classification of cases tends, if anything, to underestimate the amount of 'family' work undertaken.

[14]This matter is discussed again in a different context in Chapter 14.

[15]The situation on this housing estate is described in Chapter 14.

[16]Examples may be found in B. N. Rodgers and J. Dixon, *Portrait of Social Work*, O.U.P., 1956.

12. RESIDENTIAL WORK

[1]Since then considerable efforts have been made to deal with the problems presented by both premises and staffing and the school is being reopened.

[2]Eve Kennedy, 'Church Provident', *Moral Welfare*, July 1958, pp. 81-85.

[3]In 1963 the National Council for the Unmarried Mother and her Child started an investigation into the provisions for the residential care of unmarried mothers and their children.

[4]Details are given in Table X, Chapter 10, above.

[5]The questionnaire circulated from the Church of England Moral Welfare Council to 136 superintendents of homes and two outdoor workers working from shelters, referred to above, included a question about the adequacy of the complement of staff allowed for. Not all superintendents replied but 31 said that it was insufficient and a further 12 said that the number could be regarded as sufficient only if extra help were available at holiday times and week-ends. In 15 homes the superintendent had no residential help. E. Kennedy, op. cit., p. 83.

[6]See, for example, Eric Ingram, 'Living Together in a Children's Home', *Case Conference*, Vol. 7, No. 8, February 1961.

[7]This term was actually used with reference to the assistant worker in one annual report, a relic perhaps of the time when the committee employed a 'lady superintendent' who was assisted by a 'working matron'.

[8]In 17 cases this qualification was combined with a nursing qualification.

[9]Eve Kennedy, op. cit., p. 83.

[10]In the survey of Aberdeen described in Chapter 4 Barbara Thompson found that the 49 women from that city who went to mother and baby homes outside it included 14 'rootless nomads', and 35 women who had left home from a desire for secrecy or because of parental hostility, illness or other domestic difficulties. The 142 unmarried primiparae who came to Aberdeen mother and baby homes during the course of the survey included three upper class girls who wanted the anonymity of a strange town, some girls in conflict with their parents, some whose home conditions were unsatisfactory, and some, usually domestic servants, with no settled home and in need of accommodation.

[11]Jeremy Sandford, 'Society Exacts its Price', *Observer*, 12th May, 1963.

[12]Cf. the conclusion reached by the Ministry of Health investigators ' . . . on the whole opportunities to widen the girls' interests are not used to good advantage'.

[13]A special home in which proper teaching is given has now been opened in London for girls of school age.

[14]The absence of the chapel in this home was due to shortage of accommodation. The home had a noticeably religious atmosphere with religious pictures and texts prominently displayed. Prayers were said every morning round the breakfast table.

[15]The issues raised here are discussed further in Chapter 15.

[16]The chaplain to one home shared in the breakfast washing-up after the monthly celebration of Holy Communion.

13. EDUCATIONAL WORK

[1]Above, p. 138.

[2]See p. 181. This worker has since left the area.

[3]Cf. Margaret Gray and Edna Whitehouse, 'Teachers and Teen-agers', *Marriage Guidance*, December 1961, which draws attention to the enormous increase in married women on school staffs and contends that many girls 'were grateful to be able to talk to an adult whom they preferred to be a member of staff who knew them as people'. 55% of the 563

assistant teachers in the girls' schools in the sample investigated by the Newsom Committee were married women; 24% of the 1,857 assistants in co-educational schools. Central Advisory Council for Education (England), *Half Our Future*, Table 26, p. 249.

[4]Of the 49 clergymen interviewed 20 said that they were in contact with their local marriage guidance council. Some of these spoke very well of marriage guidance work, others were more doubtful while a third group said that they would like further contacts but had not time to make them. Ten said that they had no contacts, some because of lack of time, some because they were doubtful about the work. In a number of interviews the question was not discussed, perhaps because it was known that there was no local marriage guidance council in the area.

[5]Quoted from the constitution of a diocesan board of moral welfare.

14. MORAL WELFARE AS CHURCH WORK

[1]When drawing the sample we excluded those incumbents known to be chairmen or members of the Board of Moral Welfare or the local committees and any others whom we knew to have a particular interest in the work. This procedure has since been criticised as giving a less favourable picture of the relationship between moral welfare workers and the clergy than was actually the case but our object was to examine the position where there was no official contact. In the event it turned out that one or two whom we interviewed had some connection with moral welfare work of which we had been unaware.

[2]It is impossible to be more precise as the majority of the incumbents interviewed had kept no records of these contacts and were speaking entirely from memory.

[3]This is not the real name of the estate.

15. MORAL WELFARE WORK TODAY

[1]Birmingham Council of Christian Churches, *Responsibility in the Welfare State?*, 1961, p. 13.

[2]A story from another area shows that at least some clients were aware of the Church background to moral welfare work. The mother of a Protestant girl, pregnant by a Roman Catholic boy, went to the Roman Catholic worker for help and demanded the adoption of the baby by a Roman Catholic family. The girl was, however, referred back to the Church of England worker in the same area. She and her mother made a number of extravagant demands from this worker and refused to co-operate in any of the plans suggested. The day after this interview the Anglican worker received a telephone call from the Roman Catholic agency to say that the girl and her mother had been back there saying that 'they (the Church of England) would not do anything for them', and the mother had finally left the office in a rage declaring that she was 'going to see what the atheists can do for us'.

[3]A probation officer in another county told us that 'fundamentally there

295

was no difference' between his scope and opportunities as a Christian probation officer and a church worker.

[4]This point of view may be recognised and respected by other social workers, as was shown in a conversation we had with a statutory social worker in a northern county borough who remarked bluntly, 'Moral welfare workers invariably have a sense of vocation, they must have, look at their salaries,' but added that this, together with their church connections gave them a stable background to their work.

[5]In the words of the 1957 annual report of a diocesan association in another part of the country, 'With the co-operation of the parish priest, the work can become evangelistic.'

[6]P.E.P., *Planning*, No. 225, 13th September, 1946, 'The Unmarried Mother', p. 10. See above Chapter 3, p. 54.

[7]As explained in Chapter 12 these were the only type of Anglican home in the two dioceses surveyed.

[8]The Morison Committee found that, 'Of 670 whole-time [probation] officers first appointed in England and Wales in the period 1st January, 1958—31st October, 1961, no fewer than 302 (45%) were direct entrants'; and that, 'of all the whole-time officers appointed since 1946, rather more than a quarter were untrained on taking post.' Report of the Departmental Committee on the Probation Service, Cmd. 1650, March 1962, par. 269. The position in the child care service as set out in Sylvia Watson's article 'Manpower in the Child Care Service,' *Social Work*, January 1964, has already been referred to, p. 99 above.

[9]Once or twice we were rather disconcerted to be told by a local official, whom we were interviewing in the hope of getting an independent view of the situation, that the moral welfare worker had been consulted about the interview or had supplied the figures asked for in the questionnaire.

[10]An official in a medium-sized county borough told us that he was 'very favourably impressed' by the moral welfare worker in his area who seemed 'fresh and up-to-date in her ideas'. This, he continued, was in marked contrast to his previous experience in a similar sized town in another county where 'moral welfare did not come into the picture much' and he 'had the impression of a religious rather than casework approach'.

[11]Cf. the contention of the county welfare worker quoted earlier in the chapter that to the families with whom she was dealing the moral welfare worker's church connections were hardly understood and made no real difference. There are evidently differences of degree of perception between clients as well as in the attitudes of workers.

[12]This was shown in the widespread interest in a conference organised by the Association of Social Workers in 1959, the subject of which was 'Morals and the Social Worker'. The Association subsequently printed a report of the proceedings.

[13]Cf. Noel Timms, *Social Casework Principles and Practice*, Routledge & Kegan Paul, 1964, p. 26. 'Of the disciplines that have contributed to casework the most widely used has been that of psychology, particularly psychoanalysis.'

[14]It is discussed in a social work setting by Professor T. S. Simey,

National Children's Home Convocation Lecture, 1960. *The Concept of Love in Child Care.* Three articles by Margaret Tilley, 'Casework and Morality,' *Crucible,* January 1962, 'Religion and Social Work,' *Social Work,* April 1962 and 'Fashion and Values in Social Work,' *The Almoner,* March 1964, deal with the issues raised in the above paragraph.

[15]We came across isolated examples of work started under church auspices to deal with situations of special need, such as the work in the Cable Street area of Stepney carried on by the two women workers on the staff of St. Paul's Church, Dock Street.

[16]E.g., 'The work is simply that of a special agency of the Church of England for the service of the family.' *Not So Odd,* recruiting pamphlet issued in 1959 by the Church of England Moral Welfare Council. Cf. 'She [the moral welfare worker] is, in effect, a family caseworker employed by the Church.' *Moral Crisis—the Church in Action,* C.E.M.W.C., 1950. 'The moral welfare worker is concerned with the family, and like other social workers, she might more properly be called the 'family caseworker'. Rev. W. P. Wylie, *The Church Cares,* published for the Moral Welfare Council by the Church Information Board, 1955.

[17]Cf. the rather different emphasis of the discussion of the same point in the Report of a Commission appointed by the Lord Bishop of Manchester to survey the moral welfare work in his diocese and its relation to the Church's other activities in the social field. 'Through her moral welfare organisation the Church seeks to be an instrument of the compassion of our Lord in the realm of personal relationships. It is therefore logical that the Church should provide a remedial casework service for those who are in difficulties as a result of stress and tension in marriage and family life but, owing to practical needs and social pressures, by far the greatest proportion of the overall social work is at present in the field of illegitimacy.' Diocese of Manchester, Moral Welfare Work and its relation to the Church's other activities in the social field. Report of a commission appointed by the Lord Bishop of Manchester. Published by the Manchester Diocesan Conference, 1962, pp. 9-10.

[18]Chapter 5, p. 96 above.

[19]Op. cit., p. 47.

[20]The Younghusband Committee found that at the time when they made their investigations, local authorities were administering 29 mother and baby homes, while 106 were provided by voluntary organisations.

[21]A survey of Church of England moral welfare homes made in 1958 revealed that 380 superintendents and assistants were employed in that year in the 136 homes listed in the Church of England Directory of Moral Welfare Work. This was more than half the total number of workers employed in England and Wales by Church of England moral welfare associations. At this time there were 263 outdoor workers and 44 organising secretaries, so that in all 687 workers were employed.

[22]Accommodation provided under Part III of the National Assistance Act. Section 21 of this Act makes it a duty of local authorities to provide (a) 'residential accommodation for persons who by reason of age, infirmity or any other circumstances are in need of care and attention not other-

wise available for them', and (b) 'temporary accommodation for persons who are in urgent need thereof, being need arising in circumstances which could not reasonably have been foreseen or in such other circumstances as the authority may in any particular case determine'.

²³We were interested to note that at an Organising Secretaries' Conference held in September 1961, the view was put forward that moral welfare workers should concentrate on their role as caseworkers, and not aspire to be educationalists as well.

16. POLICY ISSUES

¹'The Justification of the Church's Engagement in Social Work, its Dimension and Mode of Operation,' *Theology*, Vol. LXIV, No. 493, July 1961, p. 266. Cf. 'In Christ, God's outreach to the world has become flesh and blood. Through and in the Church this has to become manifest, and therefore its proper reasons and mode of existence are, *missio* and *diakonia*.' Hendrik Kraemer, *A Theology of the Laity*, Hulsean Lectures, 1958, p. 162.

²Bishop of Middleton, op. cit.

³Moral welfare work is not the only kind of social work carried out in the name of the Church, although it was the only kind of work with which we were directly concerned. Other examples are the homes for old people run by the Church Army and the work of the Church of England Children's Society, to which the criteria of efficiency and effectiveness compared with the corresponding statutory services also apply.

⁴See pp. 56 and 88 above where the local health authorities' reactions to Circular 2866 are discussed.

⁵*Moral Welfare*, October 1959. One statutory official whom we met wanted to know what the Church was doing spending money on social work (which by implication his department could do better) 'when their vicarages are tumbling down'.

⁶Report of the Working Party on Social Workers in the Local Authority Health and Welfare Services, par. 1039, p. 300.

⁷For further discussion of this definition see Quentin Edwards, *What is Unlawful?* Church Information Office, 1959.

⁸F. R. Barry, Bishop of Southwell, *Asking the Right Questions*, Hodder and Stoughton, p. 65.

⁹Congregations are often asked to pray for doctors and nurses and others who care for the sick; seldom, if ever, are they reminded of the need for upholding those such as probation officers, child care officers, mental health workers, resident staff in approved schools and remand homes and others carrying out similarly exacting work, who care for the socially or morally sick.

¹⁰Cf. Professor Dorothy Emmet, 'Ethics and the Social Worker,' and Noel Timms, 'Ethics and the Social Worker—a comment,' *The British Journal of Psychiatric Social Work*, Vol. VI, 1962, No. 4.

¹¹Barry, op. cit., p. 69.

¹²E.g., *The Family in Contemporary Society*, the report of the group

convened at the request of the Archbishop of Canterbury in preparation for the Lambeth Conference, 1958. It is unfortunate that the discussions initiated in connection with the preparation of this Report do not seem to have been continued.

[13]That in some areas the coverage is no more than nominal was brought home to us by an almoner who had recently moved into one of the survey dioceses from another area, where, she asserted, there was no moral welfare worker at all.

[14]Cf. *Responsibility in the Welfare State?*, Birmingham Council of Christian Churches, 1961. Although the proposals set out in this booklet have not been implemented as was originally hoped they appear to have possibilities.

[15]Above, Chapter 5, p. 99.

[16]Home Office Circular No. 204/1963.

[17]This appears to be what is envisaged in the Diocesan Report already cited.

INDEX

Children and Young Persons Act, 1963, 98-9, 250, 270
Church, 1, 2, 3-4, 5, 6, 9, 13, 15, 18, 27, 28, 36, 37, 62, 81, 86, 87, 102, 112, 120, 122, 123, 139, 186, 193, 196, 208, 213, 240, 241, 243, 248, 250-1, 252, 255, 256, 257, 260-72
Church Army, 26, 28, 108, 127, 187, 191, 192, 198, 227, 277n
Church Assembly, 2, 3, 45, 108
  Board of Education, 211, 258
  Board for Social Responsibility, 1, 2, 3, 69, 217, 238, 258
Church Congregations, 99, 225, 227, 231, 269
Church of England Advisory Board for Moral Welfare Work, 25, 238
  Children's Society, 187
  Council for Women's Ministry in the Church, 113
  Men's Society, 146
  Moral Welfare Council (later Council for Social Work), 1, 2, 3, 47, 51, 53, 54, 55, 58, 62, 64, 65, 66, 67, 68, 69-70, 80, 81, 102, 137, 148, 193, 206, 212, 214, 217, 220, 238, 249; Handbook, *The Committee Member*, 148; Quarterly Leaflet, 57; Training Commission, 59, 60
  Purity Society, 4
  Temperance Society, 220
  Youth Council, 211, 213
  Social Workers, 222-3
Church Times, 109
Church Work (other than social work), 108, 118, 298n

Clergy, 13, 48, 60, 64-5, 174-5, 183, 185, 189, 190, 191, 204, 214, 217, 227, 229, 232, 233, 238, 239, 240, 263, 265, 270, 281n
Clergy Sample, 5, 208-210, 218-26, 295n
Clewer House of Mercy, 18
Cole, Miss J. M., 41
Committee of Social Investigation and Reform, 38, 39, 40
Contagious Diseases Acts, 23, 25, 276n
Contraceptives, 32, 82, 287n
Convocation of Canterbury, 28
Cooper, Daniel, 19, 26
Copec, 36-7, 279n
Coram, Thomas, 11, 12, 13
Criminal Law Amendment Act, 1886, 23, 95

Dalston Refuge, 15
Davidson, Randall, Archbishop of Canterbury, 45
Davidson, Edith, 45, 49
Deaneries, 128, 129, 132
Dingley, Robert, 14
Dioceses, 3, 20, 28, 46, 127, 138, 256
Dioceses Surveyed, 89, 169, 192, 202, 207, 212, 214, 238
  Northern, 5, 128, 129, 131, 137, 153, 155, 156, 158-9, 171, 173, 174, 185, 208, 212
  Southern, 5, 128, 129, 131-2, 137, 155, 156, 158-9, 171, 173, 174, 185, 196, 210
Diocesan Boards,
  of Education, 139, 258
  of Finance, 238
  of Moral Welfare — *see* Moral Welfare
Diocesan Conferences, 238

Lee Abbey Camp, 211
Liverpool, 29, 42, 43, 50, 82
    University, 61, 111, 112, 115
Local Authorities, 39, 56, 59-60, 88, 89, 94, 95, 122, 130, 138, 150, 195-6, 240-41, 244, 246, 252, 255
    Children's Departments, 2, 92-3, 94, 95, 97, 175, 182, 183, 193, 221, 256, 262
    Children's and Child Care Officers, 93, 94, 184, 241, 245
    Education Authorities, 203
    Family Social Workers, 186, 289n
    Family Welfare Services, 2, 97, 253
    Grants to Moral Welfare Work, 154, 156, 159, 183
    Health Authorities and Officials, 56, 89, 90, 91, 92, 93, 131, 146, 174, 186, 196, 241, 262
Lock Asylum, 14
London, 11, 12, 13, 21, 42, 226
    County Council, 131, 132, 226, 228
London Course, 5, 61-2, 102, 114-15, 142, 245, 246, 268
    Students, 114, 115, 118, 120
London Female Penitentiary, 15
London by Moonlight Mission, 19
London Quarterly Review, 19

'Magdalens', 9
Magdalen Hospital, 14-5
Manchester,
    Bishop of, 5
    Diocese, 271
    University, 79, 105

Marital and Family Problems, 2, 176, 219, 227, 229, 250
Marriage, 84
Marriage Guidance, 63-4, 146, 284n, 295n
    Local Marriage Guidance Councils, 63, 184, 185, 211, 212, 214, 221, 257, 258
    National Marriage Guidance Council, 63, 64, 212, 250, 265
Married Women, 53, 92, 105, 158, 176, 199, 201
Marine Society, 16
Maternities, Extra- and Pre-Marital, 74, 75
Medical Officers of Health—*see* Local Authorities, Health Officials
Mental Health, 90, 189, 225
'Michelhurst' Housing Estate, 129, 190, 226-34, 269, 272
    Worker, 227, 228
Middleton, Bishop of, 260
Moloney, Sir Thomas F., 42
    Committee on Young Offenders, 42
Moral Welfare, 6, 31, 54, 58, 73, 104, 108-9, 114, 118, 122, 123, 129, 131, 139, 151, 193, 210, 250
    Adoption Work, 58, 138, 141, 179-81, 187, 188, 241
    As Church work, 3, 41, 42, 54-5, 60, 87, 189, 191, 217-33, 237-44, 277n, 297n
    As Social Work, 41, 110, 244
    Definition, 2-3, 149, 219-20, 237, 273n
    Diocesan Organisation:
        Boards and Councils, 3,

Pastoral Work, 223-4
Penitentiaries, 15, 18, 19, 20,
26, 249, 280n
Church Penitentiary As-
sociation, 19-20, 24, 28, 275-
6n
Police, 183
Women, 249
Political and Economic Plan-
ning, 54, 55
Poor Laws, 10, 16, 17, 39, 56
Poor Law Commission,
1832, 10, 11, 16-17, 18
Population (Statistics) Act, 1938,
74
Probation Officers, 184, 185-6,
210, 221, 245, 246, 250, 258,
289n, 296n
Prostitution, 13, 16, 22, 66-7,
83, 110, 249
Prostitutes, 9, 13-14, 83,
248-9, 264, 275n, *see also*
Moral Welfare Work with
Putative Fathers, 10, 11, 17, 18,
50, 177-8, 250

Reformatory and Refuge Union,
20
Registrar General, 33, 75, 76,
81
Religious Houses, 9
Rescue Work, 22, 27, 38, 39,
40, 280-1n
*Rescue Work—An Enquiry
and Criticism*, 38-40
Rochester, 28, 47
Roman Catholics, 109, 144,
145, 174, 175, 205, 233
Russell, Dr. G. L., 50

Saint Agnes House, 29, 47
Saint Monica's Refuge, 29, 48,
278n

Saint Thomas' Hospital, 9
Salvation Army, 26, 277n
Sex,
Assaults, 182
Departmental Committee
on Sexual Offences Against
Young Persons, 40, 42-3
Morality, 37, 84-86, 122,
238
Ratio, 84-5
Shaftesbury, Seventh Earl of, 20
Smith, Theophilus, 19
Social Services, 221, 223, 239,
258
Statutory, 151, 183, 252,
264, 265-6, 271
Social Work, 2, 32, 81, 115,
118, 120, 123, 139, 140, 150,
151, 239-40, 248
Christian Responsibility
for 224-5, 265-6
Social Workers, 59, 60, 96, 191,
200, 221, 244-5, 250, 263,
266-7, 288
Southwark, Diocese of, 42, 43,
211
Southwell, Bishop of, 5
Stead, W. T., 23, 24, 276n
Steel, Ena M., 55
Street Offences Act, 1959, 68,
83, 214, 249
Student Christian Movement,
207
Suicide, 22, 264
*Ought Suicide to be a
Crime?* 88

Taylor, Dr. Dorothy, 57
Tennant, Mrs., 18
Theological Colleges, 64, 210
Thompson, Barbara, 78
Unmarried Mothers and their
Children, 2, 10, 13, 16, 17,

For Product Safety Concerns and Information please contact our EU
representative GPSR@taylorandfrancis.com
Taylor & Francis Verlag GmbH, Kaufingerstraße 24, 80331 München, Germany

www.ingramcontent.com/pod-product-compliance
Lightning Source LLC
Chambersburg PA
CBHW070600270326
41926CB00013B/2370

* 9 7 8 0 4 1 5 6 0 5 8 1 6 *